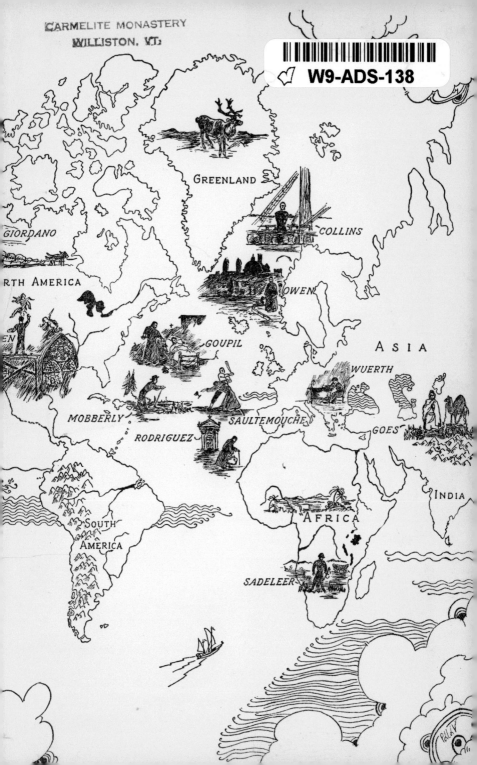

# BETTER A DAY

Edited by John P. Leary, S.J.

---

*Better a day, O Lord*, IN THY COURTS THAN A THOUSAND
OTHERS; I HAD RATHER STAND AT THE
THRESHOLD OF THE HOUSE OF
MY GOD, THAN TO DWELL
IN THE TENTS OF
SINNERS.
*Psalm*
*83, 11*

NEW YORK · THE MACMILLAN COMPANY · 1951

| | |
|---|---|
| Nihil obstat: | Joannes M. Byrne<br>Censor deputatus |
| Imprimi Potest: | Joseph D. O'Brien, S.J.<br>Praepositus Provinciae Calif. S.J. |
| Imprimatur: | ✠Joannes J. Mitty<br>Archiepiscopus Sti. Francisci in Calif. |

To    Our Lady, Queen of the Society of Jesus

# Preface

"HOW BEAUTIFUL are the feet of those who bring the good news of peace." Peace! The word has come to have an almost fantastic sound and mocks the sore longing it stirs in us. It is a thin, piping note out of some idyll of innocence that is heard for a poignant moment through the echoes and clamors of wars fought and wars to come.

Most of us today are appalled at the prospect of what lies in store for us. All the tragedies, the failures and wrongs of the past are waiting to be righted. And yet these heaped-up burdens instead of being a challenge, rousing us to a keen sense of enterprise, make us rather feel our deplorable inadequacies in the face of these responsibilities.

Peace is the cry of our time. A mere ceasing of brute conflict is not enough, or a set of circumstances where no man fights because he is afraid to fight or unable. We want to be anchored to something too strong for any eventuality to undermine. What are the answers to life's basic concerns: happiness, security, eternal salvation? Men die for these answers, these truths. The white-checkered slopes of Tarawa, Iwo Jima, and the Valley of the Saar are but a few minor indications of how fiercely we struggle to preserve and advance the Cause. Even minus the flourish and rhetoric which so frequently accompany recollections of this kind, we still cannot forget the stillness as millions lie buried together around the world because they sought with the valor and vehemence of men to wrest the world from evil and conflict.

Their burial grounds are witness to how immense the desire for peace really is and how futile it is likewise to think of its ever being fully realized in this world. For peace is indeed from within, the treasure that lies buried, the pearl of great price.

Yet men have always been confronted with these same issues.

You will hear them saying: What is the world coming to? Where will it all end up? Do things make any sense at all?

Wise men know the answers, at least some of them. They know that in final analysis peace of mind is a personal thing. It springs from an inner knowledge and conviction that in the service and praise of God alone is the key to happiness . . . the only security policy that has an absolutely iron-clad guarantee.

We have gathered here in these pages the lives of fifteen men, harbingers of peace, men as close to the world as people could be, without being of the world. They were not priests, not contemplatives. They have been picked almost at random from literally the four corners of the world, America and Africa, Europe and Asia. They have encountered practically every conceivable situation of significance that has occurred in the last four hundred eventful years. Their lives of self-effacement, of courage and perseverance in most strenuous difficulties, entitle them to honor beyond what we can give.

To the groping Secular and even to the Mass-a-week Catholic the Jesuit Brother is a rather unimposing figure, neither teacher nor preacher nor dispenser of the Sacraments. You look at him and see that he is a prayerful man, however, and you think how essential prayer is if one is to be saved. You see also that he is a consecrated man, vowed to God with the triple bond of being poor, being pure and being submissive. Just about there he ceases to be different from outsiders. His is a religious vocation, but in a way a lay vocation, too, since he must spend his life doing the prosaic and the ordinary just like the man down the street.

For sometimes forty, fifty, even sixty years these quiet, remarkable men go about their business, carrying on the tasks that men everywhere must carry on, the tasks that can eventually pall the spirit if a person is wanting the one thing necessary. They are aware of the vast solidarity that knits men everywhere together, and so they perform the ordinary with unwavering diligence; they have elevated the commonplace by a pure and simple intention, making out of the humdrum a new Nazareth. Supernaturally, therefore, their influence is incalculable.

You will see them marching to open the door for some visitor or to cook, to clear a jungle or to climb the gallows, always with dispatch, just a part of their day's work, so completely has the heroic entered into their lives.

Our only regret lies in our knowledge that we are bound necessarily to fail when we try to transmit such immensity of spirit as is manifest in the lives of these men, our amazing Jesuit Brothers, whom we so proudly hail.

We are hopeful, however, that lives like these, lived in such obscurity and self-denial, will afford some inspiration to people who are weary of simply hearing ideals talked about. For when all is said and done, human assemblies, our legislatures, our political and social institutions depend completely upon the people who make them up.

No real or lasting change for the better can be superimposed, fixed by a mere law, prescribed. It must come from within if it is to endure. The Jesuit Brothers typify profoundly the type of workaday character, elevated by motive and God's Grace, who can restore a measure of sanity to the world and with it the peace which Christ came to give.

The Brother has learned interior peace that does not rest upon the contingencies of time and circumstance, the millennium perhaps or some golden era. For him there is only one GOLDEN ERA and it glitters with a quite unearthly splendor. He is humble enough to be sane, and realistic enough to appreciate, that life at worst is suffering and hell, at its best, suffering and paradise, but always suffering, never complete satisfaction in anything short of seeing God. So even when the world has seemed almost literally to fall down on his shoulders he has maintained his calm, a spirit of detachment, that vastly single-minded orientation of all he has and is and does, to God.

These men are men of Faith in a world which has lost faith in God and hence also lost faith in itself.

THE EDITOR

# Acknowledgements

It would be difficult to express our appreciation to each of the many kind associates and helpers who have assisted in the preparation of this work. However, the Superior of the Jesuit Theologate in California, Father Hilary Werts, and the Spiritual Counseller, Father Edward Hagemann, deserve special mention for their interest, advice and encouragement.

To the many librarians and religious Superiors throughout the world, who have supplied us with information, periodicals, books and pamphlets, we express our thanks, especially to the librarian at Alma, Father Francis Sheerin, Father Edmond Lamalle of the Historical Institute of the Society of Jesus at Rome, and Father William Repetti, archivist at Georgetown University, Washington, D.C.

The map used as the end paper is the work of Jesuit scholastic, William Ryan of Sheridan, Oregon.

We are indebted to Father Bernard Kranz, S.J. of Berlin, Germany, and Father Jorge Perez, S.J., of Bogota, Colombia, for long hours of translation and to Father Russell Boehning, S.J., of Spokane, Washington, for clerical work.

To these and the many others who have been of help we extend our heartfelt thanks.

THE AUTHORS

# Contents

# Little John

BY WEBSTER PATTERSON, S.J.

*Brother Nicholas Owen, S.J.* (     *–1606*)
Declared Blessed 1929

It WAS MIDNIGHT. A lone rowboat pulled slowly up the Thames. Two men sat in the stern as a third plied the oars.

The oarsman paused and cocked a sharp ear toward the opposite shore. He picked out rumblings muffled by distance: barking of restless watchdogs; the dull clop of horses bearing late carousers to their quarters; the distant roar of water rushing through the piles beneath London Bridge. Then a voice, clear and unmistakable, from a nearby wharf: "The horses are ready," it called softly from the darkness. The oarsman stood up and looked toward the landing.

On the wharf a mite-sized man stepped quickly from the shadows. He waved a light and disappeared again into the darkness.

"Stand by, Little John," the oarsman called after. He signed farewell and once more dipped his oars in the water. The boat pushed on. High tide and the river was all in motion, swirling, gurgling and bubbling. Waves slapped sharply against the prow. Past long black piles they glided; between anchored ships that groaned and creaked upon the unsteady, swelling waters. Fog rolled in heavy banks, curled and gathered in the creases of the cloaks drawn tightly about them.

The objective this night was the Tower of London. It loomed above them, a huge bulky specter rising in the steaming mists. The Tower, really several towers, was girt by two massive walls and a wide moat, slimy and muddy at low tide. The latter would prove a formidable obstacle to anyone attempting an escape. Outside help and a good strong rope would be necessary. Even then, chances for success would be very slim. Guards abounded. The Tower was high; the moat treacherous. A dangerous risk, to say the least.

These factors Father John Gerard carefully considered as he waited anxiously in his cell this night in 1597. Weeks of plotting, passing secret notes, and the time had come. Little John directing, two other Jesuit Brothers helping, a boat, a rope, the aid of

Arden, a fellow prisoner, . . . with these, God willing, the thing *could* be done!

This night the guard was bribed. The two prisoners were allowed to spend the night together in the Cradle Tower which lies nearest the moat. In the cell's ceiling a trap door, unlocked with a knife, stood prepared. Twelve o'clock and the door was quickly opened. The prisoners climbed stealthily to the Tower's roof.

Between stone parapets they scanned the mist-shrouded river and the moat below. A lead ball with string attached was hurled across the moat. The cord hurtled behind in a long white arch and disappeared in the darkness near the bank of the Thames. The Brothers were waiting. A rope was attached, hauled up and made fast to a bastion of the Tower.

Arden swung across first, hand over hand; then Father Gerard followed, face downwards, arms and legs wrapped around the rope as he descended. Suddenly the rope slackened; a jerk, and his body swung around beneath the rope and hung limply. Arms, still weak from torture, clung frantically. He slipped, all but fell into the dark waters below. He prayed, struggled desperately, all the while praying. Inch by inch he forced himself to the other side. Grasped firmly by Brother Lily he was hauled into the boat. Quickly they pushed off and rowed back down the river.

Meanwhile on the wharf Little John watched and waited for the returning rescuers. He paced the dock, peering anxiously into the misty blackness. Carefully he had made the plans. But something might easily go wrong. Suddenly, a splash of oars and the boat with its rescued prisoners loomed up through the darkness.

"Long John," he called as the boat drew near. (This was a nickname of Father Gerard.)

"Little John," the priest smiled weakly. "God be praised, it is you."

Father Gerard threw his arms warmly about the little Brother as he was lifted from the boat and carried to his horse.

As the first streaks of dawn were breaking over London Bridge, a little party of horsemen, led by Little John, clattered through the deserted streets of sleeping London . . . to freedom and to safety.

Seven years before Nicholas Owen, known as Little John, had first met this unusual young priest who took such chances in his quest for souls. Though Little John was but a youth at the time, a carpenter by trade, Father Gerard had even then impressed him deeply. Unusually tall, black-haired, of swarthy complexion, with piercing eyes and a hawk nose, there was something striking about this strapping Jesuit whose priestly dignity shone through the worldly disguises he generally wore.

Clad spotlessly in velvet hose and satin doublet, adorned with silver lace, rapiers and daggers of gilt and gold, he never seemed complacent in the role of the noble gallant he was often forced to play. Beneath the laughing, reckless manner Nicholas saw the same burning love for Christ and the same zeal for souls that he would discover in every Jesuit he was to meet on the English mission. This was the spirit they all had in common, that magnetic attraction which irresistibly drew him to offer his own life for the same cause; not as a priest, for that he felt God did not ask, but rather as a Brother, a helper to the priests in their dangerous work.

Clad in his dull green cloak, caped with tawny velvet, the London carpenter one day presented himself to Father Persons, Jesuit Superior, and begged to be admitted into the Society of Jesus. He had no illusions about the life that lay in store for him! Like the young English Jesuits at Liége, he was presented with a list of challenging questions:

Are you ready to undergo a hard persecution?
Are you contented to be falsely betrayed?
Are you prepared to be hurried away to prison?
Can you sleep in straw and live on a hard diet?
Can you lie in chains and fetters?
Can you endure the rack?

Can you be brought to the bar and hear yourself sworn against?
Can you patiently receive the sentence of an unjust judge?
Can you face a painful and ignominious death?

These were the things a Jesuit in the time of Elizabeth must be prepared to undergo. With God's grace he thought he could endure them, for the sake of His crucified Master. He made his offering; the decision was final. Come what might, he had thrown in his lot with Christ.

It was on a winter's evening that Little John, as his fellow Jesuits had affectionately named him, stood at the main entrance of Hinlip Manor. Hinlip was the country seat of the Abingtons, one of those staunch old Catholic families that still remained in the English country districts. Located three miles from Worcester, this handsome old mansion with its rambling wings and tall chimneys stood proudly on a small knoll: the whole was unequalled for size and magnificence throughout the countryside. It had, in fact, become somewhat of an eyesore to neighboring Puritans who coveted the rich lands and fine buildings of the elder Abington.

Hinlip's oaken door resounded loudly as Little John lifted the heavy brass knocker and beat firmly on the wrought-iron receiver. Echoes vibrated dully through the hall. There was the sliding of bolts and the click of a latch. The door swung open and against the dark interior appeared an elderly, dignified man clad in dark brown doublet and loose cloak. He eyed curiously the little man standing without, covered with dust, a carpenter's bag of tools slung over one shoulder.

John Abington suddenly seemed to recognize the visitor, clasped his hand and warmly welcomed him within. The door swung silently behind them. It was a long high-ceilinged hall they entered, wainscotted around three sides, with a great stone fireplace blazing brightly at the far end. A huge log crackled fiercely, sending showers of sparks racing up the chimney and arching down on the stone floor before them.

In the flickering shadows of the fire, he seated his guest comfortably and then settled back to discuss the urgent matter at hand. He had heard of the Brother-carpenter, he explained. He had long petitioned the Jesuit superior for just such a man for the purpose he had in mind. It was the least he could do for the persecuted priests of England. This huge building, with its endless rooms and halls, would be an ideal place of refuge from the fury of the persecution. But hiding holes must be built and for this he needed a skillful and clever builder, one that could be thoroughly trusted. This was the task he set before Brother Nicholas known as Little John.

Nicholas' eyes gleamed with admiration as he sat there listening to the fighting old squire describe what things he and other faithful Catholics were ready to do for the English priests. The faith still burned in England! With God's help they would not give up the fight so easily! There was yet many an English Catholic like the gallant old Squire Gerard who resisted every attempt to make him conform to the new religion. Rendered helpless by an attack of gout, the Squire was carried to the Protestant church and dumped in a pew during the Sunday sermon. Undismayed, he proceeded to sing Latin psalms with such gusto at the top of his voice that he drowned out the preacher and had to be removed.

Such Catholics, John Abington assured him, were not rare in Lancashire. They were not so numerous as in the days of his father; but the spirit of the Catacombs had returned to England. The faithful once again burned with the pristine fervor of early Christianity. Catholics no longer slept during the Sacred Mysteries, or chose their priest for his speed in celebrating. Each offering of the Mass, they knew, might well cost the life of the priest who celebrated. Members of a family fell on their knees whenever a priest entered a household, and his hands were kissed as those of a future martyr.

As the old Squire spoke, it seemed to Nicholas his own heart would burst with thanksgiving to God for the grace He had given to this gallant Catholic nobleman, so willing to risk life and all he had for the priests of England. Many, it was true, had fallen away in the persecution; but the intimate bond between the priest and those who remained true to the faith was so much the closer. It cost something to keep the faith in these trying times! Sacrifice increased its value. And Little John yearned intensely for the day when he would be worthy to suffer something for Christ and the faith that meant so much to him.

It was after supper that John Abington took the brother on his tour of inspection. Nicholas measured and noted the salient features of the house as they proceeded. He intended to begin his work that night. Thick walls, countless rooms, winding corridors and numerous chimneys offered many possibilities to the observant eye of the little carpenter. A gallery, whose walls were covered with richly carved wainscot, ran around the entire interior at the top of the house. Behind these walls he observed the possibility of constructing secret chambers, so built that their entrances would appear as part of the wainscotting. He noted carefully staircase landings, the thickness of chimneys and how a tunnel might be devised to lead a priest to the outside of the house unperceived. These and many other possibilities suggested themselves to his observant eye. But there could be no delay. The work must begin immediately.

Little John was seated on the floor when Mr. Abington found him the next morning. Bricks torn from the nearby chimney lay strewn in wild profusion about him. Streaked with soot, red-eyed and weary, he sat looking at the fireplace before him. He was tucking away his tools in the bag he always carried as the elder Abington entered.

"Perhaps you can tell me, Sir, where lies the entrance to the hiding hole I have just constructed."

Little John smiled as the Squire furrowed his brow and stared intently. Carefully John Abington inspected the fireplace, poked his head up the flue and examined the masonry around the chimney. Each part he tested, hoping to find some section weaker than the other that might provide him with a clue to the opening he wanted. But each part seemed just as firm and solid as the other. At last with a shrug, he turned to Little John, admitting defeat.

Laughing, Little John quickly kicked aside the kindling in the pit and scraped the soot diligently from the flooring. A well-defined crack about two feet square suddenly appeared. Edging in his fingers carefully, he pulled out a small trap door that revealed the opening to a tight chamber beneath the fireplace. The bricks in the trap door, he explained, were mortared fast to planks of wood. No longer could the place be used for an actual fire. But provided some burnt wood were kept to allay suspicion, the place would not easily be discovered. It was not a masterpiece, but it might save the life of a priest in case of emergency. This was all he asked for now.

Little John's career had begun. A skillful and prudent maker of hideouts? Such a man was invaluable to the Catholic families of England. Knowledge of the Brother spread quickly. Not many had the talent for such work as his; fewer yet were sufficiently trustworthy. This latter quality was especially important. Only after a man had proven himself was he taken into confidence and entrusted with the construction of secret chambers. The hiding place of a priest was a matter of the greatest secrecy, known only to the builder and intimate members of the family. Its location was seldom disclosed even to servants; never to outsiders. Upon this knowledge might depend the lives of both priest and family. Loss of property, imprisonment and death were the penalty for its disclosure. And many was the Jesuit who chose torture rather than reveal his place of refuge.

Dust-covered and weary, at times drenched with rain or chilled through with snow, Little John would be seen tramping up the front driveway of some country mansion, a bag of tools over one shoulder, his hands rough and worn from continuous labor. He would set to work, patching a roof or repairing a floor for the master of the house. Just another wandering carpenter, so thought the servants.

But it was at night that his real work began. While the rest of the household was fast asleep, Little John was hard at work in some cubbyhole, burrowing through ceilings or tearing up flooring. Often the thickest walls had to be broken into and large stones carried out. This was a task requiring much strength and endurance, not easily accomplished by one with so small a body. Due to this over-exertion, he contracted hernia from which he was to suffer much in later life. He always worked alone; to trust another might easily mean betrayal, disaster. These hidden compartments were a closed secret with himself. He alone was their architect and builder. Time alone would be proof of his skill. Hidden and inviolate these rooms would remain . . . many of them for over three hundred years . . . their presence unsuspected by succeeding generations. Nothing but the shattering force of Nazi blitz-bombers could have torn the hidden secrets from these ancient English mansions.

One chamber was constructed in a staircase landing. It slanted artfully into the masonry of a tower. From the outside, the place appeared scarcely large enough for a man's leg. But when a particular board in the landing was removed, a fairly large opening was disclosed. This was the entrance to a tunnel which turned into a wall and ended in a secret chamber capable of holding several men at one time.

The entrance to another hole was built in a false cupboard. When a certain peg was removed the cupboard swung down and out to reveal a hidden chamber behind it. Still another was put in the side of a chimney, the entrance being disguised with brick and mortar. A false smoke funnel was attached so that food could be passed to the priest concealed within.

Entrances were never the same; otherwise, the discovery of one would be a clue to all the rest. Each was a small masterpiece built on an entirely different pattern. To construct so many and such totally different chambers required the greatest skill and ingenuity on the part of the builder. Even skilled carpenters and masons were unable to detect them, though they might search a single house for a week. Exasperated after sounding walls and pulling up flooring, they would finally leave in disgust; yet a priest often lay hidden but a wall's thickness away from them. When the pursuivants at last departed, their intended victim would emerge from his hiding place, cramped and half-starved, but thankful that God had spared his life a little longer. "By this, his skill," wrote Father Gerard, "many priests were preserved from the fury of the persecutors; nor is it easy to find anyone who has not often been indebted for his life to Owen's hiding places. I myself have been one of seven that together on one occasion escaped that danger in a secret place of his making."

Much to the displeasure of Cecil, Elizabeth's scheming Secretary of State, Little John seemed to be everywhere, but none were able to trap him. Under his Lordship's very nose the priests now worked, but vanished before any could lay their hands on them. It was the builder of hiding holes that must be caught! His name had already become a legend. Cecil fumed and raged; but still no one could find him.

Catholics mentioned his name with a certain awe and marked the special Providence that seemed to watch over him. This, they believed, accounted for the extraordinary success that always seemed to accompany his hiding holes. They noted how he received Holy Communion upon beginning the construction of any new chamber; and how he prayed constantly while the work was in progress. It was this spirit of prayer, and his wonderful patience, they believed, that won for him the special protection of Divine Providence. The Brother builder became more and more in demand among the Catholic houses of England, travelling throughout the land, and working in all the principal shires and country manors.

For many months, in the guise of a menial servant, Little John was companion to a young Jesuit later to become famous in the annals of the English martyrs. Cultured and brilliant, this talented priest had once been the idol of Oxford and the favorite of London society. Queen Elizabeth herself had been charmed by his eloquence on one occasion, and had personally praised the eloquent scholar. But the day came when "Campion, the Seditious Jesuit," was dragged through the mud of London streets to a martyr's death at Tyburn.

Little John was in the crowd that day. Edmund Campion stood upon the gallows, his lips moving quietly in prayer. A rope dangled loosely from the crossbeam. Below the gallows, a great crowd of heads surged restlessly in the cold glare of a December sun. Smoke curled skyward as the great steaming cauldron hissed and bubbled. On the executioner's block, a knife lay prepared. All was ready.

Campion was silent now. But the challenging words he had spoken at his trial yet rang out for those willing to hear: "If our religion do make us traitors, then we are worthy to be condemned . . . but in condemning us you condemn all your own ancestors, priests, bishops and kings . . . all that was once the glory of England."

As the rope was fixed around his neck, he raised his arm in final priestly blessing. The roar of the crowd was in his ears; before his eyes, hundreds of jeering faces. One last prayer, a snap of the rope, and the executioners began their bloody work. Campion, the Jesuit, was no more.

One voice in all that seething mass was brave enough to rise in protest, the voice of Campion's faithful servant. The priest had committed no treason, he boldly protested! The execution was unjust! Let all hear and know the truth: for his religion alone did Campion die!

The effect was swift. Little John, the "traitor," was quickly packed off to prison and buried in a loathsome dungeon. A heavy iron chain was bound to his leg. He was stretched on the rack, and deprived of food. Sick and weak already from his natural infirmities, he suffered still more from the lice-ridden filthy cell into which they cast him. Yet all this he patiently endured, even adding a hair shirt by way of voluntary mortification. Words, long forgotten, returned again in all their forceful clarity:

Are you prepared to be hurried away to prison?
Can you lie in chains and fetters?
Can you receive the sentence of an unjust judge?

He had said he could. It was now that the Master took him at his word. His grace would not be wanting.

But God had further plans for Little John, and he was soon released from the Tower through the help of Catholic friends. His work was not yet accomplished for the priests of England. More dangerous living, concealment, disguise, betrayal, labor, weariness, prayer at night, lay in store for him.

Dust rose in white puffs and swirled about his legs as Little John tramped heavily along the country road. It was a much older Nicholas Owen who this time approached the great front portal of Hinlip mansion. Advanced years, ceaseless hard labor and the horrors of the torture chamber had left their tell-tale marks on the Jesuit carpenter. He now walked with a limp, the result of a broken leg, once badly set, rebroken, then set again.

This time Nicholas was not alone as on his first visit to Hinlip. With him came Fathers Garnett, Oldcorne and Brother Ralph Ashley. The persecution had increased in fury since the discovery of the Gunpowder Plot, the attempt of a few hot-headed Catholics to blow the well-powdered Lords sky-high while they sat assembled in Parliament. By capitalizing on this incident, Cecil had succeeded in branding all priests as traitors, the Jesuits in particular. Pictures of the Jesuit Provincial, Father Garnett, now hung in all the streets of London as that of a common criminal. Travel had become too dangerous and the little band of Jesuits was forced to seek refuge at Hinlip until the storm subsided.

Nicholas smiled to himself as he thought how Cecil had twice unwittingly released him from the Tower. After that second imprisonment he had immediately set about to help Father Gerard who still remained imprisoned. Together they had carefully planned that escape and with the help of God had successfully carried it through. God indeed had protected His own.

But as Nicholas this time approached Abington Hall, a heavy feeling of sadness oppressed his soul, a premonition, it seemed, of the suffering His Master would soon ask him to accept. His own time would come; he felt sure of that. And that time could not be too far off. When it came, he knew no torment would be spared the infamous maker of hiding holes. Cecil, he felt certain, would see to that. And indeed the Lord Secretary was even then preparing the plans that would lead to Owen's ultimate capture.

It was evening when Robert Cecil, Earl of Salisbury, closed the door of his study and slipped the latch against possible intrusion. He walked over to the window and looked out, lost in deep reflection. The street below was deserted, save for a lone peddler's horse that went stumbling along the wet cobble-stones with a dull blunt clatter. As dusk descended, banks of fog swirled and eddied around London's steep slate roofs and smoking chimneys.

The wizened, hunch-backed Secretary turned to his desk and picked up a paper, fingering it thoughtfully. This was the information he had so desired. If the informer could only be trusted! Hinlip had long been suspected, but the evidence had always been lacking. If Garnett and Owen were there, as Humphrey assured him, there was now the immediate possibility of exterminating every priest in England!

With deep satisfaction, Cecil's mind dwelt on the pleasant prospect before him. This time there would be no slip-up, no chance for escape. These directions, addressed to Sir Henry Bromley, would see to that. He unfolded the paper and read:

### DIRECTIONS FOR SEARCH AT HINLIP HOUSE

In the search, first observe in the parlour where they use to dine and sup. In the east part of that parlour, it is conceived there is some vault, which to discover you must take care to draw down the wainscot, whereby the entry into the vault may be discovered; and the lower parts of the house must be tried with a broach by putting the same into the ground some foot or two, to try whether there may be perceived some timbers, which if be, there must be some vault underneath it.

For the upper rooms, you must observe whether they may be more in breadth than the lower rooms, and look which places the rooms be enlarged, by pulling up some boards you may discover some vault. Also if it appears that there be some corners to the chimneys, and the same boarded, if the boards may be taken away there will appear some.

If the walls seem to be thick and covered with wainscot, being tried with a gimlet, if it stick not on the wall, but go through, some suspicion is to be had thereof. If there be any double loft over two or three foot, one above the other, in such places any may be harbored privately. Also if there be a loft towards the roof of the house in which there appears no entrance out of any other place or ledging, that must of necessity be opened and looked into, for these be ordinary places of hiding.

Cecil refolded the paper and signed it with his seal of approval. For once, searchers would be prepared to suspect every possibility. His crafty eyes narrowed. He had only to wait.

Early Sunday morning Sir Henry arrived at Hinlip with an armed body of one hundred men and a warrant to search the house. When suddenly this small army appeared, thoroughly equipped with swords and crossbows, the household was thrown into utter confusion. Little John and Brother Ashley immediately rushed the two priests into hiding holes, with a few scant provisions that were hastily gathered as they entered. Mass vestments, missals and sacred vessels were snatched up and quickly hidden. There was no time to lose. Already the pursuivants were pounding on the front door, demanding entrance. No time remained for Nicholas and Brother Ashley to gather their own provisions. One apple was all they had between them. Scarcely had they disappeared within their own hiding hole when Sir Henry and his band burst into the hall. Immediately they spread throughout the house, running pell-mell through rooms and corridors, looking behind doors, peering under beds, all with the greatest noise and commotion. But it soon became evident to them a more systematic search would be necessary.

The hundred searchers were divided among various parts of the house and given exact instructions in procedure. Hour by hour, day after day, the merciless probing went on. Every part of the vast building echoed with the sound of pounding hammers. Wainscotting was torn from the walls, chimneys probed, and every room and hallway sounded and measured. No nook or corner of the rambling mansion was missed by the preying eyes of the priest hunters.

Little John had done his work well. Try as they might, the searchers could find nothing. But the situation with the Brothers had become desperate. The one apple, all the food they had, was long ago eaten. For six days now the search had continued, and Sir Henry's men gave no indication of giving up until the hidden Jesuits had either been found or starved to death. The priests also, Nicholas felt sure, must have exhausted their small supply of food. Only one chance remained. After fervent prayer, Nicholas discussed his plan with Brother Ashley. They both agreed and recommended themselves to God.

Waiting an opportunity when the hall was deserted, they quietly stepped out of their hiding hole and carefully slipped the door shut behind them. They had been careful to see that their discovery would not betray the priests who yet remained hidden in another part of the house. It was not to avoid starvation that they had determined to give themselves up. By sacrificing themselves, they hoped to save the lives of the two priests who yet remained safe. The searchers, they hoped, would be satisfied with taking them and depart.

Heroic as their action was, it was all in vain. Soon after, the searchers hit upon the hiding place of the priests and dragged them forth. Their time had come. The end was near.

"It is incredible," Cecil wrote later, "how great was the joy caused by this arrest throughout the kingdom, knowing the great skill of Owen in constructing hiding places and the innumerable quantity of these dark holes which he had schemed for hiding priests all through England."

For years the Secretary, already with blood-guilt on his hands, had waited for this opportunity:

"No dealing now with a lenient hand. We will try and get from him by coaxing, if he is willing thus to contract for his life, an excellent booty of priests. If he will not confess he shall be pressed by exquisite tortures, and we will wring the secret from him by the severity of his torments."

Too long Cecil had been frustrated by the clever carpenter. Unthinkable that a mere artisan should toy with England's Master! With incredible skill for almost twenty years, Little John had taken priests by the hand, led them along subterranean passages to places of safety. For almost twenty years he had hidden them between thick walls, buried them in secret chambers, entangled them in a thousand windings and mazes to escape the fury of Cecil's men. But now the tables were turned.

"Is he taken, that knows all the secret places?" said the head of the Privy Council. "I am very glad of that. We will have a trick for him."

Nicholas was first placed in the Marshalsea Prison under observation. By watching him closely they hoped to conjecture as to his secrets. But Cecil was baulked by the Brother's prudence. From a man of such discretion, Cecil soon saw, nothing could be gained through these means. He was thereupon transferred to the Tower of London where the torture could be conducted with the maximum of skill and industry. Owen could not long endure the terrible Topcliff rack, Cecil felt confident. He would soon be made to reveal his secrets!

In the company of Wade, Keeper of the Tower, Little John was led to the place of torture. Attendants went ahead with lighted torches, for the place was underground, gloomy and dark. Along winding passages and through cavernous halls the grim procession wound its way, penetrating ever deeper into the vast underground crypt. On the massive stone walls, lighted by the flickering flare of passing torches, Nicholas could see the various instruments of

torture which would be used upon him: iron shackles, worn on
the feet; manacles, fixed to the arms; iron gloves, in which the
hands of the victim are fastened with the most intense pain; the
Scavenger's Daughter, an iron ring which compresses the hands
and feet and head into a circle; and most terrible of all, the rack,
in which pulleys and wooden wheels draw members of the body
in different directions.

The sight of these instruments of torture lying prepared for
him, the silence and gloomy darkness of the subterranean vault,
the grim, merciless faces of men bent on tormenting him with the
most excruciating agonies, his natural sickness of body . . . all
of these combined to form one overwhelming accumulation of
horror that would have broken his spirit had it not been for the
sustaining strength of His Lord and Master. Alone and friendless,
abandoned completely to the will of his enemies, surrounded by
the most terrifying circumstances, he could turn to no one for
help or comfort in his hour of agony.

Even in those days of refined cruelty, it was forbidden by law
to torture a man suffering from internal injuries. But Wade was
determined to wrest the secret from his victim and scrupled at
nothing. Knowing the brother suffered badly from hernia, Wade
fastened iron bands around his victim's body. This would ensure
the maximum of torture and prevent the possibility of premature
death from natural causes. He shackled Little John's hands in iron
rings and fixed them high off the ground to a great upright beam.
Hanging thus in the most intense agony, Nicholas prayed, repeating over and over again "Jesus," "Mary."

Wade and the jailors stood about urging him to confess. "Tell
us, Little John, where are your hiding places! Only one word
and you will be free! Riches and honor will be yours for the asking!" They coaxed. They promised rewards. They threatened
worse torments. The pain was terrible in his hands and arms, breast
and shoulders. The sweat poured from his body. He fainted, was
revived, then fainted again. Not one word would he give them.

"He hung in torture seven hours together," later wrote Father

Gerard. "And this, divers times, though we cannot as yet learn the certain number. But day after day we heard of his being carried to the torments."

Through it all he resolutely refused to answer the least of Wade's questions. Patiently he suffered; patiently he prayed. Frustrated by his victim's constancy, the Master of the Tower grew furious. He ordered the executioners to distend his body still further. Add fresh weights to his legs! This man *would* confess! He was determined!

Under this last terrific pressure the iron band itself broke and the Brother's bowels gushed out with his life. In the midst of horrible torments, he breathed forth his soul to God.

Years later in Rome, a group of young Jesuits listened earnestly to a white-haired old priest as he talked of his days during the English persecution. From this gallant veteran they learned firsthand the secrets of the torture chamber, the things they must be prepared to suffer to follow in the steps of the Master. He himself, they knew, still bore the effects of the rack and the scars of torture. He spoke of secret chambers, Jesuits in disguise, and of a midnight escape from the Tower of London. But it was of Little John they loved to hear. Spellbound, young Jesuit hearts took fire as they listened to him tell of the Brother-martyr.

Cecil, he said, charged that Little John killed himself to escape the torture; that he had stolen a knife and ripped open his bowels when left unguarded. This was the slander published by the Privy Council to conceal the fact of the shameful murder.

The old priest grew tense as he spoke of this vicious calumny. He rose from his chair, his hands clenched shut and his body trembling. Bitterness surged within him. The angry word, long suppressed, rose to his lips. He struggled!

The great room was still. Not a finger stirred, not a cassock rustled.

But the word was not spoken. Father Gerard dropped back into his chair. His voice came soft and kind as that of a gentle confessor:

"No," he said, "the truth was this: Little John lived a saintly life and his death was answerable, and he a glorious martyr. God assisted him with so much grace that in all his torments he gave not the least sign of relenting, not any sign of impatience, not one word by which the least of his acquaintances either did or might come in any trouble. Against these things, his enemies could not so much as feign the least instance to bring forth with their forged slander, but set out a bare lie without any color or likelihood at all.

"In his life he was so famous and much esteemed by all Catholics that few in England, either priests or others, were of more credit. He was the immediate occasion of saving the lives of hundreds of persons both ecclesiastical and secular, and of the estates also of these seculars.

"How many priests may this man not have saved by his endeavors in the space of seventeen years, having labored in all the shires and chiefest Catholic houses of England?

"Verily, I think no man can be said to have done more good of all those that labored in the English vineyard."

He rose to go. Eyes filled with awe and respect followed the aged man down the long dark corridor.

"Your young men shall see visions and your old men shall dream dreams."

# Gold Is Where You Find It

BY MICHAEL McHUGH, S.J.

*Brother Carmelo Giordano, S.J. (1860–1948)*

THIS IS A STORY about Alaska, and a half pint of a man who did his share of hard work up there on top of the world. Giordano, Carmelo Giordano, is his name. A stubby bit of a fellow he was, more under than over five foot. Yet by the time he was ready to drop his tools and pick up his life's pay check, this jolly *paisano* from the Bay of Naples had put in well over his quota of work hours on the hardest mission in the world.

Giordano was a good worker, well liked and respected by his neighbors in Sant' Anastasia. He hadn't cared to take a wife and settle down in the village though. Seemed to be looking for something bigger. He was twenty-four when he thought he'd found what he was after in the Society of Jesus. They were a big organization. Had missions all over the world. That's what he'd like to be . . . a Jesuit worker brother in some foreign country . . . that is, if they'd take him in. Well, the Jesuits were glad to get him. There was plenty of need for missionaries, especially brothers. And in a matter of months, Giordano had his chance to volunteer for wilderness duty.

The wilderness he chose was the Rocky Mountain Indian country, U.S.A. That was in the year 1886 and the Northwest Rockies were almost the last outpost on the American Frontier . . . but not quite. Alaska was the last. That then was for Giordano.

In '87 the Jesuits filed mission claim along the Yukon and grub-staked Giordano and two fathers to go in and do the mining. They went in the miners' way too . . . up and over the Chilcoot Pass and down the rivers . . . but that was years before the gold rush of '97 made the Klondike and Dawson City famous and fabulous.

The Jesuits weighed a solemn anchor in Seattle's Elliott Bay and threaded their way north through Puget Sound. First stop-over was at Victoria to outfit for the trail trip. Then on to Juneau, and Skagway, where they said good-by to the deck and hit the trail.

Leg and back work from here on in. Shoulder pack up the steep

Chilcoot . . . wading thigh-deep, inching step by step through glacier-fed torrents . . . and down the quick drop to the head-water lakes. Then in a boat, link by link, along the chain of lakes and rivers into the heart of Alaska.

And about this boat. Just a thin skin of canvas stretched tight on a wooden frame. That made it light to pack . . . fine for the overland trail. But also pretty flimsy for the rough passage down the rapids. And here were no experienced gondoliers from Italy's ivory waters. Just two priests and the stocky Brother. Still they had what it took . . . courage and strong faith. And they needed both.

The first day out . . . after Brother had split and whittled enough saplings for a frame, and wooden-pegged the joints to-gether, and tugged the canvas tight, stretching a spare bit aloft for sail . . . they launched out gingerly onto the deeps of Lake Lindemann. Two at the oars, one on the helm and, they hoped, a helping-handed angel perched on the prow to point the way. Well, angel or not, there were leaks to be staunched, a whip-saw wind that tattered the slapping sail and shivered the frail shell smack against the cliff wall. Once safely out of the lakes, they were into the rock-foaming rapids. There were worries still: the lonely blood-chilling wolves at night, and mosquitoes . . . all the time . . . mosquitoes. Then, occasionally, the bloated, beaten re-mains of men who had tried the trip ahead of them . . . and had not made it. These they buried with a prayer in the heavy sand of the river bank and then pushed on.

There was plenty of room for discouragement. But they had hope too: the prospect of a church to be born and nursed into life, a cross to be rooted, seeds to be sown in these frozen acres which till now had lain barren. With such hope a part of them, they got to their goal . . . through the rapids, past White Horse, past the gold fields, and the shanty lean-tos, where grizzled miners grew rich or gray in the hunt for nuggets. Past all that to their destination . . . a frozen bit of river bank in the heart of Alaska. Here they began to build their dream . . . they piled log upon log, chinked with mud and moss, for cabin-churches, they scraped together the wood and shared the food to keep them through that first winter, they coaxed out the natives, labored to work the throaty language. Slowly, like the spring thaw along the frozen Yukon, they brought the warmth of God's love to His forgotten children.

But that is what I want to tell you about Brother Giordano. I want to tell you of his small part in saving God's Eskimo and Indian children in Alaska. His work was not to teach or baptize, he couldn't carry the graces of Mass and Communion to hungry souls, his was not to take God's part in wiping away the stains of sin. But he did save souls. The work of the priest could not have been done without the work of the Brother. The glory of Brother Giordano is in his tools . . . the axe-handle worn smooth, the palm worn rough, the tattered prayer book, dog-eared and thumbed, the medicine bag, first aid and only aid in many an accident, the few pots and pans, the wood-hungry stove . . . these are the brother's trophies, these his claim to glory.

But don't get the idea that Giordano was a wizard with tools, a magician at any and every job. Sure, he was handy. He had to be. And he was willing to work, willing to learn how. But genius, you know, is found like gold, rarely. Giordano was no genius.

Take the matter of medical work, for instance. You saw his first aid kit a while ago. Now maybe you say to yourself Brother Giordano must have been a doctor. Oh, he'd have snorted a laugh at that. He was no doctor. The most this stubby-thumbed Brother was good for was maybe to patch up a shotgun wound or sled a broken-boned native to a doctor or . . . and here his eyes would glow with memories . . . keep fighting that everlasting war against sabotage in the native digestive machinery. That last job was something of a problem, don't think it wasn't, and to meet it Bro kept a big bottle of castor oil on hand. But that was just the trouble. What good was a ladleful of light castor oil for these hardy Eskimo insides, trained from infancy to resist the heavier on- slaughts of fish and seal oil? Besides, castor oil didn't taste like medicine. They loved it, smacked their thick appreciative lips over each dose and opened wide for more. Very pleasant to the palate indeed, but quite ineffective. Well, doctor or not, Brother Giordano hit on his remedy. When the Eskimo . . . always a good actor . . . would drag himself painfully up to Bro, face screwed up tight, give-away eyes sneaking hopefully at the big bottle on the shelf, and groan, "Belly no work, big hurt," well, Bro would just mix a warm mugful of Epsom Salts. A dose of that could cure the belly-big-hurts in a hurry.

But more serious Alaskan sicknesses were his to nurse. Here medical skill was needed, which Giordano did not have. But he did have a cool reserve of common sense and brotherly concern, enough to carry him and his patients past many a scare. This one, for instance.

It happened after supper. The Father had not eaten his usual share of bread and beans, just sipped tastelessly at a cup of tea. Had a heavy headache, he apologized. That overnight trek to the sick Indian family had been hard on him. He'd got hot and dry keeping up with the racing dogs and had drunk a lot of ice water from the creeks along the way . . . He'd just finish his office here by the open stove and then get some sleep. Well, Brother was tired too. Splitting and hauling a couple of cords of stove wood had gnarled knots into his spine.

Suddenly, Father slumped to the floor. He was all shivers; his forehead was on fire. Brother pulled him to bed, got out the medicine kit and spare blankets. Next morning though, the fever was higher. Worse still, the sick man's mind was wandering . . . babbling far away dreams . . . warm mornings in Italy . . . sunshine on the white cottage walls . . . bright blue sunshine bathing the body . . . green trees. . . .

Snap out of it, Brother! Don't you get dreaming too. All that is far away. No Italy here . . . just you, all alone in this lonely Alaska. And the only friend you have here is dying.

For the other priest, the Father Superior, was miles down the river by now. He couldn't be reached till next spring. The few natives around were no help; Giordano didn't know the language yet. And there was no medicine in that small kit for what might be typhoid or pneumonia. And that brain fever. . . .

Days and days of this drifted into weeks, and then, on New Year's Eve, the wasting priest stirred and gasped weakly, "Brother, I do not expect I will see the New Year tomorrow. You will find the old boat . . . break it up . . . make me a coffin. . . . In the spring, the ice will be gone, there will be long days . . . and good trails. Take me down the river . . . bury me where the Fathers will come. Good-by, Brother, pray for me. . . ." And he slipped into fevered dreams. Brother did pray. In his fear and loneliness he clung to God and Mary for help, praying like a child. Then wrapped in his blanket he watched by the bedside till he dozed.

Brother woke stiff and chilled. A cold wind riffled his thin blanket. No wonder. The cabin door was blown wide open. A figure huddled on the doorstep. "Father, what are you doing? You will be frozen." He dragged him back to bed, and got a fire roaring. "That will kill him for sure. It must be 50 below out there."

Strangely enough, it didn't kill; it cured him. A few more hours into the new year, Brother was wakened again. "Brother, I am hungry." That was good news. Half a fried grouse was devoured with appetite, and soon the other half. A hind quarter of bear steaks bartered from the natives kept the recovery coming, and within the week, their crisis of the first winter was over. Brother Giordano felt a sense of weakness tug at him, of desperation whenever he remembered that first winter. Those bleak days, his utter inability to do much, the fright and desolation of tending a dying, delirious man. But there were more winters to come, and more crises too.

Like that other case of mind sickness some years later. There were by that time more Fathers and more Brothers in Alaska; more missions too, and they still hadn't enough men to fill all the gaps. So one of the Fathers had to bach out at an isolated Eskimo village through the weary winter. Now, being cut off from his companions, from confession, from common table talk . . . that was bad enough. But, when, in early March, even the native villagers, taciturn at best, loaded their sleds and mushed away to the seal hunt . . . well, that dropped a heavy shroud of cold white silence over the lonely priest. There was no one near for miles and miles of still snow, except one old man, half deaf and too feeble for the hunt. There was nothing for the Father to do but scratch away compiling his dictionary-grammar of the dialects. With nobody talking, he could hardly even do that.

Soon he began to feel and hear the awesome silence, it started to pound in his ears. The strain got taut, and finally, one winter night, it snapped. Stumbling out of bed in a daze, he scattered up those long hours' work of notes and manuscript, flung all into the mocking, laughing fire. Then, half dressed, he staggered out into the snow and across the tundra wastes.

Luckily for the priest, his one companion in the deserted village missed the smoke from the Father's cabin next morning. Investigating, he found the empty disorder, saw the zigzag tracks in the snow, and followed. He caught up with the wandering man close by a running stream. Out of his head, the sick man sloshed into the cold water. The native managed to drag him out, and get him back to the village.

Day and night the faithful Eskimo watched by the Father's bedside, soothing and feeding him, till the tribe returned. Then they gently sledded the invalid overland to the nearest mission station. Getting back among the Fathers and Brothers saved him. There was no medicine for a lonely mind like Giordano's laugh. Busy, hustling, bawling out his off-key tunes, Brother fanned alive the dimming coals of sanity to a merry blaze that warmed the frozen heart.

Though he worked no miracles in medicine, Carmelo Giordano did wave his magic wand over a stubborn stove, creating kitchen miracles out of the monotony of beans, flapjacks, and fish. Give him a fair enough oven, too, and he really put on a show. A warm slice of his homemade bread called forth honest admiration. But Brother would bawl out a laugh and tell all over again about the first time he tried baking bread in these drafty shacks. It was too cold to get the dough to rise. So what did he do? Why, he just took the batter, bowl and all, to bed that night under warm blankets. And the next morning? An upset bowl and his own big feet right in the middle of the wasted batch.

But talking about stoves and cooking brings up this story on Brother. He was stationed at a mission with a young priest new to Alaska, just in from the outside. This *cheechako* had a still sensitive skin to the deep drop of the winter thermometer, and he also had a sympathetic heart for those cute little Alaskan puppies. Well, one well-below-zero morning, a healthy litter of huskies were yipping and squealing for Mamma. Thought the tender-hearted: These poor little pups are freezing, I'd better warm them. He scooped the half dozen up, popped a squirming panful into the oven . . . and closed the door. Some minutes later, Brother stomped in, wondering where that sizzled hair smell came from . . . and found out. Baked pups!

Then there was the brother who took over the cooking chores from Giordano . . . and handed them back within the week with a confession: "Brother, I made a big mistake. Our tomcat that got lost last week . . . remember? Well, yesterday I cleaned the water barrel. There was something at the bottom. I fished it out. It was Tom. And I've been cooking with that water all week."

But Giordano had his own blunders to blush about. Like the summer they were pioneering a new mission post and were still in a tent, had no cabin as yet. But they did have mosquitoes. . . . Alaska doesn't have summer without mosquitoes. And Brother said to himself, I'll get rid of those pests. So he built a circle of heavy smudge fires around the tent. That mostly suffocated Brother and the priest trying to eat supper inside, still the smudge did get at the mosquitoes. But the smudge also got at the tundra moss and soon they had a running fire fight on their hands. They barely managed to pull stakes in time to drag the tent to safety. The fire kept spreading; they saved their gear by heaving it across a small creek. But the sparks jumped the creek and flamed up afresh on the other side. So through the water they waded, snatched up the scattered equipment, heaped it smoking in a burned-out spot, and stood helplessly watching the fire run freely up the valley. That fire burned on for thirty miles . . . there was no way to stop it . . . till the mid-July rains doused it down for good. Long before July the mosquitoes were back.

Wheneverafter the matter of mosquito smudge was slyly suggested, Brother retreated beneath well-bushed eyebrows. Let bygones be bygones, he'd grumble. Especially his.

Still that mosquito mishap was light loss compared to a fire that hit the missions years later. They were out of the tents then, and had slaved together a snug cabin-church combination of tight spruce logs.

Well, the winter was cold that year. They say the thermometer kept close to 50 below a good deal of the time. And that's where it was the night Father hung his wet socks close to the glowing stove to dry, rammed the fire-box chock full of wood, and tumbled between his blankets. About midnight he tumbled out in a hurry . . . the socks had caught fire; the floor was blazing. Dry spruce and the hungry fire dug in greedily. No time to save a thing, not even to grab shoes and pants. Out the door he shot and across the snow for help from the Eskimo neighbors. He shouted them awake, but they were scared and wouldn't open up . . . they thought it was a ghost or the devil himself. There he was, shivering and stamping and bellowing in long woollies and no shoes, helpless to save his burning church. When finally he persuaded them to open up they peeked out through the cracks, realized the blazing fire, and managed a pair of shoes and pants for him. But it was too late to save his church. Steaming wet ashes were all that was left. His clothes, supplies, books, language records, vestments, altar, even the Blessed Sacrament . . . nothing left. The fire gutted him completely.

That was a stiff jolt to the young Alaskan church. But . . . God knew what He wanted. Only thing to do was pitch in and rebuild.

Giordano did a lot of such building and rebuilding during his years up there. From the first day in, when he pegged that boat together with a handful of tools, to the quarter century later, with materials and men more numerous, Brother hewed and hammered in rhythm with the growing mission.

Don't imagine though that Carmelo Giordano was Alaska's one and only master builder. He was a willing workman, but Brothers like Horwedel and Cunningham were the mission builders. Now Giordano could snake down enough spruce from the hills to snub into place for a cabin. But Ed Horwedel logged his own timber, tooled a mill to saw, rip, and trim the lumber, then hammer-and-nailed it into boats, churches, schools, and homes for a full generation of Alaskan mission history.

There was Brother Cunningham too. Cunningham Construction Company, he could be called in the early days. For nearly every shack, barn, boat and sled on the many mission posts bore his trademark for construction or repair. He did slow work, they say, but steady and solid. Well, he should have. . . . He was over fifty when he volunteered for Alaska service in the Society of Jesus and he spent a full dozen years there till his heart could keep up no longer with the work he wanted to get done. I don't wonder, either, for he's the one they talk about harvesting the precious crop of short summer hay, this way. He had no team, no wagon, just three hungry cows, and a field of scythed green hay to be got in. So he'd bind it into bundles, balance a bundle on his shoulders, and pack the hay three hundred or so yards to the barn.

Cunningham was a tall man. And when the Eskimos came to the mission store to swap fish for tobacco or calico cloth, they would maneuver to have this lean Irish Brother, not the short Giordano, measure out the material. Fingertip to shoulder was the standard length, and with Brother Cunningham as the yardstick, the shrewd natives managed a long measure.

The same Brother had rigged up a code of flag signals to keep the Eskimos up on their calendar. For Sundays and Church days, he'd run aloft a white flag with red cross, the stars and stripes would fly on a national holiday, and a blue flag meant Friday . . . no meat. Well, once, Brother Cunningham bagged a brace of geese and wanted a place to hang them, safe from the dogs. The pole was free, so up they went. Hey, a new signal, shouted the natives. Brother must be inviting us all to the mission for goose dinner to-night. They all came, and finished the geese.

The Irishman had other troubles with the natives too. He could not get the hang of their language. Giordano could, though, and did. In fact, he was counted among the best at mastering the complicated idiom of the Ten'a tongue, which won the missionaries' respect as the most elusive of the dozen dialects they met among the Rocky Mountain and Alaskan Indians. The little Italian Brother was a handy guide and interpreter on the sled runs to the native villages. But Brother Bernard Cunningham was lucky to learn enough Ten'a to call a dog.

Giordano's easy tongue was no small advantage either, and he put his ability to good use. Once an Indian came to the mission to sell some fish. The fellow had two wives, both clucking after him, jockeying about like a pair of jealous hens. The harassed Indian attempted a joke! "Brother, look at me. A wife should sew the man's clothes and boots, yet I have two wives and my boots are torn and ragged." "Well," replied Brother, "it's your own fault your boots are torn. You have two women, they fight each other all day, and neither will sew your boots. If you had one wife, she would be happy to mend clothes, boots, and do all you need. By your own fault, you will go barefoot." The argument took, the advice was followed, and the boots were sewn.

But there were some native tricks that got by Giordano despite his gift of tongues. The missionaries had the practical custom at infant baptisms of making a gift to baby of enough calico for a dress. Proud parents bring in baby to be baptized, receive the few yards of cloth, and go away grinning. Next week another family brings in a baby, gets the baptism and the cloth, and departs. More grinning. "My," muses Brother, "babies surely look alike." Next week another family, another bab—"Say, that baby!" Brother does some checking, finds that one well-baptized baby has earned a lot of calico for the grinning aunts and uncles.

But the natives weren't the only ones with funny ways, these missionaries had them too. Like the long black skirt they wore. One of the priests at the mission used to keep his cassock on all day; the other changed after Mass to more convenient work clothes. It happened once that the black-skirted father tripped on his robe, slipped down the river bank and into the water. The natives ran for Giordano with the startling news, "Brother, come quick, long dress make fall. Father's wife is drowning." The dripping priest didn't see what was so funny about it, but that did not dampen Giordano, and he wrung waves of laughter from his ever-after overtelling of that story.

For Giordano was a jester, a born-to-tease practical joker. Laughter was free. For him the joke was the thing. He played them on the Fathers, he played them on the Eskimos and Indians, he even tried tricks on his dogs.

The husky has a bushy tail. Brother had a package of assorted water dyes. Would not these bushy tails be beautiful in color! So yellow, blue, green, Brother painted the tails of the wondering dogs. For his lead dog, "Garibaldi," a bright red color was selected and applied. When the pack saw 'Baldi, his tail dripping red, they took it for blood, closed in upon the poor husky and almost massacred him before the artist could drop his brush and reach for a club. Brother did not laugh as he scrubbed off the dye. A joke was a joke, but he needed his dogs.

There is Giordano for you . . . there his life of labor and laughter. A real Alaskan missionary, working to make the world's hardest mission just a little less hard for his fellow missionaries.

So for two dozen years he fished for salmon, shot for game, gardened for food, cooked, baked, kept house, making a home of a cramped and cold log cabin. He mushed his team, portaged poor trails, went snow blind, burned with frostbite. He nursed diseased bodies and comforted souls through the fever of sickness; he buried the dead in the frozen earth. He taught his clumsy woodsman hands the mysteries of river-boat machinery, he shared his sometimes scanty supplies with needy missions, learned to cinch up his belt in hunger and reluctantly pocket his companion-pipe to stretch rationed tobacco. He labored with log and plank to build cabins and churches, then saw spring floods swirl his work to the sea. What a life! He prayed and pleaded to steady the quicksilver morals of the natives, then saw white man's lust for flesh and gold wipe away the example of years.

He disciplined his own young and selfish wants, harnessed his energy into a full-teamed pull for God and His missions. He gave of himself to be a liveable partner in the often maddening monotony and winter-long isolation of tight-circled, forced companionship. He taught the new missionaries, put up patiently with their icy indifference to his hard-earned and trial-proven lessons. And he learned to be patient with himself, with his too easily tiring body, so often failing him when there was so much to be done. Patient with that easy habit of practical jokes, that so frequently frayed the nerves of his suffering fellows. He learned to be patient in his prayer, desolate as tundra, when God didn't care to talk. Patient too with obedience, when God did talk, but hidden then behind men, very human, mistake-making men.

Yet no hero he, for there was little in that life of laughter and labor that was worthy of heroic headlines. He wasn't called to give his life in any one burst of blazing glory. Like young Brother Paquin . . . told to take a sled of supplies a day's run down the coast. But this was his first winter in Alaska—and the weather is treacherous. A blizzard caught him midway along the trail, and that's where they found him, days later, frozen to death. A martyr of obedience, you might call him.

Giordano's destiny was not that, not a few months of work and then a martyr's death. No, his was a quarter century of daily grind in the mockery of martyrdom that is the average life. And even at that, his quarter century is a meager bit of what he may have hoped, say to spend forty years, to give his full lifetime, to end his life still working on the mission he helped to make. That at least would be a little crown of glory. A crown of disappointment was his instead.

Superiors decreed: Brother Giordano will return to the States. No need to tell you how he felt leaving this home he had built in his chosen wilderness. The jolly little man was sad inside as he clambered up the gangplank and stood against the railing watching his land fade through the mists.

That was obedience. God called, you answered. No excuses, no alibis, no sentiment could stand in the way.

God kept calling and Carmelo always answered—for the next two dozen years of school and parish work in the Pacific Northwest. Then, when the little man at seventy-five was getting tired, the Jesuits opened a house on the Olympic peninsula above Seattle where their young priests along the Coast might receive final spiritual training. A quiet, secluded spot on the edge of town. Still, too, save for the bonging of the clock in the old town hall.

Here the little man grew old. Ticked off his rosary of years. Went on endearing himself to everybody who knew him, went on puttering in his rocky garden, building his shrine to Our Lady, went on past his golden jubilee.

One can still see him tottering down the gravel path in the evening, the mist creeping in across the waters and a faint glow of dusk catching up the stout figure, vigorous even in his decline. The oversized shoes flap and shuffle, his cassock is too large for him, worn and patched, a few strands of scattered hair lift softly in the evening breeze.

He switches on the halo lights at his shrine and a glow of pride creeps into his eyes. He made this. And suddenly you feel a reverence for such as he. You glimpse the vast singleness of purpose; the stature of the little fellow breaks upon you. As he shuffles up the path toward the house, you hear the clock. The time is passing on.

# A Strong City

BY JULES J. PRATS, S.J.


*Brother Joseph Castiglione, S.J. (1688–1766)*

JOSEPH CASTIGLIONE put his brush on the table. He was tired from painting all day. Besides, the studio was becoming too dark from the evening shadows. Rising painfully, he walked out upon the balcony of the Imperial Palace.

He stood there leaning against the grilled railing, an old man, clothed in the long black robe of a Jesuit, gazing quietly at the evening sun, a dark crimson in the West. The cooling shades of the dusk stirred him strangely, for the fragrance of the air, opening suddenly a chamber of the past, brought him back to the time when he had stood, fifty-two years before, upon the prow of a merchant ship carrying him into the mystery that was China.

Then, how intently his dark young features had studied the sky, the waters, the speck of land looming larger in the weird green of the China Sea. A great thought was dancing in his mind and when he felt its whirling urge, he wondered if it were not too fantastic to dream of—the conversion of the Emperor of China. His cassock rippled gently in the tranquil breeze as he had stood in the fast fading light, his eyes glued to the coast. What Xavier died longing for, he was to possess.

The long months of sea voyage, the stench of the hold, the nausea, the still tender memories of recent separation, Italy, laughter, familiarity, love—were all behind him. This new world waited for the touch of his hand. There was a time when, boylike, he had dreamed of fame as an artist in Europe. Michelangelo—Da Vinci—Castiglione—it all fitted in so well. He, the genius of the continent, trained by the most brilliant and masterful artists of Milan for portrait painting was expected to take his place beside them and add lustre and glory to their renowned school. Instead, he became a lay-brother in the Jesuit Order and consecrated his talents to the service of the Divine Artist. He had caught the vision of sacrifice, of an oblation beyond hours, canvasses and oils, and so in the year 1715, he had set sail with Brother John de Costa for the Empire of China.

Years before, Francis Xavier, dying alone on the little island of Sancien, had turned his last gaze upon this vast and hidden country which he had so longed to convert. At the end of the century, Mateo Ricci and his companions set foot upon its hostile shores. Their learning and piety attracted the Emperor and soon they were made favorites of the Imperial Court. It was to continue this mission that he and Brother John were now sailing on the China Sea toward this land of destiny.

Cool night air broke into his reverie. Standing on the balcony, he was looking back over fifty-two years of service, hidden and obscure, seemingly so wasted, so futile. Softly, his face, now worn and wrinkled, broke into a quiet smile and his failing eyes sparkled momentarily as is the wont of the old in recollection of some chance memory, some glimpse of what was, some insight of events long since passed.

"And I thought that I would convert the Emperor," he exclaimed in a whisper.

Joseph laughed again to himself; then, turning back slowly into the studio he sought one of the reclining couches and lay there wearily. He was old. His work was about finished. It was time to ease up and await the angel of death. He was thinking realistically, now. The slanted roof-tops of Peking, the city he had desired so earnestly to convert, caught his wandering eyes as he looked through the huge gilded doorway into the twilight. Rising gaunt and black in the fading day, the city and the noises from the streets below—the clop-clop of wooden sandals on the cobbled stones, the cries of vendors, the sing-song of gentle voices, and the spilling laughter of running children at play—made his mind retrace itself again to the past, to the day when first he had walked upon the soil of the Orient.

It was a cold morning in December when Joseph arrived with Brother John before the gates of the Imperial Palace in Peking. White snow lay two feet deep in the streets and covered the sprawling domes of the hundreds of shrines and temples. White mist poured from their nostrils as they breathed heavily in the bitter chill and stamped their feet to keep warm in the frozen silence. Imperial guards were marching slowly up and down in front of the great dragon gates when finally they stopped expectantly. The guards halted and looked severely at the two worn travelers.

"What you want?" one of them rumbled.

"We are missionaries," exclaimed Joseph.

"Go away!" he said angrily.

"We would like to see the superior of the Christian mission," explained Joseph, undaunted by the threat of the guard's brandishing sword.

"Go away!" he repeated harshly and started to push them toward the city gates.

Father Parrenin, the Jesuit Superior, had been watching the skirmish from the east balcony of the Palace. When he saw the predicament of the two black-robed travelers, he hastened down to the gates. Quite gently he explained to the guards that they were the long-expected helpers assigned to the mission. With much ceremony and profound bows the guards apologized, and soon Joseph and Brother John found themselves being led through snow-filled gardens of the Palace to the mission headquarters. As they walked, carefully, for the close-packed snow was slippery, Father Parrenin spoke excited words of welcome. The two missionaries were greeted with even more excited cries when they entered the Jesuit house. After the first enthusiasm had died away, a warm meal of fish and rice with red wine was served to them and as they ate hungrily, their fellow Jesuits plied them with questions of home and the Europe they had so willingly and yet reluctantly left.

When they had eaten and were warmed a little Father Parrenin told them both:

"You must report to the Emperor as soon as possible. I will take you."

Joseph prepared a little speech for the Emperor. Next day he found himself in the august presence of K'ang-hsi. Kneeling respectfully with Brother John and Father Parrenin as was the custom, Joseph said:

"We have come, mighty Emperor and Lord of the Chinese, to your honorable kingdom to preach the gospel of the Lord of Heaven to you and your people."

The slanted eyes of the Emperor smiled pleasantly, shrewdly, as his long-nailed, yellow-skinned hand rubbed his bearded chin.

"You are welcome to our unworthy realm."

Joseph's young face lit up. K'ang-hsi, noting this, was attracted to him.

"What is your talent?"

"I am an artist, Majesty. I paint."

"A painter!" exclaimed the Emperor. "You are something new to us. Before we have had from your continent mathematicians, astronomers and architects. And now a painter!"

Joseph glowed with enthusiasm. He felt he was making headway already with his great plan. He had told no one of his dream.

"You will remain with us here . . ." continued the Emperor, "in the palace; and take your place among the great artists of China."

Joseph bowed low.

"I am honored and unworthy of your favor."

This was what he had hoped for. Now he could set to work to paint—each stroke of the brush would be a prayer ascending to Heaven for his Imperial Majesty, for China—and he hoped it would not go unheard. Brother John was assigned to assist the astronomers of the Empire.

The days passed into weeks and winter faded into spring. Joseph began to realize that all was not sweetness and ease in this work for the Emperor. His training in Europe had made him a painter of portraits; the art critics of China preferred nature subjects, especially the tree, in all shapes and forms. Joseph could make masterpieces with oil paints; K'ang-hsi liked water-colors. The artistic soul of Joseph rebelled at being forced to channel his art into grooves for which he had no liking and no inclination.

Again, he was required to make his shadows extremely light, since the Chinese artists did not use the contrast of light and shade. They taught him to paint in the Chinese fashion and laughed uproariously at his first efforts. With a condescending smile they told him that all the points he had neglected in the flowers, leaves, skins of animals, dress, Chinese hands and long nails, were exactly the details in which Chinese art was strictly precise. Joseph felt the heat of despair rising furiously in his soul over these chains, these formalistic nativisms imprisoning his natural genius. But for the sake of his great purpose—the gaining of an Emperor's soul—he would have to bide his time and make his sacrifice.

A year fled by. It was becoming more unbearable. He felt as if he were a dog on a leash, who must go wherever his whimsical master led him. Even on Sunday he must paint, scarcely given time for his prayers. The crushing melancholy that seized him brought temptation—he should abandon this mission as useless and return to Europe where he could paint as he wished, satisfying his genius. The illusion passed and he prayed in the little chapel of the mission that he should never again falter.

On a wintry day five years later, K'ang-hsi while hunting in the imperial parks near Peking, was overcome by a sudden illness. A few evenings later he died, leaving the throne to his fourth son, Yung-Cheng. The young Emperor favored Joseph as his father had done, yet never condescended to speak with him in person. It was the next Emperor who showed even greater attachment to Joseph. Ch'ien-lung was the ablest administrator and wisest ruler that China had had for many centuries.

One Sunday morning Joseph was sitting at his easel and painting, Chinese fashion, the picture of a fountain in a European garden. Ch'ien-lung approached and stood behind him, watching. As the fountain took shape he became curious.

"What is it, Joseph?"

Joseph put his brush down.

"A fountain, Majesty."

"How does it work?"

Joseph explained exactly how a fountain worked.

"Can you make me one for my gardens?"

"No, Imperial One. I know nothing of physics."

"Then one of your Brothers can do so. I will send a eunuch with you to mission headquarters to inquire."

So Joseph found himself standing in the presence of his Jesuit Brothers while the eunuch declared his mission to them.

"I must bring to the Emperor the man who can make this fountain. It is the will of the Son of Heaven."

The Jesuits were embarrassed. The only one who knew physics was Father Benoist, but they weren't at all sure that he could make a fountain. All eyes were turned on the priest. With a shrug of his shoulders and a calculating gleam in his eyes he nodded his assent.

"I'll try!" he said. "But you, Brother Joseph, will have to draw up the plans. I have no skill there."

Joseph consented and not many weeks later the gardens of the Emperor enclosed a magnificent stone fountain. It was made in the form of a clock, the head of some animal marking the hour, and as the hours passed, one by one, water flowed from the mouth of the animal to which the hour corresponded. The Emperor was delighted and commanded Father Benoist to fill his garden with fountains. To furnish the necessary water supply for these toys of the Emperor a gigantic reservoir had to be constructed.

The Emperor was amazed at these accomplishments. And Joseph was glad of the Emperor's delight. The warmth of their friendship grew.

The missionaries next were asked to lend their genius to beautify further the Emperor's summer palace. When Brother Joseph walked slowly into the grounds of this superb showplace of Chinese royalty he was almost overwhelmed by its magnificence and beauty. It was a gigantic city of huge parks and gardens of multi-colored flowers with a million inhabitants. In the parks, picturesque little valleys of green grass and shrubbery lay in their natural beauty between artificially erected hills. Symmetrically spaced grottoes and pavilions, painted a brilliant gold and red, shone in the streaming sunlight on tree-lined shores of blue lakes. Arched stone bridges crossed over tiny streams of glistening water. The hills were covered with trees of every kind and shape. And as Joseph looked over the whole resplendent picture he noticed white pathways weaving in and out of the gorgeous beds of flowers. The buildings had gray stone walls with roofs of green, red and blue tile. An air of opulence and splendor, antiquity and oriental luxury, was everywhere. In the middle of one of the parks, lay a calm rippling lake, and in its center, an island with a small palace of one hundred rooms.

Joseph thought that nothing more of beauty and splendor could exist. But to his amazement, on the first night he was there, a great display of fireworks lit up the neighboring palaces, the gilded boats and canoes on the lake, all the surrounding trees. The sky was bright with many colors of various shapes and designs. He held his breath at the spectacle. The Chinese without doubt had a flare for pageantry even though he did not quite agree with their ideas.

And so, here in this sumptuous palace, Joseph and the missionaries toiled summer after summer according to the whims of Ch'ien-lung. They seemed to be getting nowhere, and Joseph was becoming discouraged about ever converting the Emperor who showed, nevertheless, a genuine interest in the missionaries but only for their learning and talent. His discouragement might have degenerated into real hopelessness at his inadequacy had not another desire come and occupied his heart in place of the first transient dream.

While he went on painting what he considered outrageous scenes of nature and a blasphemy against true genius, the lesser magistrates of the realm were renewing by imperial edict the persecutions of the Chinese Christians. It was not the first time he had heard of these terrible injustices and sometimes bloody attempts to force the converts at the point of the sword and with the threat of horrible torture to abjure their new-found faith.

Even before his coming, from as far back as 1583 up to the year 1616, there were fifty-four different persecutions in the various provinces of China. When Joseph had arrived in 1715 a bad one had broken out and he had winced at the sight of so much tragedy as he watched the faithful Chinese being led through the streets in chains—to prison, to torture, and inevitably, if they did not give up their faith, to death.

When Yung-Cheng came to the throne, he entirely proscribed the Christian religion. All missionaries except those who were at Peking were exiled from the Empire. More than 300,000 Christians were without priests, destitute of all spiritual aid and comfort.

When Ch'ien-lung ascended the imperial throne in 1736, he granted pardons to all political prisoners of the previous reign, and Joseph remembered how he had hoped along with his companions that the new Emperor would annul the anti-Christian laws. But he did not do so and persecutions continued to rage.

It was during one of the worst of these that Joseph began to see how he could replace his shattered dream of conquest of the imperial soul. Since he was a favorite of the Emperor, he could intercede for the suffering Christians and have the unjust laws against them abrogated. An opportunity soon presented itself. The prime minister, Matsi, a friend of Father Parrenin, sent a message to the missionaries urging them to formulate a petition for the official reëstablishment of their religion. They came in person to present it to the Emperor. But one of the mandarins of the court influenced Ch'ien-lung to deny the petition and to issue further decrees against the Church. Joseph trembled as he heard the proclamation read from the balcony that overlooked the huge central square.

"As for the Europeans whom we have allowed at Peking, because of their skill in all the sciences, and above all, in Mathematics, the Tribunal of Rites orders that they do nothing to attract to their religion either the common people or the nobility of the Chinese Empire."

With this edict the persecutors released anew their pent-up fury. Joseph could not believe that the Emperor was responsible, so he thought of a means of interceding with his Imperial Majesty. Again

he had not far to look. The missionaries had been denied access to
the Emperor's presence—with the exception of Joseph. Father
Parrenin commissioned him to present another petition to the Emperor as he watched him paint. Joseph was happy. He had reached
the age of fifty and, up to now, had accomplished nothing. This
was his chance.

The next morning, with the carefully written request concealed
in his cassock pocket, he set to work at his painting. It was not
long before Ch'ien-lung came as usual to watch him work. It was
a pleasant morning and the sun came streaming in through the
windows of the studio. Joseph's face slowly grew sad and he drew
his brush across the canvas in tired listless movements. Turning to
the Emperor, he knelt before him, took the written petition, ridged
in yellow silk, from his cassock pocket and presented it to him.
The courtiers and eunuchs who always accompanied his Majesty
in the palace trembled at the boldness of Joseph. But the Emperor
showed no signs of anger.

"Imperial Majesty," exclaimed Joseph, "I bring you this petition
from the hands of my brothers. Do not persecute our religion."

"I did not condemn your religion," said the Emperor kindly. "I
simply forbade the Chinese to embrace it."

When he had said this, he accepted the petition and gave it to
one of the courtiers; with a gentle courtesy he spoke to Joseph.

"I shall read it; don't worry. Now go on with your painting."

Ten days later Haiwang, one of the high officials of the Emperor's household whose business it was to conduct the affairs of
the missionaries, ordered them to the palace. Joseph's hopes were
soaring. Haiwang bowed deeply to Father Parrenin and all of
the missionaries as they stood before him in eager expectation.

"Your petition," he said sadly, "could not be deliberated upon;
it is simply not fitting for the people of China to become Christians
and less so the nobility."

The priest's eager eyes clouded with disappointment and Joseph's heart sank.

"But surely," responded Father Parrenin, "his Imperial Majesty knows that we wish him no evil."

"We do not forbid your religion," protested Haiwang. "We do not say it is false or bad; we leave you free to practice it; the Chinese are better off without it."

"Then what is left for us if we can neither preach nor convert them?"

"I suggest that you forget about converting the Chinese and be satisfied that you are such favorites of the Emperor. I warn you also, to take precautions to protect yourselves from the mandarins who would wish that you be banished from the Imperial Court."

"Do you not wish to help us?" pleaded the priest.

"Perhaps!" answered Haiwang—and then left them.

Discouraged but not despairing, the missionaries returned to the mission house to plan further strategy. Joseph went back to his painting, hoping for another opportunity to speak with Ch'ien-lung. In truth, Haiwang could not or would not come to their assistance with his influence. As winter came, cold November winds whipped through the streets of Peking, tearing at the great placards that had been posted denouncing the Christian religion. Orders had been issued to condemn Christians mercilessly. The missionaries appealed again to the Emperor. Ch'ien-lung transmitted their appeal to the Tribunal of Rites. The day came when the Tribunal was to give its decision in the presence of the Emperor and the missionaries.

The court buzzed with voices of the courtiers and magistrates. Joseph and Father Parrenin with the rest of the Jesuits stood quietly in a corner of the high domed hall awaiting with the others the arrival of the Emperor. Suddenly a muscular soldier of the guard lifted a huge metal hammer and struck the great brass gong with a powerful stroke. The sound echoed through the hall and all the talking ceased. Awe and silence fell upon the assembly.

The Emperor entered with the President of the Tribunal, their sandaled feet making tiny scraping noises on the polished floor.

Joseph waited anxiously for the tribunal's decision. With a show of importance and a grandiloquent Chinese bow to the Emperor and to the assembled court, the President read a memorial of the Tribunal:

"Imperial Majesty, Ch'ien-lung, mighty Ruler of the Empire of China. Worthy foreigners from the continent of Europe. We have deemed it fitting to reject your petition. We must tear out by the roots this evil doctrine which you have brought to the Empire and which is perverting the people. It was only because you have some knowledge of mathematics that the predecessors of his Majesty, Ch'ien-lung, now gloriously reigning, full of kindness for strangers, did not expel you from the Kingdom. The foreigners from other countries are naturally very ignorant; that goes without saying.

"As for the manner of governing the people, one cannot be too severe and too exact, for the purpose of inspiring respect and fear of the laws. The religion of the Europeans is skillfully presented so as to deceive people and it is very dangerous to grant it the least liberty; the results will be bad. There is no way for us but to cling to our ancient doctrines."

The Emperor looked at the missionaries with careful cautious eyes. To Joseph he gave an apologetic smile, bowing his royal head, as if to say, could it have been otherwise he would have granted the Brother's request.

"I approve this memorial," he exclaimed resolutely. "You, good Fathers, while you are in the service of the Emperor are permitted to practice your religion freely in your churches. The Chinese people, and above all the nobility, must not do so."

With this the Emperor rose from the golden throne, and the gong resounded loudly as he and the President left grandly by the way they had come. Little by little the court was cleared until only Haiwang and the missionaries stood there alone. They faced one another. Father Parrenin had lost his meekness now, or else it was transformed and set on fire with indignation.

His white hair tossed on a thundering head and those chiseled features were aglow as he began to speak to Haiwang.

"Noble Haiwang, Prince of the Chinese Empire," he cried, "we did not come more than eight thousand miles to ask permission to be Christians, to fulfill our Christian duties, to pray to God in secret. The court, the city, the provinces, the empire, all know well that we came here to preach the Christian religion and at the same time to render to the Emperor such services as we could. The imperial predecessors of his majesty, Ch'ien-lung, and above all his august grandfather, K'ang-hsi, had our doctrine examined not by a few ignorant people, but by all the sovereign tribunals . . . and all these, after careful discussion and thorough investigation, declared the Christian religion was good, true, entirely free from the least evil suspicion, and that it was certainly never to be proscribed, and that the Chinese should not be forbidden to follow it and to enter the Church. This declaration was confirmed by the Emperor and promulgated throughout the realm. Since that time our holy religion has not changed. It is always the same. Our sacred books prove this!"

Haiwang bowed his head beneath the wrath of the ancient priest. Joseph thought he saw a change in his passive face. But it was illusory.

"We do not deny that, honorable Father," said Haiwang. But Father Parrenin would not be pacified. In flaming words he continued his passionate appeal.

"Why then does the Tribunal of Justice imprison Christians? Why does it punish them? Why does it put up placards throughout the city to make apostates of those who profess the Christian religion? Why does it do the same in the provinces? If to be a Christian is to be a criminal, we missionaries are the most guilty of all, for we exhort people to embrace Christianity. And nevertheless we are told to continue our work here."

Haiwang was troubled and seemed moved by the words of the Father.

"Honorable Father, it is the will of the Emperor; the Son of Heaven has decreed it; it must be so."

"But how shall we dare now to show our faces in public?" inquired Father Parrenin, "and how can we, covered with shame and confusion, with the odious stigma of seducers of the people, serve the Emperor in tranquility? And if we return to our country, will our lot be any better? People will say to us in Europe: 'Did you not praise the new Emperor to the stars? In how many of your letters did you not state that this great prince rewarded the good, that he treated you as well as, even better than, his predecessors had done! All Europe was glad and showered benedictions upon him. But today you are exiled from China. You must then, by your evil conduct, by some glaring fault, have obliged him to drive you from his Empire.' What, O Prince, can we answer? Will they believe us when we tell them the simple truth? Look at us then in the unfortunate position of one who can neither advance nor retreat. Does anything more remain for us than to implore the clemency of the Emperor? He is our father; can he abandon us? Shall we be the only ones who groan under oppression in the midst of the glory of his reign?"

"But the matter is settled, Honorable Father," replied Haiwang, "there can be no retraction."

"Many great tribunals spoke previously," exclaimed the priest. "Why is their decision reversed today?"

Haiwang, wanting to help them, gave them some hope.

"I do not dare to approach the Emperor today on your behalf, nor the Tribunal either; but later on I will see if I can move them to change their decision or at least modify it. Until then, say nothing more."

Bowing graciously, he left them.

Brother Joseph realized he had failed in his personal plea to the Emperor. His heart would not be stilled by one defeat. Gathering up his courage that had been so shattered by the finality of the words of the Imperial Prince, Haiwang, he resolved boldly to plead again the cause of the Christians to Ch'ien-lung.

The Old Brother, for he was growing old now, began his painting one morning soon after the discussion with Haiwang. If this attempt failed; then he could do no more. Ch'ien-lung came slowly into the studio followed by his household retinue. Coming up close to Joseph he spoke in a whisper.

"You are angry, Joseph?"

"No, Imperial One; only sorrowful."

The Emperor changed the subject for fear Joseph would plead with him again.

"This picture you are painting, don't you think that line of the tree branch could be broader?"

"Yes, Majesty," replied Joseph listlessly.

"And why do you use so much shading here?"

"It brings out the tree."

"Joseph," he said a little reproachfully, "a true artist never uses this method."

"I know, Majesty."

The Emperor plied him with more questions about the painting but Joseph was so saddened by the sufferings of the Christians and his own inability to help them that he could no longer answer. The Emperor showed anxiety.

"Joseph, are you sick?"

"No, Imperial One; but I cannot paint enthusiastically when the streets are lined with placards outlawing our religion, when the prisons and torture chambers are crowded with Chinese who will only to serve the Lord of Heaven."

"Joseph, speak no more to me about this. Your sorrow touches me profoundly."

"But, Majesty, how can we serve you, after you have done this to us? When it becomes known what you have done in Europe, will there be anyone who will dare come here to toil for you?"

"I did not forbid your religion," protested the Emperor anxiously, "you are free to follow it yourselves, but our people must not embrace it."

"We have been in China for so long a time that we might preach it," replied the brother, echoing Father Parrenin, "and the Emperor K'ang-hsi, your grandfather, proclaimed leave to do so throughout the entire Empire."

Ch'ien-lung seemed to be touched deeply by the earnestness and sincerity of Joseph.

His protestations did have some effect this time, though not too much. In a few days the Emperor notified the missionaries again that he had not proscribed the Christian religion. This was a pronouncement of momentous importance in the present persecution, but it was made known only to the missionaries and the persecution of Chinese Christians continued relentlessly. At the suggestion of Haiwang, the missionaries promulgated a note in the official imperial newspaper, which was circulated throughout the Empire, thanking the Emperor for his statement that the religion of the Christians was not officially condemned. The Emperor said nothing after this and slowly the persecution abated, and martyrdoms halted for a while. His dream had partially come true. He, Brother Joseph Castiglione, had stayed the hand of a man before whom millions fell in fear.

The years passed and still Joseph painted, always in the way that the Chinese wished and above all to please the Emperor. Slowly he became venerable; his seventieth summer rolled around. It was an ancient custom in China to honor men who had reached such years in life. Parents, relatives and friends were supposed to visit on such days, pay their compliments and offer gifts on which were traced the Chinese characters for longevity. When Ch'ien-lung learned that his favorite, his great friend, had come to his seventieth year, he wished to honor him for his long faithful service by a brilliant, public spectacle.

The Emperor sent to him a rich gift made up of six pieces of silk, a beautiful robe and other costly presents. Among these, ranking first in honor, was a scroll upon which were written four characters in the Emperor's own hand. It was a eulogy of Joseph. The gifts were prepared in the imperial palace, placed on a table draped in yellow silk and covered with magnificent and costly drapery. Eight men in imperial livery bore them on their shoulders, to the accompaniment of martial music played by twenty-four musicians. Four noblemen on horseback preceded the procession. In the rear rode a high nobleman of the court with a personal letter of the Emperor, congratulating Joseph.

The parade came from the summer palace of the Emperor to the Jesuit Church in Peking, where Joseph had gone for a short rest from his duties in the imperial studio. When it arrived at the gates of Peking, armed guards stood at attention and soldiers cleared the streets for the procession to pass. Crowds of Chinese thronged the way of the parade, eagerly guessing who it was that the Emperor was honoring. Finally it appeared before the church, which had been decorated with silk banners and garlands of flowers by order of Ch'ien-lung. The gifts were presented and received with great show of Chinese politeness and many bows. It was a triumph for Joseph as a friend of the Emperor. In his heart he knew that he had done nothing, for his two great dreams —the conversion of the Emperors and the protection of the Christians—were shattered, and he was old without much time left. Persecution had again sprung up from time to time, and he had been powerless.

Six years more had passed since this great tribute, and Joseph relaxed now on the cushions of the couch. It was dark but the moon had ascended in the blackness, a bright disk of light, flecking pale silver on his wrinkled features. He sighed. There was still that painting to finish. A few more strokes of the brush and it would be completed. He chuckled. What a useless life he had lived. But it was the way God permitted it. He had seen for some time what God wanted. If His only Son had been an apparent failure, then why not he? Was the servant greater than the master? He knew now with the strongest conviction that if the broken body of the Christ, hanging on the Cross of shame, was the symbol of tremendous failure, it had also been the supreme triumph of the ages. But how futile it did seem to paint and paint and never see the spiritual good that God used it for. And there were new missionaries now. Father Parrenin, Brother John, all had been called to the Master. Only he was left—he and Ch'ien-lung. He sighed again as he rose and walked toward his work bench. His steps were slow, his shoulders bent. He covered his picture with a cloth, for it would not do for anyone to see this one before it was finished; he resolved to complete it in the morning.

Day came and Joseph was at work again stroking the canvas with his brush. His hand was weary. It trembled. This was a picture he had not dared to paint before. It was according to his heart and his genius. He dipped in red and as he slowly dabbed the portrait, the brush slipped from his hand, clattering to the floor; his snowy white head bent gently forward, and he fell prostrate before his last work.

Ch'ien-lung came as usual that morning to sit with him. When he knelt in consternation beside Joseph, poignant horror flashed in his eyes and a pang touched his heart. Joseph, his favorite, was no more. Ch'ien-lung sent one of his courtiers for the Jesuit superior, who came in haste, bearing the holy oils. He found Ch'ien-lung gazing with a strange fascination at Joseph's last portrait.

"This picture, Father," he asked in awe, "what is it?"

The Superior looked keenly at it for only a moment. He saw the livid features, the agony, the outstretched arms, the spent frame, the skies aghast at the sight so terrible.

"It is the death of the Lord of Heaven," he said simply.

# Keeper of the Books

BY LEO B. KAUFMANN, S.J.

*Brother William Wuerth, S.J. (1906–1938)*

THE YOUNG ACCOUNTANT smiled and rose from his desk with honest ease. "Come right in. What can I do for you?"

The faces of the examiners, as impersonal as their brief cases, betrayed nothing. They had looked for a startled glance, a suspicious shuffle, a drawer furtively shut. But they must let fall no hint of disappointment. A party man disarmed by the easy smile of a lay brother was out of the question.

It was Cologne in the days of the infamous morality trials.

Perhaps it was part of Hitler's own superstitions about the Jesuits —perhaps not—but the order had come down to "frame" them with more finesse, by discrediting their legal integrity.

It was on the face of it a new and effective technique, although its pretensions, always paper-thin, have since worn themselves completely through, in the trial of Cardinal Mindszenty for "espionage and foreign currency abuses" . . . But in 1937 it could still boast of a little deception, at least by contrast with the bald hypocrisy of the "Morality Trials."

For anyone knew that the Jesuits had money dealings with Rome. They were supporting foreign missions and even their own seminary over in Holland. The new tax regulations and foreign currency exchange laws, embarrassing as they could be for all religious communities, were made to order. For bare existence sake the Jesuits would have to start cutting corners somewhere sooner or later.

Maybe the order had had its day in old-fashioned intrigue but in the technicalities of the new laws no Jesuit could hold his own against the experts, especially not this young flunky in the province business office in Cologne.

At least so the three experts allowed themselves to be more and more convinced as they gave him their coats and tightened their defenses against his sincere politeness and the young, ingratiating smile. Perhaps he was too simple to recognize trouble when he saw it.

Even the sheepish old father whom they met at the door had caught on immediately, but his various frustrated movements and inane remarks belied sufficient presence of mind to have sent an alarm ahead.

However, it would all be easy enough; but they must be careful not to overstep themselves in side issues. Let him go on smiling as long as he liked.

All would be very regular, first a few leading questions, a stern demand for proof, a request to see the files—not overbearing but official. Now a quick but comprehensive look.

"Ah yes, Meine Herren, this entry of the 14th, an evident violation . . . far worse than we had feared."

The two assistants would give the account book two officious glances through the bottoms of their bifocals. Three Nazi officials would nod in unison and straighten up like three triumphant cats waiting for the first twitch before the fatal pounce.

All was going much more easily and with far greater speed than they had dared to hope. The Gauleiter would be pleased, but there would be no point in stressing what a push-over the Jesuits had really been. Let the others keep their old ideas about Jesuit craftiness for a while. There was no advancement to be had in the new order by minimizing one's own skill and effort. If need be they could build up a fairly rational case for the Jesuits themselves.

But the stupid mouse does not even start. With his smile now only a trace around the corners of his mouth, he almost looks as if he were thinking. In a moment the disconcerting smile has broken forth again, as he reaches for the files.

The nervous old father, watching all this while, for his part, did not exactly look upon Brother William Wuerth, business secretary of the provincial's office, as a helpless mouse, and what kind of old cats he considered the financial examiners was his own business, but he did view the whole scene with ill-concealed apprehension. He knew the brother had the provincial's unquestioning confidence and that the procurator, so frequently absent in these troubled times, put everything into his assistant's hands. But right now the spiritual old man felt sure that a little bit of supernatural intervention—say a thunderbolt descending upon a certain trio of heads, or (a more Christian thought) a beam of supernatural light striking the brother just in the right spot—though not exactly to be presumed upon, would not be completely out of order either. At least some lesser grace would overtax neither the blessed spirits above nor get in the way here below. And his lips whispered a prayer as his eyes followed Brother Wuerth's deft movements through the file cards.

He took several official-looking papers from their folders and spread them out before Nazi officialdom. There was a copy of the latest foreign exchange law, now only a month old, with the pertinent clauses underlined, a certificate of permission from the foreign office, signed and sealed, a notarized account of all money transactions up to date and the thousand and one other minutiae of totalitarian red tape.

With baffling speed but really utter thoroughness Brother Wuerth went from item to item. And in the fifteen minutes or so it took him, the three officials had plenty of time to acquire an entirely new if confused outlook.

They could not decide whether to be incredulous or indignant or both. It would not be proper for finance experts to confess that they were outrun, but it would be worse still to be taken in. The worst thing of all would be to go over the papers again slowly, with the danger of having to admit that all was in order, but it had to be done.

So back they went to the beginning to start through all the papers one by one. After the first few had been checked, their frayed feelings forced a way through the expressionless faces and broke out into open bluffing and abuse. The examiners fired tricky questions; they shouted in unison, but to no avail. Brother Wuerth's composure was not strained at all, and his quick intelligence became even more mystifying than his persistent smile.

When, after a few more futile trials at other entries, complete frustration had grown painfully closer and finally certain, the leader stood up with a crisp, "Thank you, everything is in order."

Three stone faces moved to the door and down the corridor where they were met by the same mousy old father, now bubbling over with hospitality. He invited them with several respectful bows and gestures to come into the parlor for a drink of wine, assuring them in whispered tones that he had just inveigled the very best out of the brother cook. They stopped, turned a mere quarter of a turn, glared at him and walked out without a word.

As they got into the car they could see Brother Wuerth through the window leisurely putting his papers back in the files. He nodded to them with the same pleasant smile that had somehow taken on a much deeper meaning.

After the first curt order to the chauffeur there was little said in the car. There were explanations to be made to the boss, of course, but time enough for that later. If they could only figure out how the young so-and-so, who evidently belonged to an underprivileged non-Aryan class within his own order, had covered up so well, or worse yet, he had had nothing at all to cover up! They say the Jesuits were organized by an old Spanish army officer. Surely he must have added the brothers as enlisted men from the peasant classes, for orderlies at the very most.

If it had been the provincial, or the procurator himself, or at least a father, they might not have led with their chins. But wishful thinking would get them nowhere. Maybe Der Fuehrer's intuitions were right again. There was something truly sinister about the Jesuits. It was a good thing Hitler had thought better than to drag them into the morality trials.

But National Socialism would win out—first a war, then victory and a new order to last for a thousand years. The Church, always annoying and at last completely unnecessary, would be wiped out openly—in blood if necessary. And the Jesuits with all their bags full of tricks would go down with it. They sat back more comfortably in the car. Every dog had its day and the cats had their afternoons.

Two weeks later a messenger from the Gestapo offices presented a folder to the party chief in Cologne. It was a report on Brother Wuerth.

The Nazi official opened it and read:

William Wuerth, age 29, son of post office official in Merzig, etc., joined Jesuit order as a brother in 1927. Previous employment at the Mettlach branch of the firm of Villeroy & Bock. Started as office boy and bookkeeper's apprentice. Won the district competitive vocational examination held by Nazi party. Worked his way up through one confidential position after the other to top auditor. Strangely and suddenly decided to quit in 1927, in spite of blank check for advancement offered by the company.

Disappears into Jesuit order for about seven years—probably out of the country most of the time.

First reappears in 1933 in the following confidential entry of an efficiency expert in the records of a Cologne Trust Company that reorganized the local Jesuit business office: "Brother Wuerth could get a job at any time as head accountant in any big business firm he desires."

There was one final report and, of all things, from the finance office's own files, but from the time before the party had reorganized it. What was more, it was a note made by a man who had since advanced to the financial arbitration board. It read:

Brother Wuerth, the Jesuit accountant, makes an incredibly brilliant impression, and he does so in a very captivating manner.

The party bigwig leaned back in his chair and folded his hands, "Hm, very interesting, a most regrettable mistake that the examiners had not investigated more carefully first. A record must be made of possible charges of incompetency or negligence on their part, in case a need should ever arise. Certainly a less obvious approach should have been used."

But no matter now. With war more in the offing, yesterday's orders from the top had called for a change of policy. Fewer new processes against the Church were to be started, and of the ones already under way, only those that required less synthetic evidence were to be pushed.

After a few more moments of nodding reflection the official rose and put the data on Brother Wuerth in its proper place among all the rest on the Jesuits, there to await future reference in the case of Brother Wuerth versus National Socialism, just one more part of the great showdown to come.

But we know now that the first round which Brother Wuerth won so handily, proved to be also the last. For when the day of reckoning came, Brother Wuerth had long since gone to present his books to the Supreme Auditor, and the Nazi Party had gone wherever bad parties go.

And it was not, as the Nazis should have clearly seen, black magic or the Jesuitry of popular superstition that thwarted their examiners in Cologne and elsewhere. For ultimately it was only a kind and extraordinary Providence that had, among other things, endowed and prepared Brother Wuerth in no ordinary way and sent him to the Society of Jesus for its zero hour just before the war.

In the Jesuit part of the total struggle between National Socialism and the Church, the Jesuits carried the day in every encounter fought on legal grounds until in 1943, with their conquests now definitely falling back upon them, the Nazis abandoned all serious pretence to legality and sentenced the famous sociologist, Father Nell-Breuning, then emergency procurator at Cologne, to three years in prison and a $250,000 fine for "a lack of confidence in the National Socialistic State."

He had traveled from cloister to cloister of both men and women, checking the legality of every move, and the only charge the Nazis could make was that the permissions he had acquired six years before in Brother Wuerth's time to send money into Holland must have been obtained by fraud. They substantiated this charge with the amazing evidence that Father Nell-Breuning was a Jesuit and "Jesuit" according to the dictionary meant "one given to deception."

In checking the Society's own books, Brother Wuerth had also gone from house to house, but his work was done, when at the outbreak of hostilities abroad the Nazis decided on a truce at home. Otherwise he too might have been honored by the singular justice of a Nazi trial.

With or without such a distinction he need not blush to find himself in this collection of giants chosen almost at random, of saints and martyrs and heroes around the world. His ticket for general admission consists of a solid interior life, while his reservation lies not only in the great debt owed him by his fellow German Jesuits but in that he exemplifies the type of brother whose professional work relieves the Jesuit priests of much that they cannot do half so well and which, as foreign to their particular training, most of the priests had better not do at all.

How Willy Wuerth acquired both a religious vocation and his business sense is the burden of this account.

William Wuerth, the second of five in a middle-class family, was born in 1906, just long enough before the first World War to carry always a vivid impression of primitive but terrifying air raids in his native Saar. And the Saar itself with its dingy coal fields and towns contrasting strangely with the freshness of vine-covered hills seemed to leave its own contradictory marks on Willy's character.

Everything had pointed to the best in education for Willy. His teachers recognized in him a talented if restless pupil. And the parish priest, with an eye always open for possible vocations to the priesthood, was not slow to suggest to his father that such talents be liberated. As a post-office official, his father held a secure and well-paying job, and desired nothing better for his son. But all these people and circumstances had not reckoned with Willy himself. He simply refused to be educated, and that because of some idyllic notions he had about being a flower gardener. He could think of nothing worse than a school bench unless it be the swivel chair of an office.

In the classical tradition of hagiography (which in spoken English means lives of saints and holy people) such flouting of parental desires would have to be twisted around to an edifying interpretation or at least so watered down as not to be positively disedifying. But since the plain simple facts, as put down in Willy's German biography, do not easily lend themselves to a pious or even an indifferent interpretation, the incident would have to be passed off as having taken place before his conversion.

Some edifying reflections can be drawn from the fact, however, that his childish willfulness was to be the unwarranted occasion of great good later on. But since it is hardly possible that Willy was thinking of such a future at the time, full credit must be given to the Divine Providence that knows how to draw good out of evil whether it be through the mistakes of saints or the stumbling along of just ordinary folk. In any event when Willy had finished the minimum of schooling required by law, his father, undoubtedly a very patient man, set out to find him a gardening apprenticeship. But the good father's position and diligence were no match for the inflation and economic recessions of post-war Germany. The net result of his efforts was no gardening job for Willy—in fact no job at all.

But Willy was not to be beaten by a little thing like inflation, so he set out to find his own job. The same day he uncovered an apprenticeship in the office of the Mettlack Branch of the Villeroy & Bock Industries.

He must have been very realistic and adaptable, after all. For the incongruity of a sworn gardener, a lover of the great outdoors, the pruning knife, the lilacs and the tulips, turned office boy, could not have escaped him even if his friends and relatives allowed it to.

With fresh air, the sky and his own fond desires realistically abandoned or conveniently forgotten, he made his way from one position to another with a speed that can only be explained by native genius. With an eagerness that belied all former lack of ambition he grasped every opportunity for advancement, including night school and a membership in an accountant's aid association. It was at this time that he won the Nazi's competitive exam in auditing.

Even in later years, burdened as he was with the modesty and self-abasement of religion, nothing could make him more enthusiastic than a question about his many confidential assignments with Villeroy & Bock.

In fact, if things had taken their natural course, he could very easily have risen to the dubious honor of being denazified in the best of company—along with innocent and not too innocent German industrialists.

And all this before he had even reached man's estate, for he was not yet eighteen when he did a strange and disastrous thing. He became a Jesuit brother.

His active and enthusiastic membership in the local sodality is the only key we have to how or why it happened. But one vocation like Willy's would be in itself a happy commentary on the virility and effectiveness of the German sodalities that had just been reorientated to the original ideal of selection by the Jesuit fathers now fresh from the exile originally imposed by Bismarck.

With his mind made up, nothing could stop Willy, neither his present salary nor a blank check of advancement offered by the firm.

Maybe there was an element of the purely natural in it all, a sudden relapse into his childhood distaste for desks and books. In such an obvious rebellion against his surroundings there is a possible explanation for his not wishing to be a priest, but he could hardly have become a brother with his eyes closed to the fact that his business training would be remembered, and that, in all likelihood, he would end up sooner or later where he came from, in an office, behind a desk.

Further than such general surmises no one can go in that mysterious realm where free will and grace meet under the guiding hand of Providence to effect a kind of harmony in every true religious vocation, to make it the very best not only for the individual but for his order and for the whole church.

We cannot see Willy Wuerth sitting for long hours worrying and disputing about what is the most perfect religious vocation in itself, the most perfect balance between action and contemplation, and just how lay brothers can claim the *"tradere contemplata"* of St. Thomas at all—trying to share with men the fruits of divine conversation while tied down to works that might estrange them from both God and man.

But we can well imagine his sudden but certain awareness of what God wanted of him and his jubilant submission to it as the most perfect thing for himself. That is the way insight works.

One whose whole life and work was so providential would not have missed the old commonsense truth that the religious who does his best in the Order and grade to which God by interior or exterior circumstances and graces has called him need never worry that the perfect balance between prayer and work will ever be wanting to him or to the Church as a whole because of him. And aware of it or not, Willy completely avoided that great danger of illusion which is the lot of all those who seek only for the most perfect under the assumption that God could not have called them to anything else; or finding themselves already called, proceed, under the same assumption, to mutilate either their own institute or the traditional doctrine or both.

Be that as it may; William Wuerth now disappeared into the Jesuit order in more ways than the Gestapo sleuths had later imagined.

He disappeared into the kitchen of the seminary in Valkenburg, Holland, which the German Jesuits had not yet moved back to the fatherland both because they were well established there, and because a long tradition of exiles had taught them not to be too hasty.

The brilliant and lively young office worker, now fourth or fifth cook, did not immediately acquire all the virtue needed to carry on calmly and religiously under the pressures, and dead-lines, and continual frustrations of a large community kitchen. As the

Germans say, "He occasionally risked his lip and burned his nose badly." Which being rendered into impolite but expressive slang means: "He put his foot into it by shooting his mouth off too much."

But many another Jesuit brother got his start towards heroic sanctity in the same place, and many a Jesuit priest looks back with wonder at the example of incredible patience he received when, during his own month of supposedly helping in the kitchen, he did little more for the cause than add to the brother cook's eternal merits.

Brother Wuerth had to learn the hard way, but learn he did. Looking back when he was well established as the provincial's secretary he had only pity for those young brothers who had no period in the kitchen. He feared that without a lesson in this hard school of self-control they might be ill-prepared for later trials.

Not for four years did he receive his release from the kitchen stove, but in the meantime his restless mind had picked up Dutch and Lithuanian, and more important for the community, he had learned to cook.

But his time of trial was not yet over, rather it was really just beginning. He was sent next to be a bookkeeping assistant to an old Brother Altenkampf in the provincial's office in Cologne. Brother Altenkampf was set in his ways, and his methods were badly outdated. It must have been a severe test for the young champion accountant of Merzig, trained in the modern business methods of a large German firm, to lend a hand with ancient methods in their futile struggle to keep the Jesuits' international connections and property abreast of fluctuating foreign currency rates and to cope with modern tax laws.

But Brother Wuerth was no longer a novice but a veteran completely equal to his task. He kept his place as an assistant and did nothing to hurt the feelings of one who, though hopelessly old-fashioned, had "borne the heat and burden of the day." He even learned and adopted Brother Altenkampf's methods while he patiently bided his time.

And it was not too long in coming; after three years he succeeded Brother Altenkampf. With a determination and speed that were equal to his former caution and consideration, he reorganized the whole office. On his own initiative but with full approval from above, he called in the efficiency experts of a trust company to help him. It was at this time that the business expert immediately recognized Brother Wuerth at his real value and carefully noted down his opinion: "Brother Wuerth could get a job at any time as head accountant in any big business firm he desires."

After this reorganization he was to have exactly five years, from 1933 to 1938, at the work for which he was so well prepared and which he now liked immensely. They were crucial years and loaded with work. For if the Jesuits were not unaware of the gathering storm, neither were they slow to make use of the young genius that God had seemed to provide from nowhere in Brother Altenkampf's old position. Besides taking over the books for the head procurator of the province he soon became general trouble-shooter for all its houses. Whenever a procurator's office ran into difficulties Brother Wuerth had to go there to help out, or most usually to take over the whole business. Once for a whole year during the illness of the father procurator in the large diocesan seminary of St. George (taught by the Jesuits in Frankfurt) Brother Wuerth took over all the business. Every month he spent eight days there putting things in order before taking up where he had left off at Cologne. Superiors who had got themselves into financial troubles immediately sent for Brother Wuerth. With so many opportunities he developed an astonishing knack for teaching others, and Jesuits who had prided themselves in knowing nothing about business suddenly found themselves learning fast and liking it.

But with all his dealings with superiors and important fathers he never let himself begin to slip out of the sphere of his fellow brothers. He remembered those at Valkenburg especially and kept his eyes open and used his position to obtain whatever he thought they could use, from material for the carpenter shop to new equipment for the astronomical observatory. The brothers themselves knew from experience that there was nothing too little or too big for his attention where they were concerned.

Like many another Jesuit who must spend his life in more prosaic work, it had been his first and most ardent desire to go on the missions. But Brother Wuerth sublimated his loss by making it his hobby to collect provisions for the sailing missionaries and by packing the trunks himself.

Of his private spiritual life little need be said after even a bare recitation of the facts of his religious career. Such exterior work and such abounding charity could not have sprung from anything but a deep interior life. His confidant and present successor in office, who also wrote the short account of his life, cannot seem to find enough adjectives, even in German, to describe his hero's lively kindness and cheerful self-sacrifice. But he frankly admits that Brother Wuerth's life, devoted, as it continually was, to bringing order out of chaos, did not run minus the problems and the difficulties of inner conflict, and his closest friend was the first to see that the young brother had his own interior into which no one but his spiritual father could enter. Hence of his lights in prayer and private virtues he was reticent, but when it was a question of an external fault or defect he was the first to admit it and could discuss it most objectively.

And all the time he was fully aware of his worth and of the fact that his superiors considered him irreplaceable. This at an age when the scholastics or future priests are still carefully watched over as they press the hard schoolroom benches during interminable classes and lectures. Brother Wuerth was in the midst of all the important business transactions of the province, and those affairs with which he was not directly concerned he could easily surmise. Yet he did nothing that could be interpreted as trying to foster a sphere of influence for himself. Throughout it all he remained as sincerely modest as when he left the kitchen at Valkenburg. And already before his early and unexpected death he had done everything in his power to prevent his being an indispensable man by preparing, as best he could, two younger brothers to take his place.

His death came on the feast of his confrere, St. John Berchmans, November 26, 1938. It was a strange death, almost too distinctly twentieth century for one whose religious life is considered worthy of being recorded. St. John Berchmans had died so properly. He is often pictured with his crucifix, his rosary, and his rulebook in his hands at one and the same time. He actually died that way, and from causes that were very becoming. His death was brought on by a combination of the Roman fever (which must be very holy since it carried off so many saints we read of) and overwork preparing a public defense of all scholastic philosophy, joined with an order, imprudently given but carried out through obedience, of showing some pious brethren the holy places of Rome. A hagiographer could ask for nothing better.

But with Brother Wuerth it was just another accident. He was on one of his constant treks back and forth across Germany, possibly just one jump ahead of impatient creditors or Nazi examiners. He had just left Koblentz where he had worked in the procurator's office for three days. The books must have balanced easily for a change, since those who saw him last remembered that he was in particularly high spirits and probably without the lest presentiment which a holy man should have so shortly before death. He was going to Treves but this time on a motorcycle that he was breaking in for the missions. It was a miserably wet and foggy late afternoon when he ran into a freight truck and died a short while later.

There is nothing beautiful or romantic about automobile accidents. They are bloody and dirty and ugly. The crowd that gathered around, even the good Catholics among it, could have noticed little resemblance between the dying Brother Wuerth and the death-bed scenes of the saints they had ever heard of. He was not even in clerical clothes as he lay crushed and bedraggled on a concrete highway. And even if they could have joined such lofty thoughts to the almost animal pity that wreck victims evoke, their senses were glued, each to its own unpleasant object, the wail of the sirens, the smell of spilled gasoline and dirty steam, discolored and nauseating, the grimy, blood-stained features.

But as the curtain of his senses was slowly drawn back for the brother himself, the crowd around him faded, and a new group seemed to take its place. At its head he could make out what looked like a once proud old Spanish hidalgo with a round-faced Belgian youth smiling recognition at his side. The old captain was drawing up the men of his company as if, to all intents and purposes, he were actually assembling them to welcome Brother Wuerth.

The good brother was all confusion and just as surprised as the crowd on the road would have been, could they have seen what was going on beyond their ken.

He could not believe his ears when the young Belgian took his hands, remarking how privileged he was since on his own feast day he need not wait his usual turn behind more important people.

It was a strange company as they came forward one by one. All eyes were fixed on Brother Wuerth as if they had known him for a long time. They were men from all over the world, cardinals and princes, great scholars and doctors of the church, heroic martyrs and great missionaries. Each one took his hands and bade him most welcome, but he could only mumble some confusion in return. Whatever this was, and whoever they were, it was all too good to be true.

But slowly the great realization began to force itself upon him. And when an old father he had known at the novitiate embraced him with what felt more like a good slap on the back and said, "Great work, Willy. Just wait until you see what's in store for that whole creation of the Nazis," and then added, "Well, don't just stand there; we turn out like this for any Jesuit that's worth his salt," Brother Wuerth knew that it could not be far from true.

And when last of all the old leader himself came forward and took his hand with a proud and fatherly smile saying, "Well done, my brother," he finally found himself and answered "I thank you, Father Ignatius."

And even while he said it the strange company was gone, and every trace of rapture with it. Waves of pain swept through a body still desperately clutching for life. He fought to focus his eyes on the blurred faces bending over him, but the effort was too much. With more confidence than he had ever dreamed of, he settled back to await his Master and Judge.

Back at Koblentz the large delegation that accompanied their pastor and his assistant from Merzig for the funeral was a great consolation for Willy's parents. The large assembly of Jesuits from all over the province was also a wonderful honor and comfort.

But for the assembled Jesuits themselves there was little comfort in numbers. Knowing the reluctance of superiors in allowing travel for the best of causes they could see in each extra face only further proof of how much the province owed Brother Wuerth and how much it had lost.

They laid him right beside the cloister of their old friends from St. Ignatius' day, the Carthusians. Maybe the Carthusians, wholly contemplative as they are, could have seen it all more clearly although the Jesuits were men of faith too. But faith alone can never see too clearly. It could and did assure them that all would come out right in the end, but it could not demonstrate that the work of their irreplaceable man, just when the Nazi persecution was at its worst, was no longer really needed.

True, they had many things yet to suffer. The Nazis would plan to gather them all into one concentration camp—for purposes we need hardly guess. A number of them would be there already, some to drag themselves forth on V-day, others to remain. But out of all the material ruin the German Jesuits arose not only intact but strong in spirit with their prestige enhanced immeasurably. When the cards were down all could see.

Ironically enough Hitler's morbid fear of Jesuitry would itself furnish the turning point. The German in them was indignant

when, after being drafted along with everyone else, they were suddenly discharged as unworthy soldiers, but the Jesuit in them
broke forth into one of Brother Wuerth's disarming smiles. There
just wasn't anyone, after all, who could balance books, like the
Master Accountant who lived upstairs and before whose scrutiny
every deed on heaven and earth was made manifest. A shame
Hitler hadn't known that in advance!

# Accidental Aureole

BY THOMAS J. FLYNN, S.J.

*Brother James Kisai, S.J.* (*1533–1597*)
Declared a Saint  1862

SAINTS DO NOT HAPPEN: they are not simply a product of heredity, environment, or the conditioned reflex. They are the workmanship of an artist who creates and coaches the personalities he chooses; they are planned, set apart, and especially loved. It is not sufficient to look upon them as supremely integrated individuals, or heroes in the combat of life, or religious geniuses. It is nearer the truth to say that saints are the pivotal personalities around whom swings the Divine government of nations, epochs and the movements of society.

Who are they though? The Church does not and cannot make a mistake when she reveals to us their names. And it is here that the hagiographer enjoys an illumination which no other biographer can possibly claim. For he knows with serene certainty the most important single fact about his subject: he knows that he so lived that he saved his soul, and that from his earliest to his last day he was the object of a mysterious, infallible and loving Divine predestination. In the light of this fact, all the elements of a life fall into focus and take direction. Without it, any biography must always perforce remain incomplete and up in the air. For it is not up to us to pass final judgment on any man. It is up to God to do that, and, thanks to the Church, He has told us what his final judgment is in the case of saints.

That is the most important single fact we know about St. James Kisai. He was a saint. His life was exceedingly obscure, as almost befits a Brother, usually so little in the public eye. Yet with slim clues and the sure witness of the Church, we have reason to believe that the outline of his life gives some insight into his destiny.

## THE BOY

The air was alive with the silver tinkling of tiny bells. Along the shore cruised silken-bannered scallops of jostling holiday-goers and in the hills wandered festive groups out to enjoy the cherry-viewing time. Boys in masks and costumed wings of hawk and falcon called to one another as they darted in and out of crowds. Women in richly brocaded kimonos, their long black hair piled high into a gleaming knot and entwined with flowers, made circumspect progress on wooden platform sandals, one hand dawdling a colorful paper parasol in graceful arcs as they leaned on the arm of husband or consort. The men, short hair shaved on the top for ease in wearing the military helmet, and elegant in the stiff folds of fine robes, smiled at the women's birdlike cries of wonder and delight.

The boy, Kisai, suddenly drew up short. On the path below he saw two parties meet, each waiting for the other to give way. On the left was a gilded palanquin, borne by four carriers in homespun, and from inside emerged the painted face of a Kuge, court noble and effeminate relative of the shadowy Mikado. Blocked in front of him, tautly astride a fiery little thick-necked horse, was a Samurai and his retinue of three. The Samurai sat motionless, his fine-cut lips curved in a contemptuous smile as he eyed the ornate palanquin. Then the Kuge spoke quick words to his carriers, and waved a languorous fan as he was lifted aside to let the Samurai pass by. The boy's eyes followed the horsemen in admiration. Theirs was an iron discipline: Bushido, the Way of the Warrior! Well, it was necessary in these degenerate and ruinous times. The distant Mikado, living in the crumbling palace at Kyoto (Miako), was little more than a legend. Even the Shogun was General supreme in title only. Japan had become but a welter of atomistic fiefs warring on one another. Trickery, disloyalty, deception were the accredited weapons of soldier, Samurai and General; it was every man for himself. Kisai was seventeen, but he was sure there was little chance of his rising to the rank of Samurai. Yet his parents were affluent enough for those apocalyptic days, and they insisted on his regular attendance at the school of the bonzes. And he was an apt pupil of the monk's lore. They instructed him in calligraphy and pictorial design; he learned the rudiments of flower arrangement (difficult art!) and, most arduous of all, had become initiate in the esoteric cult of cha-no-yu, the Tea Ceremonial. It would be a long time before he were master of that, but at least he had learned the outlines of its labyrinthine ritual.

Still, his mind was weighted with pity at the mass of his fellows laden with an intolerable feudal yoke and with little chance of enjoying the esthetic delights of taking tea. Two-thirds of the crop forfeit to the landlord; that was the bitter rule. That is, if anything could be salvaged from the ubiquitous scourges of bandit soldiers and bandit bonzes. Bonzes, whose twin avocations were war and beggary! Telling their beads, giving oracular or fantastic answers to religious questions, fingering the sword underneath the voluminous black and white robes, and all the while watching for the hint of an opportunity to gain. Could it be that such men truly represented another world?

On a blue day Kisai would be awakened by the streaming sun as it touched off the faint firecracker explosions of the morning lotus popping their folded petals. The way to the temple school led through intricately patterned fields of rice and wheat and soya. On an arched stone bridge he would pause to scan the quick carp in the jade green waters beneath. Could it be that, like men, they too were caught up in the endless cycles of life and death? On the other side he admired the cunning composition of a carefully landscaped garden: clipped firs balanced with maples and trimmed pine, studded with shining pools, encasing a rash of rose and gold azaleas that filled the eye with flame. And there, over against him, loomed the vast and shadowy temple. What curious and intricate symmetry! A long series of stone slab steps precisely bordered by a dense green hedge, leading into lacquered red pillars supporting heavy beams carved in fantastic design, crowned by rolling, thickly-shingled, upswept eaves.

The temple garden was somber with weighty stone lanterns. And inside, the sacred place was troublous with shifting shadows through which one could catch the gleam of walls adorned with golden idols, demonic in mien or sometimes transfigured in meditation. And there, in a deeper recess, silent and implacable, rose the huge cross-legged Buddha, inscrutable gaze turned inwards and placid hand clasping the lotus of enlightenment.

Who could interpret the far-fetched parables and undecipher-able narratives of the bonzes? When they parried his naive questions the boy was annoyed by the mockery lurking in their smiles. Older men were not hesitant in ascribing to them dark practices and he began to discern that everywhere a parody of virtue brought but a parody of respect. Let that be as it may, still, Chuko, loyalty to family and ancestors, was his ideal; nothing was more fundamental than that. And his religion was Shinto, for that was the religion of Japan. As the boy understood it, Shinto consisted in worshipful reverence of nature and ancestors, ancestors who were or mingled with gods, the Kami and Hotoke. But his bonze teachers, of the Zen sect of Buddhism everywhere so popular in Japan and notably so here in his province of Hizen, had explained to him that Confucianism and Zen crowned and completed Shinto. Zen! It meant, liberation through nondiscrimination. A trenchant formula. What is non-discrimination, the boy had asked. The answer was oracular: it was the renunciation of ideas, distinctions and questions. "You ask: what is life and death, what is bondage and suffering? You would not ask these questions if you understood, and if you understand you do not understand these questions." Nirvana, the Outer Bank, the Great Affirmation: it was to this that Zen proposed to lead one. Experience without discrimination. It was hard to understand, but there it was, the doctrine of the bonzes! A pervasive and corrosive scepticism and the final renunciation of intelligence, was that the teaching of Zen?

These were hard problems for a boy. Better to bend his mind to practical things such as the four virtues of the cha-no-yu. Urbanity, purity, courtesy and imperturbability. They were hard to acquire, but not so hard to understand. Manners made the man, and here was a fixed ideal for Nipponese manhood.

There were temptations. He had friends, young men from nearby littoral estates, who had undertaken the dramatic career of piracy. They told of exciting raids on Korea and down the coast of China as far as Shanghai. Well-armed, in concert and sufficient numbers, it was not too hard to swoop down on a town, raze and pillage it and seize women and hostages. And better far, they claimed, than enduring the harsh penury of Japan. Wealth and adventure, if one would take one's life between one's hands!

No, said Kisai. Something better would come. If only some great leader would arise to restore the Empire! He did not know—how could he?—that two of the greatest names of his country's history were already alive, still younger than himself. In Owari the brilliant but eccentric young Nobunaga was already on the point of driving his tutor to suicide from exasperation. And in the same province a farm boy of thirteen, cutting wood and carrying water, would one day dream of becoming the Caesar and Napoleon of the Orient, Lord of the World. Even the farm boy's family were nonplussed by his boundless energy and invention. Not a few called him "Monkey" because of his unprepossessing physiognomy and penchant for playing Tarzan. The world would hear more of him under several other names, the last being Taikosama and Hideyoshi.

It was 1549, a memorable year. For on August 15 the Gospel of Christ was first heard in Japan, ancient stronghold of the gods. The accents were halting but of shattering power, and the voice was the voice of Xavier.

### THE CHRISTIAN

No other people in the Orient delighted the Apostle as much as did the Japanese. He was filled with admiration for their quick intelligence, courtesy, curiosity, and iron resolution. Later Jesuit missionaries would write that Japanese seminarists seemed able to learn as much in three months as many European seminarists could in three years.

Yet Xavier's progress was slow and disappointing. He knew but little Japanese and relied completely on the linguistic talent of his companion, the Jesuit Brother Fernandez. He did not tire of repeating that no people would make better Christians than the Japanese. Yet everywhere he found this great people enthralled to Satan. There were prevalent in Japan, he noted, three terrible

vices: (1) idolatry (2) sodomy and (3) infanticide. They infested
the social structure from top to bottom and were far more fearsome than the economic slavery in which the empire lay. Xavier
knew that a strong man who has long been master of a house cannot be easily dislodged. The Kingdom of Christ would progress in
Japan only with labor and frightful sacrifice.

We do not know when St. James became a Christian, or through
whom. *Dei gratia praeventus* says the Bull of his canonization,
through the anticipatory action of divine grace, he was converted
by one of the first companions of Xavier. Who? Was it Brother
Fernandez himself, or the most noted of all the missionaries of that
epoch, Brother Luis Almeida? Almeida at the age of thirty was already a celebrated name among the merchants of the Far East.
Then he had suddenly renounced his wealth and become a Brother
of the Society. Since he was also a skilled physician, Superiors
made use of him in the province of Bungo, where the local daimyo
contributed land and he employed some of his former wealth to
build a thriving hospital. In this hospital, records show that Almeida treated nearly sixty thousand infirm, himself in charge and
specializing in surgery of ulcers and fistulas. From all over Japan
came patients to the hospital and annexed maternity ward. But
from this and other social works, the Jesuits discovered to their
sorrow that proportionately few converts resulted. The people
were dominated by feudal daimyos and were reluctant to do anything without their consent and approval. It soon became evident
to the Jesuits that real progress could be made only by working as
much as possible from the top down. From that time on, Almeida
had become a *perpetuum mobile*, incessantly contacting feudatory
powers and winning their favor for the new religion.

It meant endless disputes with the bonzes. But the Brother was
not slow to utilise European knowledge of the natural sciences;
deficient as it was, even the Physics of Aristotle was immeasurably
superior to the fantastic cosmogonies of the bonzes. Tact, learning, doctrine, self-devotion, prayer: they won admiration, then
a trickle of converts, then tens, then hundreds. Powerful protectors

of Christianity arose, such as the daimyos of Bungo and Arima. The Portuguese traders insisted on making much of the despised missionaries. And Portuguese trade was itself not something to be despised. It meant above all the introduction of firearms for protection and conquest of hostile dynasties. With the blessing of Portuguese trade, more than one daimyo began to see possibilities of making himself master of Japan.

It was evident too that the missionaries had close connections with these sought-after merchants. It began to appear that in some ways it was not disadvantageous to become a Christian or, at least, show them favor. Add to this that if the new doctrine be assayed in contrast with the cynical mythologies of the bonzes it showed in quite a good light. In the new crop of Christians then, not all were of equally deep, and some were of artificial growth.

It could have been Brother Almeida who converted James. More likely it was the most fabulous of all Japanese Coadjutor Brothers, the nearly blind, ugly, clowning, minstrel singer, Lawrence. It could have been that one day on the corner of a muddy street Kisai paused a moment and mingled with the curious crowd surrounding the ballad singer. There was a skilled recitative of the legendary birth of Yamota, land of the gods, the battle prowess of the Samurais of Taira, and the unbelievable story of Momotara in the Island of the Devils. The zither and his stories gave the Brother entrée all over Japan. And then, at the end of some old tale, when the faces of his audience were relaxed and pleased, that practised voice would assume a new tone, and a subtle change worked in the fat and comical form. "But now I will tell you not a story, but the truth. The fact is that the Kami and Hotoke are men, not gods. There is but one God, the Creator of the World, and he has sent His only son to earth, whose name is Jesus Christ. . . ." The audience became tense, unconvinced. Then a new Lawrence appeared, patient and supple in reasoned dispute, profound, yet cautious. Sometimes his adversaries would lead him onto dangerous ground. The cunning Brother would assume a didactic air: "The question is too difficult and complex to be treated this evening. . . ." That night he would consult with a Jesuit priest companion. The following day brought the theologian's response.

It could have been Lawrence that converted James. We do not know. But we do know that the man who converted him, and the day of his conversion were remembered with thanksgiving when finally he hung on the cross.

## THE MARRIED MAN

James Kisai had no inkling that his marriage would one day end in divorce. Like many a married man, his honeymoon had been cloudless, and he had believed it would last forever. The priest who had married the two Christians had explained that this Sacrament was for life and their soul's sanctification. They had been blessed with a son, and to his boy the saint had explained the gift of God. It was, he said, a gift to whose reception penalties were attached. Christianity was still a fringe religion, a marginal and despised sect. Former friends were not slow to make mention of tendencies towards treason. How could one be loyal to Chuko if one claimed that outside Christianity there was no salvation? The first auditors of Xavier had wept when he told them that many of their forefathers were in Hell. The amused and non-committal smiles of the bonzes changed to hate when they had discovered the absolute intransigence of the new religion. There were but two ways, said these new foreign bonzes: Christ's way and the devil's way.

The doctrine was as strange as the appearance of the preachers. Japanese legend tells us how the European Jesuits looked. Father Organtino, who was to be St. James' Superior, a veteran of many years and of much influence in the Empire, is described as making the following impression on Nobunaga's court: he "was a man different from ordinary men; he was more than nine feet high, head small, color red, eyes round, teeth like those of horses and whiter than snow, his hair and beard of rat color, his age appeared to be about fifty, his coat appeared to be made of cotton; . . . on his head he wore a vulgar looking bonnet; in his bosom he carried a perfume which diffused odors all around. His mode of salutation was by putting his feet together, placing his hand on his breast, and bowing low." And Father Luis Frois, the celebrated historian of that epoch in Japan, was "ten feet and-a-half in height, his hair and beard were yellow, and his dress the same as Urugan" [Father Organtino].

Emphasizing the strangeness of doctrine was the violence encouraged or permitted by the foreign missionaries. The bonzes were openly denounced for their depraved lives, and on occasion some over-zealous Christians took it upon themselves to invade and destroy the temples of the gods. Profaning the Kami and Hotoke! Was it not treason? It became apparent that this new religion, if allowed to progress unchecked, would sweep away the most sacred of Japanese traditions. The bonzes were the dedicated guardians of these traditions. So it was that Kisai, newly baptized James, and his wife became accustomed to the climate of threats, warnings, and a sudden stone crashing through the wicker walls of their house at night.

Would the little community of Christians never grow? They had lived underground so long, surviving by fits and starts. Then, perhaps one Sunday morning after Mass, when the priest had come out to pass on the news, they had first heard of Nobunaga. His was a name to change the whole destiny of Japan. Reports said that he was a military genius, that province after province had fallen under his sway. He was restoring the prestige of the Emperor and the Shogun, and, miracle of grace, he was favorable to Christianity!

Himself an unbeliever, disavowing the immortality of the soul and intent only on his own apotheosis, Nobunaga was nonetheless the unrelenting persecutor of the bonzes whose doctrine he condemned and whose conduct he stigmatized as the prime cause of the national disorder. It was to be the mature judgment of the Jesuits that this man was the unwitting tool of Providence in the spread of Christianity in Japan. From the beginning he admired the foreign Fathers, the purity of their lives and splendor of their doctrine, the tireless courage and learning with which they pursued the goal of evangelization. He kept them at his court and sought their advice. Nor were their connections with the Portuguese traders unnoticed; all in all, they were powerful allies in his war against the bonzes.

But even with growing favor for the Gospel, there was no lack of suffering and misesteem for Christians. Japan was a pagan land, weighted with an immemorial pagan cult. As the years passed, the pagan Kisai became the seasoned Christian, James, singly intent on an inner life. It was then the blow fell.

His wife apostatized. She confessed that she had never really been convinced of the new religion. When the old daimyo had been won over, she and nearly all the families of the region had followed his example. But his son, the new daimyo, had never allowed himself to be baptized. He was, moreover, suspicious of Nobunaga's ambition and his affection for the Christians. Her family insisted that she was in truth a traitor to her own heritage by renouncing Shinto. And the ties of the old cults were strong. . . .

James reasoned with her, wept, prayed. She was resolute. What of their son? He was grown now, off, we may conjecture, following the wars with some Christian prince. At any rate, the father knew he was now outside his jurisdiction. For if he were not, we may be sure that James would never have taken the momentous steps he now took. He separated from his wife in legal divorce and then went to the Jesuit Fathers and offered them his services for the remainder of life.

### THE MAITRE D'HOTEL

One would not suppose it, but it was almost a key job. What use could the fathers make of this middle-aged, exquisitely mannered man? He was skilled in the arts esteemed by the Japanese; he was docile and self-effacing. As time went on they got to know something of the mystery of an intense inner life, preoccupied with the profundities of sin, predestination, suffering and the terrifying conundrum of the Cross. They put him in charge of the

Jesuit house at Osaka, the wealthy port of the capital of Japan, Kyoto.

It was in accord with the adopted plan. Osaka, and Kyóto which was only nine miles distant, were major cities more populous with nobility than any comparable region in the Empire. And since it was genealogy more than all else that this nation prized, capturing the high-born meant also capturing many of their less blue-blooded compeers. It was the concern of the missionaries first of all to set up a *visible* Church, with regular dispensation of the sacraments and a native clergy. Their mission theory held that a city seated on a hill cannot be hid, since it is plainly visible. The Church must be that city, and not otherwise than through the regular establishment of ecclesiastical administration. When the pagans saw this thriving life, then they would come in coveys to inquire. But as long as the Church remained underground she was not visible except to a few who were poor and misprized. She must emerge into the light of day and grow. And to this end, the coöperation of the masters of this completely feudal society was indispensable.

It became the lifework of St. James to administer the house at Osaka with that requisite ceremony necessary to attracting the cultured Japanese. In his hands lay the duties of landscaping and interior flower arrangement. Any untoward lack of balance, proportion or design would provoke the disdain of those trained from earliest youth in this art of sha-do. And the Tea Ceremonial, more than anything else, would there be the entrée to the Gospel.

James would lead some interested Samurai down a long narrow corridor and up a polished stairway of carefully worked larchwood into a spacious court, then beyond through a rich lobby that opened into the tea room. As he swung open the door, with one swift appreciative glance the Samurai would assay the appointments of the little chamber. On the far side, the mirror-bright ebony hearth duplicated the interior, and to the left, poised on a wrought-iron tripod was an elegant tea-pot, under which on finely ground cinders of egg-shells glowed in precise pattern some little geometrical coals. The coals were of a special type, burning to the very end and giving off no smoke. When the guests were seated on the tapestry carpet the exquisite ritual would begin. Immaculate napkins, immaculate covers and service, setting off an exotically frugal repast. To each guest James would tender the tea with grave and smiling courtesy. In prescribed forms, the conversation would begin. It progressed, and new topics emerged: one admired the rare workmanship of the great painter Sesshu; surely only Motonobu could rank with him in mastery? James, himself an artist, warmed to the subject. And then at last, there was an opening for a new gambit: What did the noble Samurai think of mysterious Destiny which had kept to these last times the great enlightenment about the God who was Creator of the Universe and with Whom men were happy after death? This God has an only Son, Jesus, Who Himself dwelt on earth and showed men the way to eternal life. . . .

He was captivating, this urbanely courteous Christian.

Evidently, thought the guests, this new religion did not mean regress into barbarism. They would come again and bring others. Under the skilful manipulation of James, his fellow Catechists and the learned priests, converts began to multiply. In the year 1581, after years of disappointing labor and thirty years after Xavier's arrival, there were 150,000 Christians in Japan.

### THE PATRON

When Nobunaga, friend and protector of the Jesuits, was trapped and slain in his palace at Kyoto through the treachery of a retainer, the Fathers and Christians at Osaka and through the land were filled with consternation. Reports of civil war reached them and of the ambitious maneuverings of Nobunaga's top generals. The household at Osaka was seized but not harmed. Then, in a few months, one name became more and more dominant. It was Hideyoshi, former sandal-bearer and then almost Chief of Staff to Nobunaga, who was to be the new ruler of Japan.

The Fathers held their breath and waited. They knew that

Hideyoshi had once saved the life of Brother Lawrence when he disputed with a bonze before the court of Nogunaga. They were mountingly apprehensive as in a series of swift moves Hideyoshi mastered section after section of the Empire. Everywhere men were awed by this ugly duckling, the only man not of noble birth in Japanese history to make himself undisputed dictator. Astute, patient, well-informed, he was an adept at strategy who had learned his art in long campaigns, and, even more significant, he was a diplomat of charm and force. Better than any of his peers he had come to realize that a conquered enemy remains an enemy, while a conciliated enemy frequently becomes a friend. And in time another quality, masked at first, became evident: he was even more ambitious than Nobunaga.

At the first reports of the Regent's benevolence the household at Osaka was cautious. The memory of the frightful carnage of 1580 in the pitched battle between Nobunaga and the soldier-bonzes entrenched in the castle of Hongwan-ji, but a few miles away, and the rumor that these menacing monks were again on the move gave the Christians uneasy nights. Yet soon the first report became certainty: Hideyoshi was friendly to the Jesuits.

James would not forget the day when the Regent dropped in for an unexpected visit to their house at Osaka. Through the stiff folds of his gorgeous robes he could discern the small but powerful frame hardened by years of campaigning. His features, falling into a long thin mustache and beard, were unprepossessing. Nothing caught the attention save the flashing, fiery eyes. Report said he was unlettered; yet he moved through the complicated cha-no-yu with accomplished ease. And there was no lack of cordiality. He knew of Christianity and admired its code. Turning to James in the foyer he had asked of a picture of the Savior "Who is that?" "Why the crown of thorns?" and had studied the picture long.

He was interested, no doubt; but could they ever really explain Christ to such a man, completely sunk in the life of the senses and devoured by pride? On leaving the house he had made a memorable avowal to Father Gregory Cespedius, the Superior: "I know you are excellent men, and of a far purer life than the bonzes. I like everything in your religion, except one thing. That is the commandment of having only one wife. Were it not for this, I would become a Christian myself." After his departure the Father re-told the incident between himself and the canny Brother Lawrence. Once after an instruction by Lawrence, Hideyoshi had joked with him: "Here's what I'll do: I'll become a Christian on one condition. Do you know what I mean? Women." The biting irony of Lawrence's reply was not wasted on the Regent: "Condition granted. For even if your women bring you down with them to Hell, still you will have been the cause why many will be able to live a good Christian life."

At Osaka, not far from the Jesuit house, Hideyoshi kept over three hundred concubines, and elsewhere too he was plentifully supplied with them. Yet on this matter he was quite severe with the nobles, and even put some bonzes to death. Nobody was a more constant source of amazement to the Regent than Don Justo (Takayama Ukon), whom the missionaries styled "The Pillar of the Church in Japan." He had been one of Nobunaga's best generals, and an invaluable ally to Hideyoshi. What was the source of his continence, his nobility of life and strange spiritual serenity?

Sometimes of an afternoon James would take a stroll across the city to watch the construction of the huge Castle of Osaka. There Hideyoshi kept sixty thousand men busy in continuous shifts day and night digging foundations and moats for the colossal fortress planned to enclose one hundred acres. Frequently enough he could see the Regent himself, clad in tiger skin and surrounded by his retinue, overseeing operations with ferocious tyranny. Any disorder, excessive talking, or noticeable slip meant immediate punishment of foreman and all involved. Watching the feverish activity, the unmitigated servitude, James was struck with a premonition of fear. This man intended to make himself absolute master of every soul in Japan! And not only Japan. Already he had preparations under way for the invasion of Korea, to be used as a beachhead for the conquest of China itself. Like China, the Philippines, now under Spanish rule, were, said Hideyoshi, the possession of the Emperor by immemorial right. It was his destiny to recover them for their rightful owner.

Only slowly did the full scope of the dictator's projects reveal itself. He ruled the daimyos with an iron hand, kept the army out of mischief by saddling it with vast construction projects as well as with the invasion of Korea, extorted crippling taxes from farmers and artisans of all classes, moved governors about in such a way that their power was checked and balanced, and embarked on a lavish building program that would make his name live in history. At the same time that the huge Castle of Osaka was under construction the Regent was restoring the Emperor's palace at Kyoto and near it was building a fortress of proportions hitherto unknown in Japan. On this pile, too, work went on day and night, engaging more than another sixty thousand men. Meanwhile, he was erecting a magnificent temple at Nara; while in Fushima, a few miles outside Kyoto, men were engaged on a great palace for his own use. Not content with this, he forced the local nobles to increase real estate values by building similar establishments. In Kyushu, southern Japan, from the beginning the stronghold of Christianity, he had gained almost complete mastery. The historian Charlevoix sums up the picture of that time:

Everything then smiled upon the missionaries: never had they been more in credit. The Imperial armies were commanded by Christians, and the revolution just accomplished in Kyushu had given as masters to the provinces of which the Regent had disposed in virtue of his right of conquest Lords who were either zealous partisans or declared protectors of Christianity. But, on the other hand, the Christian "Kings" were no longer sovereign, and it is certain that the *coup* which degraded them shook the foundations of the Church in Japan. . . .

"The Christian Kings were no longer sovereign": so that if the Christians should lose favor with one man, all was lost. The price for the final unification of the empire was the untrammeled authority of Hideyoshi.

### THE PERSECUTOR

Even in retrospect the missionaries had difficulty in understanding the onslaught of the persecution, so sudden was it, and such a complete reversal. Multiple causes have been alleged by modern historians. The most simple explanation is favored by some non-Catholic scholars. In essence, it runs as follows: The missionaries were children of their times. Philip II, King of both Portugal and Spain, was a Catholic sovereign who favored this religion in his domains. If Japan and/or China were brought under the Spanish political yoke, it would be an easy matter to Christianize them. This was as it should be, for Church and State should be united. Anything less was undesirable, and, at the most, merely tolerated. Besides, what allegiance did a Christian owe to such a unregenerate pagan ruler as Hideyoshi? Hence it was incumbent on the missionaries, for both the temporal and spiritual welfare of the countries they evangelized, to act as a sort of fifth column. In fact, they were willing to do so. We have a document drawn up by Father Alonso Sanchez, S.J., on July 26, 1586 (just one year before the edict of persecution), and signed by the Bishop, Religious Superiors and Governor of the Philippines, in which it is proposed that missionaries be contacted so

that they may give information to the Spanish armies about what they know of the country, its strength, and its military forces and supplies, and whatever dangers or reasons for caution they have in mind. They will also serve as interpreters and persuade the Chinese to allow the Spaniards to enter in peace, and to hear and receive the preachers, and to accept the religion sent to them by God. . . .

Naturally, Japanese intelligence intercepted this and similar proposals. When the evidence mounted, Hideyoshi saw that in favoring the missionaries he was in reality nourishing a viper in his bosom. So even though it meant foregoing the blessings of Portuguese trade he was forced to ban them. This was the provocation for the terrible edict of persecution in 1587.

This explanation is plausible, but it contains only fractional truth. When, shortly after the death of the twenty-six martyrs of Nagasaki in 1597, the cause of their beatification was introduced at Rome, the Auditors of the Roman Rota called witnesses to inquire into the reasons for the persecution. More than twenty-two accredited witnesses testified that "not from political reasons, or rivalry, or any other private reason was the mind of Taikosama [Hideyoshi] inflamed; but that he condemned them to the cross because of the hatred he bore the Catholic Faith." The Bull of Canonization of these martyrs, among whom was St. James Kisai, goes on to say that the Roman Rota after careful investigation were convinced of the truth of this testimony, and that moreover it was confirmed by subsequent miracles.

The reason for this concern as to the true cause of persecution is that, according to the classic treatise on Martyrdom written by Pope Benedict XIV, among the canonical conditions for the authentic aureole of martyrdom is the norm that in general it is not licit to provoke the persecutor, and that also the persecutor must be led on by hatred of the faith or of some other good work commanded by reason of faith in Christ. It is not necessary that the persecutor openly allege his hatred of the faith (after all, how few are willing to do that!), it is sufficient that this be his true motive, no matter what pretext he assigns. And if the persecutor thinks that he is punishing a true crime, at least the lying accuser, who brings it to his attention, must be led on by hatred of the faith.

It is worth noting that the case of the Japanese martyrs in this regard was especially scrutinized by the Congregation of Rites. The fact is that the edict of persecution in 1587 itself stated that "Japan is the kingdom of the Kami, so that it is not right for the Christian religion to be tolerated here. Moreover the preachers of this religion destroy the temples of the Kami and Hotoke and sabotage its laws." And some ten years later when the martyrs were herded onto carts for the terrible six-hundred-mile journey to crucifixion at Nagasaki the placard borne along the way in front of them and signed by Hideyoshi stated that they were being put

to death for propagating Christianity which had been forbidden
years before.

We may wonder how many of the complex circumstances leading to his death St. James knew. No doubt he learned something
from the Fathers of Jacuin, Hideyoshi's personal physician, a
honey-tongued former bonze, the greatest single enemy of the
Church in Japan. For over ten years this evil man, one of whose
principal tasks was to procure concubines from all over the Empire
for his master, had not tired of calumniating the Christians in
public and in private. When some Christian women of Arima and
Omura had declined his offer to join Hideyoshi's harem, Jacuin
had made capital their refusal, citing it as an instance of the general disobedience of Christians, and of the contempt in which they
held the Regent.

At the edict of banishment in 1587 the Fathers in consultation
had decided that rather than abandon the nascent Church, planted
with so much toil, they would stay on and work underground and
take their risks. James, of course, elected to stay with them. The
Jesuits, then about 134 in number, had changed from their clerical
garb to ordinary Japanese attire. They went through the motions of
obeying the imperial edict. They did not preach openly. For the
most part, the 140 churches ordered closed by Hideyoshi remained
closed. But the converts still came, and even more quickly. In one
year alone, 1589–1590, they baptized 20,570 adults in addition to
many babies.

We can only conjecture the duties of James, *Maitre d'Hotel* at
Osaka during these eventful years. We know that his catechising
was not a little responsible for the many baptisms there. The Jesuits
were filled with respect for this graying, unobtrusive steward of
their household. What a Brother he would be, were he not beyond
the regular age-limit. Well, even without the vows, he did all the
work of a Brother. Nothing was more remarkable than the singular
instinct which led him to almost uninterrupted meditation on the
Passion and Death of Christ. Why was it this subject, more than
any other, which attracted him so much? Perhaps it was some deep

sense of the tragedy of things, the terrible price Satan exacts for sin, a haunting awareness of the temporal and spiritual miseries crushing his own people, and a premonition of the fearsome times to come in which Japanese Christians would suffer more for their faith than any single nation has ever suffered.

As time went on the Fathers grew to think of him as typified by a single predilection, shuffling around the house in his grave and quiet way, a little book of the Gospels in his hand, turned open to the passages on the Passion. He himself had written out the book in his beautiful script; and opposite each page were illustrations of the text, done with that fastidious artistry he had learned as a boy. Sometimes when the visitors were gone and the house was in order, he would pause at an upper window. There, down below the house and stretched out to the horizon was the gleaming surface of the bay. That incessant shuttle of boats loaded with immense granite slabs and great timbers from the provinces of Northern Japan was from Sakai. It was material to complete Hideyoshi's Castle. Turning back into the courtyard and looking northeast he could catch sight of the huge beams of the Castle's three-story dungeon, coated with heavy plaster, and above, the roof of the great fortress shone like a sea of copper, which it was. . . . The enormous gates, covered with iron, were faced with menacing iron studs. It was a lowering memorial of the puissant wrath of the persecutor.

What had led him to mitigate his first edict? The Fathers said that he had not; it still stood and could be re-invoked at any time. But at present it was advantageous for the Regent to wink at the work of the missionaries. One reason was that he still needed Portuguese trade, especially in firearms. He was attempting huge armaments, and the invasion of Korea was already underway. Another reason was the need of conciliating some of the Christian daimyos in his army; they were of proven worth and indispensable in the work of conquest. Still another was the imposing person of Father Alexander Valignani S.J., the legate of the powerful Viceroy of the Indies. Hideyoshi right now could not afford to alienate such a figure.

Things had stood this way, delicately poised, when the Franciscans arrived in 1593. On more than one occasion James walked over to their new Church, Bethlehem. They had built it in the teeth of the Emperor and his edict, and were preaching to swelling crowds. They were Spaniards, and had none or only rudimentary knowledge of Japanese language and customs, but the gray-robed, bare-footed poverty and evangelical simplicity had soon attracted an enthusiastic group of translators and catechists, many of whom they enrolled in their Third Order.

At home, James had frequently heard their arrival discussed. They had come in the political capacity of ambassadors from the Governor of the Philippines, and one of their main assignments had been to break the Portuguese trade monopoly. For the Spanish and Portuguese, though technically united under Philip II, were old-time enemies. A few Spanish adventurers in Japan were unremitting in their effort to disparage all things Portuguese. They did not hesitate to point out that the Jesuits too were from the Portuguese Province and naturally allied to the Portuguese traders and methods. They openly questioned the purity of the Jesuits' motives in the court of the already suspicious Regent.

But the Franciscans were zealous men, who had long been eyeing the field of Japan, and were more than a little attracted by the prospect of martyrdom there offered. Their venerated Superior, Father Peter, had undertaken the embassy with reluctance. He would have preferred to enter Japan another way, but no other opening was visible. He felt that the Friars had a doctrinal and devotional coloring to give Christianity in Japan that was different from what the Jesuits offered, and perhaps more attractive to certain Japanese temperaments. He was not wrong; for even the dictator himself had been impressed by the uncompromising simplicity of the Franciscans. They insisted on wearing their robes and preaching openly in the full tradition of St. Francis. The five holy

Franciscan Martyrs of Morocco were their ideal. And their success was marked.

Nonetheless it was only by a ruse that they had obtained Hideyoshi's permission to visit the interior, Kyoto and Osaka. They had played on his vanity, professing curiosity about the great buildings he had there erected. But once there, they had proceeded immediately to build a church in both cities. Friendly Japanese warned them of the folly of openly provoking the wrath of the Regent in his own province and capital. If they must preach, it would be better to go north into some of the remoter provinces, where the Regent would not so readily notice them. The Jesuits, too, had taken sharp issue with the Friars on this matter. They admired their courage, they said, but it seemed to them after over forty years' labor in this mission that it was simply foolhardy to endanger the long and careful project of building a native Church because of a few men's quest of martyrdom. Admirable enough for the martyrs; but what of the more than 250,000 Christians that would be left without pastors if the decree of banishment were once more and effectively re-invoked? Many unseasoned converts, newly baptized and surrounded by a pagan milieu, would certainly relapse into idolatry. Was it right to endanger so many souls in a Church so young?

This was the reason, said the Jesuits, that they had doffed their cassocks and taken to the life of the catacombs. They themselves would far prefer a sudden martyrdom to the daily uncertainty, secrecy and deprivation they had so long endured. As modestly as they could they pointed out that the Franciscans really had no right to be in Japan. Pope Gregory XIII in 1585 by his Bull *Ex Pastorali Officio* had reserved to Jesuits exclusively the right of evangelizing Japan. This, said the Fathers, had been done *consulto*, with full deliberation, because the Holy See did not wish to expose the infant Church to the markedly different traditions of the different religious Orders. That was advisable and desirable in Europe and elsewhere; but in Japan it had been the decision of the

Holy See that it would do more harm than good for a few years to come.

The zealous and learned Franciscan Superior, Father Peter, had replied to these arguments that they were indeed aware of the Bull *Ex Pastorali Officio;* but in the Philippines he had consulted theologians who had disputed its precise force, or pointed out that, after all, the Franciscans had been given full permission to evangelize the West Indies. And was not Japan a part of the West Indies? Here arose the old squabbles concerning longitude and latitude and the partition of Pope Alexander VI. The Spanish and Portuguese had not ceased to dispute about it. And the rivalry was not only commercial. The Franciscans were Spanish and they preferred the Spanish methods which had evangelized Mexico and Peru after first conquering them for the Spanish crown. And to be perfectly honest, they were more than a little dubious of the Jesuit theories of missionary "accommodation." They were not at all sure that it was right for missionaries to adopt so many customs of pagan provenance, to allow such latitude to a culture of idolatrous worship, to abandon religious garb and seem to compromise the Gospel for pagan ears. . . .

The Fathers had told James that as they listened to Father Peter's reply to their objections they had realized with sorrow that the dispute was too deep for easy settlement. It was a matter of different nationalities, different temperaments, and different prudential judgments. But afterwards on the hill of crucifixion at Nagasaki Superiors of both Orders begged pardon of one another for their intransigence and any injury each might have caused the other.

### THE MARTYR

*San Felipe!* A doubly fateful name that would ring the death knoll of twenty-six Saints. To Hideyoshi it suggested two related images. For when the rich galleon *San Felipe* had in October 1596 run aground in the port of Urado, a port of Tosa, and had had her back broken on a sand shoal because of the malevolent maneuvering of two hundred little armored boats dispatched by Hide-yoshi, the Japanese had coolly appropriated to themselves the remainder of the cargo, worth some 600,000 crowns. In vain had the Spanish ship captain aired his vehemence. He was, he stormed, under the protection of Don Felipe II, Philip II "King of Castilla, León, Aragón, the two Sicilies, Jerusalem, Portugal, Navarra, Granada, Cerdeña, Corcega, Murçia, Jaen, the Algarves, Aljecira, Jibraltar, the Eastern and Western Yndias, and the islands and mainland of the Ocean sea; archduke of Austria, duke of Borgoña, Bravante, and Milan; count of Abspurg, Flanders, Bretaña, Tirol, etc." Beware his wrath! thundered the arrogant Spaniard. The Regent's envoy, Masuda, was intrigued. "These territories, how did King Philip become master of them?" The answer was astounding, and fated to inflict on the Church in Japan a wound from which she was to bleed for nearly three hundred years. For foolishly attempting to overawe the Japanese, the Spaniard had replied: "First of all the religious entered these regions as missionaries and preached their religion; then the soldiers simply followed up their work and subdued the people."

It was the last straw. Hideyoshi's long-smouldering hatred broke into devouring anger. Missionaries that were in reality a fifth column for Philip! It was news that simply confirmed the incessant accusations of Japanese and Spaniards that reached his ears. He swore that he would not leave a single missionary alive. "They will learn what it means to play with me!"

Weeks later, when the long death trek from Kyoto to Nagasaki had begun, James recalled again and again the unpredictable, tortuous, almost arbitrary chain of events that led to his being one of the twenty-six condemned men in the carts. Why was he chosen, when there were so many others begging for the privilege of giving their lives for Christ? He, who was not yet even a Jesuit? He had been too old, he thought; but Father Organtino said he was sure the Vice-Provincial would receive his vows before the end. He smiled. They would take him now because there was no chance of his doing any damage afterwards. He would be on a cross.

But of so many thousand Christians in Japan, why himself? It was a question he could not answer, that he was almost afraid to ask. On the long journey, Father Peter, the Franciscan Superior, never tired of warning them to pray, not to give way to pride at having been singled out for such a grace, not to count themselves blessed until they had persevered to the end. The end! It was now less than three weeks away; they had been on the death journey seven days.

The snow was blinding to look on; mile after mile of it, except when they passed through a small town of curious, hooting, or more often, awed inhabitants. They were to make a tour of the imperial cities in order to frighten and intimidate Christians. They were to be made dismaying examples. Yet to the exasperation of the officials and the bonzes almost the exact opposite was occuring. Christians everywhere wanted to join them! They were treated with respect and even consideration by their guards.

James' feet were covered with chilblains; his left ear had been a dull steady ache since the lobe was severed in the public square in Kyoto. The wind, sweeping down from Fuji and in from across the Inland Sea, pierced him to the marrow. He was getting old, sixty-four. His eyes wandered over the carts ahead and behind him. There were nine of them, each drawn by two horses and containing three prisoners, except for the last, which had two. Ahead of him were the Spanish Franciscans, three of them priests. Behind were their fifteen helpers, catechists and interpreters, members of the Third Order. Next to last were the three Jesuits, Paul, John and James. Last were the two sent by Superiors to help the martyrs along the route in whatever way they could. The guards had tolerated them for a while; then they questioned: "Who are you —Christians?" "Yes," came the resolute answer, "we are here to help these innocent men." "Very well," replied the Captain in anger, "then get in and try it yourself." Curious Providence! Now by accident they too were destined for the aureole of martyrdom at Nagasaki.

By accident! in memory he attempted to retrace the tangled web woven of intrigue, luck, malevolence and oversight during these last four weeks. To the sceptical eye the whole affair was nothing but accident. It had just happened that he and John and Paul were alone in the house at Osaka when the guards finally closed in. It had just happened that Hasegawa, the Governor of Osaka, already under suspicion of graft, had felt impelled to demonstrate his loyalty to the Regent by doing more than he had been told. For the dictator had nowhere indicated his wish to corral the Jesuits; on the contrary, it was the Franciscans who were the special objects of his dislike. The first sweeping resolve to liquidate all missionaries had subsequently given place to milder counsel: he would punish only the Friars who dared to tweak his beard in the capital city.

If anyone were to be thanked for James being on this cart, it was Hasegawa; and if anyone were to be thanked that not more Jesuits than three had been condemned it was Ushioye, Hasegawa's son. For in good faith Ushioye had believed that he could save the Franciscans by logic. After all, he argued, the Jesuits had converted far more than the Franciscans all these years, and were doing the same work as they were now, although in an underground way. Why single out some for punishment rather than others? It should be both or none at all. The alternative, he reasoned, must be none at all, for it was foolish and excessive to punish all the missionaries. But his logic was deficient; instead they had taken some of each.

Even then it was an accident that they had taken only three, and these three. If Hasegawa and Ushioye, his son, had not been so anxious to round up Jesuits for the holocaust, though from different motives surely, they would not have trespassed on the jurisdiction of the Governor of Lower Kyoto by entering his territory. As it was, just because Hasegawa wanted the Jesuits persecuted, the Governor of Lower Kyoto had decided to teach him to stay in his own bailiwick by refusing to touch the Jesuits. So, for all his pains, Hasegawa had taken only the three Jesuits in Osaka.

But when the soldiers came for the arrest, why were there only three? An accident, again. The old Superior, Father Organtino, and Father Rodriguez, the official Court Interpreter, had departed shortly before with many misgivings. They were torn by their own desire to stay and face the persecutors with the chance of dying for Christ and the repeated importunities of their flock. Their friends had argued that the warrant was only against the Franciscans, the Jesuits were but lightly or not at all involved. To stay on at Osaka, however, as if nothing were amiss might provoke Hideyoshi beyond all measure into a total persecution of Christianity as such. Better to lie low until the storm blew over, as it had ten years before. It was not licit to endanger the whole nascent Church just because they personally courted martyrdom. So the Fathers had departed with reluctance, insisting that they be at once informed if their names were on the list of proscription. For in that case discretion would be of no avail, and they could never deny their faith.

With what a lot of consultation, excited coming and going, and grapevine rumors had those last weeks been filled! If Father Superior should decide that Paul would stay . . . If the Governor interprets the warrant like this . . . If James himself should like to do some work for Father Organtino at Sakai for a short while . . . The labyrinth of hypotheses was endless. It was almost humorous. For as a matter of fact this was the way it had turned out, and it was no accident at all, because in careful detail it had been eternally planned. From the beginning God's wisdom had decided on the sacrifice of these three Jesuits, six Franciscans and seventeen laymen, no more, and no less.

They were a strange, helter-skelter crew. A cook, a carpenter, five married men, a former bonze, two children of twelve and thirteen, a doctor, boys nineteen and sixteen. It was, James knew, the mystery of Predestination. He turned over in his mind that enigmatic text of St. Paul:

So it is that we read, I have been a friend of Jacob, and an enemy of Esau. What does this mean? That God acts unjustly? That is not to be thought of. I will show pity, he tells Moses, on those whom I pity; I will show mercy where I am merciful; the effect comes, then, from God's mercy, not from man's alacrity. Pharao, too, is told in scripture, This is the very reason why I have made thee what thou art, so as to give proof, in thee, of my power, and to let my name be known over the earth. *Romans 9:13–18*

He trembled, not from the icy wind, though the wind was cold enough. The cart gave a sudden lurch as it hit a deep rut in the road. The rope cut into his frozen hands tied behind his back. How much longer? Less than a week they said, they were coming closer to Kyushu, where he was born. They were lucky, at that. Orders were that they should have nose and ears cut off before beginning the journey, but the Governor had taken it upon himself to sever the left ear-lobe only. Surprisingly enough, too, they had received something to eat, through the good offices of Christians along the way. At night they were herded together, and that was good, for soon the twenty-six criminals were lasting friends. James admired the Franciscans, their moving exhortations to humility and prayer, their love of the Church's song. Some of the Japanese tertiaries too had good voices, and often as they passed through a little town one of them would intone the "Benedictus" or the "In gratiarum actionem," learned from Father Peter and his companions. The townsfolk would receive the concert with strange reactions. Pagans were puzzled at the singing, smiling jubilation of the condemned men on carts. Was this a picnic or a death march? But the town Christians, serenely ignoring the restrictions of the guards, swarmed about the martyrs begging remembrance and promising prayers.

At James' left, Paul Miki began to preach to the assembled crowds. As he listened to the torrential force and eloquence of the younger Jesuit, now on the eve of his Ordination, the graying Japanese realised that if this man were allowed to live he would be famous in Japan. No one of their group could match Paul for the combination of fluency in Japanese and mastery of doctrine. He had made a special study of the nine current national sects and had written refutations of each. The Jesuits had looked forward to the brilliant career of Paul, soon to be one of the first Japanese priests.

More than of James, who was old, and of John, who was young and comparatively untrained, Father Organtino had bemoaned the loss of Paul. Why in the few days he had been in prison in Osaka he had baptized six of his jailers! Of Samurai rank, and trained in the seminary from his eleventh year, even as a scholastic Paul was venerated in Osaka. Yet it was not the native brilliance or even charism of eloquence that James admired most in Paul. It was his singleness of mind, total devotion to the Lord and Captain Christ who wished to gain ascendancy in this ancient land of Dai-Nippon.

Of course the young John Soan, standing at his right, did not have Paul's rich background. He was only nineteen, the Jesuits' sacristan and part-time catechist. But in his spontaneous gestures, in the quiet inflections of voice, lay what ardor and purity of soul! As James watched the young John his mind was plummeted in mystery. Incomprehensible. Why was he, James, after all these years to pronounce his vows as a Jesuit with this angelic scholastic? Nineteen and sixty-four—their ages were disparate enough; but their minds were the same, their destinies identical. They were to be crucified.

He trembled again. Was it the devil playing with him, trying to trap him into a terrible pride, thinking that he was to have the same death as Christ? How did he know that he could endure another week of this frightful journey? How was he sure that suspended on the cross he might not beg and fight to be released? There had been before, there would be again, men who apostatized in the very act of martyrdom. He prayed.

Come, Lord Jesus. The journey wore on, hour after hour, day after day. Many had developed deep colds and coughs; their limbs ached from the relentless jolting of the carts over the iced and rocky roads. Once when they paused for a few minutes—as they neared the destination more and more of the martyrs attempted to walk—the three Jesuits had seen the large frame of Father Peter seated on a rock and shaken with sobs. Paul was their spokesman: "Father! do not let the guards ridicule you. They think you are afraid of death." But the ardent Friar had turned to them in courtesy: "It is not the prospect of death that saddens me. But when I came to this land I had planned and hoped to establish a Province of Franciscans here, a thing which I shall never do."

In Kyushu the news of their arrival preceded them like fire. The crowds multiplied, and in some places they lined the way. The Jesuits were everywhere among them, trying to curb the enthusiasm that threatened to provoke Hideyoshi all the more. In anger, the Governor of Karatsu had threatened that they might find fifty crosses prepared instead of twenty-six. This news caused mounting excitement. Who would have the privilege of dying on the other twenty-four? The bonzes were angered beyond belief. What was the meaning of so many thousands of Christians all vying with one another for the honor of martyrdom? It was sheer fanaticism.

But James knew that rather it was grace building on nature, as it always did, and not destroying it. There were no people more brave than the Japanese. They prided themselves on stoicism in suffering. To commit hara-kiri when only dishonor remained was a canon of nobility. Schoolboys quoted the verses so loved by the great Nobunaga:

> Life is short; the world's a mere dream to the idle.
> Only the fool fears death, for what is there of life that does
> Not die once, sooner or later?
> Man has to die once and once only;
> He should make his death glorious.

But Nobunaga, like most pagan Japanese, did not believe that the soul lived on after death. Perhaps that death which introduced a man into an eternity of recompense for his life on earth was not always glorious? Sin, and the mystery of iniquity: to the man who understood something of these death gave pause.

The journey was almost over; they would make the final stage by ship into the harbor of Nagasaki. On February 4 they were thrust into the suffocating hold of a ship, all except the Franciscans having their arms roped behind their backs and tied to their necks. That night they were left there shaking, almost congealed with cold. The dawn was cold and clear. Rough hands hurled them stumbling onto the deck, hoisted them onto horses and by a winding path led them up the steep hill overlooking the bay where twenty-six crosses had been prepared. It was not the scheduled hill where ordinary criminal executions had taken place. The Portuguese had bribed or cajoled officials into choosing this other one instead, chosen because of its fine view as a suitable place for a future Church to be erected in honor of Our Lady of the Martyrs. So sure were they that this day would not be forgotten in Japan.

Nagasaki, the new Rome of the Orient! It was fitting that they should die in the center of Japanese Christianity. Here, perhaps, they would do even more good in death than they had in life. Was it strange that in these last hours, some words of the Canon of the Mass went through James' mind? Remember the place where, just before the Consecration, the priest holds his hands over the bread and wine and whispers the words "Hanc igitur oblationem . . ."?

We beseech thee, Lord, that being pleased, you may accept this offering of our utter indebtedness, as well as that of your whole family. May you dispose our days in peace, snatch us from eternal damnation and command that we be numbered among the band of thy elect. Through Christ, Our Lord. Amen.

A holy host, a pure host, an immaculate host. They were almost there. James hardly had time to notice the hushed and weeping crowds. He was, says the chronicle, "numini intentus," intent on God. There were multiple incidents that last hour as relatives and friends sought to get a final word from the martyrs, send them a special greeting. Could it be that some of those white-faced women, transfixed with love and fear, were wives of some of the Franciscan Tertiaries? In front of him, the Governor of Nagasaki, Hasaburo, a former classmate of Paul Miki and here in charge of the execution, was making a last attempt to coax the twelve-year-old boy Louis to come along with him, if only he would renounce his faith. The boy had declined the bargain. There was no proportion, he said, between an eternal reward and the few years of such life as Hasaburo could offer him.

The heart of James was laden with thanksgiving as he stumbled up the hill. Just a few hours before Father Pasio, the delegate of the Jesuit Vice-Provincial, had heard the general confessions of the three Jesuits and then at Mass and Communion had received the first vows of James and John. God had seen fit to admit him from servant and handyman of the Fathers into their own family. Well, the vows would not be too hard to keep for another hour. Again he was struck with fear. Less than an hour! But he could not falter now. He prayed; he was old and weak.

The crowd was enthralled at the spectacle of the martyrs. It was a drama for the angels. Someone, noticing the modesty and devotion of the old Brother, now nearly oblivious of landscape and spectators, begged him for a handkerchief attached to his belt. They would like it as a relic. Brother James flushed violently: "No! I beg you not to try to make a Saint out of me who for so long have been a sinner." It was his enemy whispering pride and complacency even on the cross.

He had meditated so many years on the mysteries of the Passion, and for so long had made the Via Dolorosa the recurrent theme of his prayer that now at every step the distorted figure of the Suffering Christ seemed to him to grow more luminous.

The procession stopped. The crosses were laid out on the ground. They were far easier than Christ's Cross, he thought. Here was a little foot-rest on the bottom, and they had a sort of seat in the center. And instead of being nailed their arms and legs were tied on to the cross, secured at the waist and fastened at the neck with an iron collar. And unlike Christ, they were left their clothes. The crowd thrilled as the martyrs threw themselves on their knees before their crosses and thanked God. The executioners and soldiers were dumbfounded and still. The small boy Anthony laughing aloud rushed to his cross with extended arms.

Hasaburo spoke a quick word to the soldiers: Work fast! He was afraid of the restless and eager crowd. Guards with poles and clubs beat back the surging thousands. Then, almost before he knew it, James was flung to the ground and roped to the cross by his two assigned executioners. Quickly, swaying and jerking, he was lifted into the air and the cross was dropped into a hole in the ground. He was fifth from the left in a semi-circle of gibbets five or six feet apart. The iron cut into his neck, but on his right he could see Paul, and John was two further on. Paul had begun to speak, lifting his wonderful voice out over the hushed crowd: "I am a Japanese, like yourselves. I am thirty-three, the very age of Christ on the Cross. It is a great privilege to be here. We have been condemned simply for preaching the Gospel of Christ. But we forgive our executioners, as we do His Excellency who has placed us here. May he and all be brought to the grace of Baptism! Listen to me, I am about to die, and I tell you the truth: There is no other way to salvation than the Christian way. Our Lord Jesus Christ is the only begotten Son of God." His face was alight as he turned to James. "Courage!" he called to the rest: "Courage, my brothers. We will meet again in heaven soon." Then someone—it was the boy Anthony—intoned the psalm "Laudate, pueri, Dominum" and the martyrs took up the melody. Father Peter in the center spoke to the boy Louis. "My son, in a few moments you will be in Paradise." Tied and strapped as he was, the small Saint began to jump for joy.

James looked outward from the hill. He was praying for his wife and son, the Society, the Church. Over the heads of the crowd lay the harbor of Nagasaki. He could see lines of boats rocking in the tide and his eye swept tier after tier of huddled black little roofs rising up from the shore. What lay beyond?

The executioners, one for each cross, had unsheathed their swords and were grasping the long spears. He called good-by to Paul and John and the rest, his friends. From the corner of his eye he saw down at the end of the line the flash of steel moving in a swift arc. As the blade pierced his side the bystanders heard a triumphant, love-filled cry: "Jesus! Mary!"

It was the 5th of February, 1597.
St. James Kisai, pray for us.

# They That Sow in Tears

BY JOHN V. MURPHY, S.J.

*Brother Francis de Sadeleer, S.J. (1844–1921)*

Dear Rev. Father Superior,

Five years ago at the end of May I was in this immensity, on the same hill where now my wagon is. Then we were eleven, now I am alone. What sad events have happened in the mission field, which then we entered on with such a bright outlook, such a youthful hope! We forgot then that God's great works bear, all of them, the stamp of trial. We believed or seemed to believe that the blessing of early success would crown the enterprise which obedience had sent us to undertake. Alas! Numerous are the graves of my first companions. They are scattered far and wide in the African wilds at whose entrance I now stand.

Everything around me is silent. The sun sets here as on the infinity of the sea. A prayer rises up from my heart, as I think of my dead companions; of Father Augustus Law, whom I loved as a brother, of Father Fuchs and Father Terorde, men of burning zeal and inexhaustible devotion; of good old Brother De Vylder, whose memory is cherished by the whole mission. I pray also for the leaders of that time, the revered Father Depelchin and the brave Father Blanca; then for those too whom I hope to see again on African soil, the survivors of the trek to Umzila; Brother Hedley and Brother de Sadeleer. . . .

Thirty-three years after Father Croonenberghs wrote this letter, a stooped old man eased down on a chair and reached a gouty hand for a pen. The time was 1920; the place: the novitiate of the Society of Jesus at Aarlen in Belgium. He scratched out a diary, excerpts of which follow:

They told me this morning I'd soon be blind. Just a matter of a few weeks or so. The doctors are very sure.

Father Rector gave me a pretty hard job to do after he told me about my eyes. Wants me to write the story of my life. "Who'd be interested in an old African missionary tooting his horn?" I asked him. But if that's what they want I'll scribble out my remaining days of sight telling about myself. Awful waste of ink and paper, though.

My name is Brother Francis de Sadeleer and I was born on December 8th in a little town called Lede not so many miles away in

East Flanders. I had just got born when they thought I was going to die. But here I am, in 1920, seventy-six years later, writing about it. Guess I've been too ornery to die . . . so far.

My dad clerked for the village notary, a job that paid so little that my mother had to work too. They were up against it rather bad. Even as a tot of two years, they had to farm me out to my grandparents.

My grandfather was the local thread-maker in the village, so as soon as I was old enough, I was set to work spinning, a knack which has kept the rain off my head on the mission many times when they gave me nothing but a needle to mend a canvas wagon top.

At thirteen, I decided the time had come to show I was a grown man. I had gone to the village baker to get the week's supply of bread and brought my wheelbarrow home full of long hot loaves. I knew my granddad liked to have me carry them into the house two at a time, but I thought he was working me too hard so I was wearing myself out puffing in with them one by one. "Bring two at a time," he shouted out to me. "No," I roared back at him. He rushed out of the house, set me and bread sprawling with a blow on the ear. This was the last straw. I ran away, but I came back fourteen months later.

I got eaten up with boredom in that tiny village. Nothing to do but work all the time. No chance for games when you're busy all day. Not enough time or money for trips out of town either. But I could read, my imagination was a flying carpet that didn't cost anything to run, so I let it carry me all over the world.

In the evenings, especially on Sunday, I used to rummage around the house for travel stories. The only ones I found were in mission magazines. And the missionaries were always priests.

Now I have nothing against priests, in fact if I could see myself studying all those years I might be one now, but I like to work with my hands. Still there were other places to work with them besides Lede. I began to wonder if there were any other kind of missionaries besides priests.

Then one night I read a story about a mission somewhere, only this one was all about a lay brother. The priest who wrote it gave most of the credit for the success of his mission to a jolly little fellow in a cassock, a master carpenter. He was smiling all over his picture in the magazine. I read up some more on these brothers. They had just as many narrow escapes and hair-raising adventures as the priests. But I couldn't see how they converted any heathen just working with a hammer and saw all day.

A couple of years later I heard a sermon on St. Joseph. Came to find out that a carpenter is one of the greatest saints in heaven. He wasn't a priest but he converted more souls than anybody except the holy Mother of God. Right then and there I made a decision to be a missionary lay-brother. Didn't know that eighteen years would pass before I cracked my black whip over a gray-hided ox-team in South Africa.

I got an all-clear from the Jesuits to enter the novitiate at twenty-five. Went home to see my family and found my dad in the garden. He was furious at my decision to be a Brother. He wouldn't shake hands or say good-by. Wouldn't even look up from his digging.

But I can't be too hard on dad, because a few weeks later in the novitiate I put on a little display of temper myself. Most of my fellow novices were from the city. I guess I was a bit too rustic to suit them. Besides, everybody spoke French in that part of Belgium, and those nasal vowels were choking up in my throat somewhere. A large group of us were peeling potatoes. Every now and then a wet potato peel would fly through the air and hit me on the head. This was getting in my hair slightly since all I could do was shout, "Peace, Peace!" the one word I knew in French. Must have looked mighty silly.

At this point the ring-leader took careful aim and hit me on the lips with a nice soggy peel. I jumped up and swung from somewhere near the floor. I landed nicely on his face and down he went. By this time I could feel my blood pounding at my temples. I was thinking of tossing him into the potato pot, when he scrambled up and ran out of the room screaming, "Father Superior! Father Superior!" He had me hot on his trail mimicking even louder, "Father Superior! Father Superior!"

Years later I hit another man. Had to bluff a big crowd of angry natives.

We were traveling from Tati, our main mission to an outlying station called Panda-me-Tenga. A very valuable herd of goats bleated along beside us, a present to the mission, and our wagon route lurched through a wasteland of high grass and thorny bush.

The trail led through the Makalaka tribes, cunning first-class thieves. If the oxen had not folded up on me we'd have gotten through without mishap but they had to be staked out to graze right in the middle of these tribes. We set up a camp with some misgiving.

The motto of the Makalakas was "finders keepers." Except that they didn't wait till you lost something. They proved they could steal a whole herd of goats right out from under the sentry's nose. After the chief made them give the goats back, I knew it would be a point of honor to pilfer them for keeps. So I traced a large circle around the camp at every stopping-place. No native was to enter the circle.

One day a huge Negro came into camp. I pointed to the circle. The fellow looked at it and coolly stepped over. It was either my circle or my goats. I went straight over and struck him. Hard enough to make him get away from the circle. But not hard enough to keep him from threatening to return with some friends and level our camp to the ground.

Father Kroot who was with me at the time thought we were in for it bad. I told him, "Get to your horse; I'll stay here and don't worry." Then went out and sat down on a rock in the middle of the circle, laid my rifle across my knees, and lit up my old black pipe.

When the enraged Negroes came back, I went on smoking calmly, appearing not to notice them. They were screeching threats and curses. Suddenly as if at a given signal they all froze in silence.

For a moment I thought they were going to rush me. Then some superstitious fear seized them and they all scampered away.

Father Kroot was amazed. And the natives had to tell their fellows such a whopper about my witch-doctor power to cover up their cowardice that my goats and I lived in a "charmed circle" for the rest of the trip. . . .

The sun is hot on my desk this morning. Reminds me of the afternoon we left Grahamstown for the interior. That old sun really blistered the backs of the oxen that day. But we saved them and ourselves as much as we could by traveling in the early morning and late afternoon. Only way to do it in Africa.

Yes, Grahamstown was the last jumping-off place for the interior of South Africa back in '79. Located about five hundred miles east of Capetown and thirty miles inland from the coast. The bulge of South Africa starts to swing up north into the Indian Ocean at Port Elizabeth just a little way from Grahamstown.

We were in great spirits that day. A four months' adventure trip ahead of us, and all the people in 450,000 square miles to make Catholics! This wasn't going to be too hard. We would go a few hundred miles into the interior, pick out a nice spot on a river, build a mission, ring a bell and the natives would come flocking to us in great numbers. In no time at all there would be many converts, flourishing stations, even native priests.

I was a young man then, about thirty-five, and just as starry-eyed as the rest of them.

There were eleven of us, all dreaming the same dream, four Belgians, three Germans, two Italians and two Englishmen; six priests and five brothers in all. How could we know then that the next five years were to bring in a mere handful of converts, that these same five murderous years were to kill ten men, that two of those years were to pass without a single conversion? God mercifully kept the future veiled.

Would we have left Grahamstown all smiles and happy chatter if we could have foreseen that of our own eleven, dreaded malaria was to strike down Father Fuchs within a year, Fathers Terorde and Law within a year and a half, Good Brother De Vylder in five short years? Twelve years later, 1891, would find only a dying Brother Nigg and a broken-down-me still on the mission.

Pioneers don't last long in missionary Africa. Many's the time I've said, "Jesus, Mary and Joseph, I give you my heart and my soul," and wondered if they weren't going to take it right then and there. If it hadn't been for my rosary and rifle . . .

The plan was to trek the thousand miles to the Zambesi River in the winter because almost all the rain falls there in the summertime. Some places get thirty-five inches in three months. The amount isn't so bad—it's the *way* it falls. It's like somebody had stretched a tarpaulin across the sky and collected rain for weeks and then upped and slashed it with a knife right where the water bulge was biggest. You just don't poke your head out of your hut during a rainstorm.

We creaked and jolted out on the trail in four wagons—prairie schooners the Americans called them—and they were crammed with loads that would have broken their springs, if they had had springs. The white canvas top on one was tightly stretched over bales of bright calico cloth, chests of rhinestone jewelry, red, blue and yellow beads, shiny knives and colored trinkets of all kinds for barter with the natives. Out over the tailgates of another pushed bedding and furniture while within were stools and small tables, a dismantled portable forge, an extra wheel or two and assorted tools to repair the wagons at points of stress and strain.

The third and fourth swelled with food supplies for at least a year; flour, coffee, sugar, tea, salt, seeds for spring planting, fruit trees wrapped in burlap, to say nothing of plows and spades, three hundred pounds of gunpowder, bullets, axes and picks.

Shoved away in nooks and corners within easy reach rattled a hundred and one things needed on the road; pots and pans and a first-aid kit, canvas patches for wagon tops, hardwood patches for wagon bottoms, lard for cooking and axle grease, buttons and thread, umbrellas and sleeping bags. Locked up in a watertight chest under each driver were our most prized possessions—portable altar kits, hosts and a tiny barrel of altar wine.

We named the four wagons after saints: "Ignatius," after the founder of the Society, "Xavier," "Claver," and "Britto," after three great missionaries, and woe to the Jesuit up in heaven who let his wagon load of supplies go over a cliff. We never lost a wagon on the trip—perhaps if each of us had dedicated *himself* to a saint we wouldn't have lost so many missionaries.

They had me playing stage-coach driver that first afternoon out of Grahamstown, with oxen instead of horses, seven teams of them —fourteen of the finest gray beasts in Cape Colony—picked them out myself. For a while I put a native boy out front to lead them till I learned how to handle the bull whip—but when I missed the lead ox and nicked the boy, I brought him up front to sit with me and teach me the language. Used a lot of native words on those oxen that weren't too nice 'fore I knew what they meant.

Our first hurdle reared up due Northwest—Hell's Gate, the reassuring name given a certain pass through the Sour Mountains. Veteran trekkers told me it wasn't too bad unless it rained.

All we had to do was drive four heavily loaded wagons—seven ox teams to a wagon—up a twisting mountain trail with a sheer granite cliff rising up on one side and a hundred-foot drop on the other. On sharp turns four of the ox teams would be completely hidden from view around the bend. The driver, left behind on the wagon, spent his time hoping the native leading the oxen in front would not pull the wheels over the ledge. So steep and rutty was the grade that time and again extra teams had to be hitched together to yank the wheels out of the gumbo.

We had been crawling through the pass for some time when what we feared most struck unexpectedly. A sudden storm broke over us in all its tropical fury, just at nightfall. The mountain slopes began to funnel mud and water down on the ledge that was called a road. Dusk and rain blacked out everything an arm's length away. We slogged along beside the wagons, stumbling and falling, praying and hoping that we could get out of the pass before the ledge road, weakened by the rain, gave way under the weight of the oxen and wagons. Water sluicing down the wagon ruts dug us into the mud up to the axles. It was so dark we even welcomed flashes of lightning. Danger or not from metal-tired wheels, they lit up the road.

Halfway through the Hell's Gate pass, a pair of fear-crazed ox drivers almost canceled our mission plans for that year. The storm was at its height. But even its crashing noise could not drown out the cries and curses of an ox driver rolling down the mountain pass toward us. Out of the gloom quickly appeared two wagons rushing down headlong on the inside track. Without a thought for our safety they drove us out to the extreme edge of the cliff. Ox teams raced past, terrified by the storm, the stinging whips, the shouts of the drivers. Wheels scraped lightly on wheels as they whizzed by.

God has given me courage. But my common sense told me that at least one wagon was a goner. My only help was prayer. My Hail Marys and ejaculations at that moment cannot be counted. A few inches more and the whole caravan would have tumbled into the abyss forever.

As it was, ten o'clock that night found a group of bedraggled missionaries kneeling in the mud, thanking God for saving all their wagons and wondering where their Guardian Angels had found a road-widener.

Week followed week as we pushed on through the veld. We had left the terrors of Hell's Gate far behind and the back-breaking fatigue of climbing almost a mile up to the high plateau that overlooks the Limpopo river valley. We were entering the desert.

We were up against a different type of hardship here. Thirst. These "ships of the up-country"—as the ox wagons were called by the Dutch settlers—would have to be put under forced draft if we wanted to reach the Tati River alive. Treks of thirteen, twenty and thirty-six hours without a let-up were ahead of us—treks without water.

For this was Kalahari—the Sahara of the South—where to miss even one spring could be fatal. Here your life depended on the oxen.

If they died of thirst you could never carry enough provisions to get across. The irony was this. You couldn't take enough water for sixty oxen—you had to find a stream or river or oasis for them—or else.

Thirst naturally was the greatest torment for the oxen. Three full weeks they pulled, day and night, though the wheels sank over the axles in the sand and boulders set the wagons shuddering. Clouds of dust clogged their windpipes, reddened their eyes, coated their parched tongues till they bellowed for water.

Finally, completely spent, they fell. Some were shot; others were whipped up and driven on. There was no other way.

Again and again when we arrived at a river it was dry. Nothing to do but pray and dig for water.

I must confess a kind of fury seized me at these times. I have never been able to stand the sight of suffering, even if it was only an ox. Besides, carrying the success or failure of our mission under their yokes—they were our one link with life—I had to stand by helpless for hours while the broiling sun drove them almost mad with thirst. My one thought was to find water, and quick!

Seizing a spade, I would begin digging like a soldier seeking cover under heavy fire. All the rest fanned out with spades in a circle. Soon the sand was flying up from an ever-deepening pit.

As we dig down we eagerly watch for signs of moisture. The sand becomes heavy and damp—a parched cheer comes from those resting around the pit as wet sand comes up. One more spade full, and we scramble out of the slowly filling hole, calling for canteens and barrels.

But the oxen have smelt the water too. Sixty pairs of horns rush for the pit. Six men with clubs beat off the thirst-crazed animals while a seventh hastily fills buckets and pots and pans with the muddy brown water. Then with shouts and flailing clubs we cut a path through the milling bullocks.

In a moment the fever-wracked Father Fuchs is enjoying his first cool drink in days on a rough wagon bed inside a canvas covered furnace.

Four months after leaving Grahamstown we sighted the Tati River. Just opposite was the settlement by the same name. We were all dead tired; many of us drinking brackish water suffered from dysentery; Father Fuchs still had malaria; but we had reached our goal. Tati, we hoped, would be a spring-board for future mission stations everywhere in the Zambesi country.

As far as I was concerned, we could write the trip off as a good chunk of Purgatory which would come in useful later. Then, too, it was all for pagan souls.

Tati was in the kingdom of Lobengula, a native ruler who lived in his capital a few miles away—Gubuluwayo. Fathers Depelchin and Law and myself pushed on to the latter village without delay, leaving the others to recuperate and pray for the success of our appeal to the king. For by gifts and flattery we hoped to wheedle a permission from him to set up our post in his land.

We found old Lob on the verge of taking a wife—for the eighteenth time. Pre-marriage celebrations were in full swing. We presented our gifts and our petition. He accepted our presents; said he would think it over.

For days and weeks we prayed and waited for his answer. During the marriage festivities nothing could be done. It came unexpectedly one morning, two months after our arrival.

We were summoned into the king's presence.

"You are free to stay here and preach to my people—on one condition," Lobengula said.

We waited to hear some impossibility. He spoke again.

Providentially for us, it seemed that his ceremonial ox cart was ready to collapse in the yard. We all relaxed in a wide grin as he took us out to look at it.

There it stood, hood drooping, and wheels propped against its sides for support. It needed remodeling from tongue to tailgate. . . . We made our plans quickly. The king should have a wagon which no others could surpass and few could equal. Father Croonenberghs, an artist, should decorate the new canvas top which Brother Hedley, an ex-sailor, should make. I was left with the job of mending the mechanical gadgets.

We returned without delay to Tati where it was decided that we should send two wagons loaded with supplies for fixing the wagon and for a stay of some length at Gubu. I was to set out with the party and return after a day's journey to Tati. They needed me there to set up a permanent camp, while the others were finishing the royal wagon hood.

A day's walk from Tati I gave the reins to a native driver and started walking back before sunrise to get the jump on the heat. In my hurry I went without breakfast, intending to eat on what my gun could bring down.

I had gotten up that morning weak and stiff; thought I could walk it off, but that's no way to get rid of fever. After a short time I was shivering and sweating. Overcome with nausea, which the idea of breakfast only increased, I thought only of water for my dry mouth, drinking continually the slimy stuff in the holes and river beds along the way. I ate nothing all that day.

By pushing on I hoped to reach Tati by nightfall. Spending the night alone in the jungle would be literally sleeping in a lion's den.

Night caught up with me on the banks of a river, eight miles from help. Worn out all over I staggered about gathering wood for a watch-fire. The fire sputtered and sizzled. Soon a crackling blaze and the distant roar of lions cleared my drowsy head. But only for an hour.

The flames died down. I awoke with a start, my head almost between my knees. There was a rustle of leaves in the brush behind me. I wheeled around to stare into the glowing eyes of something in the darkness. I sprang up and poked at the fire. It leaped into flames. When I looked again the eyes were gone.

I spent that night putting wood on the fire, my rifle in one hand, my rosary in the other.

Daybreak brought quiet; I knelt down to thank God for my life. Though I had not slept, the fever seemed to have gone. I felt much better, but just as I was tidying myself up I got a scorpion-sting, not dangerous, but extremely painful.

Near the river, I shot two turtle-doves. After roasting them I ate one and put the other in my kit. With a drink of water I was on my way.

But I was not to get home that easy. The next mile or so found the sun beating down on me in a barren sandy plain, where there was no water. The fever returned. The sun blazed down unmercifully. It must have been about one hundred degrees out there.

For three hours I stumbled along only to fall at midday at the foot of the tree. I knew I would never last another night in the open. I decided to walk two hundred paces and rest; then walk again. Never before had I felt so weak. My throat was dry as a bone on the desert, my lips stuck together.

I reached a wood and felt cooler. The sun went down and I seemed like a new man. Throwing off my pack and stripping down to shirt, pants and boots, carrying nothing but a revolver and rifle, I drove myself on, surrounded by the growling of lions and the snarling of leopards.

"God is with me," I told myself, "God who created these animals to do His will."

At half-past ten I reached Tati and knocked on the door. "Who is there?" But I could not answer; my lips were too firmly glued together. . . .

The natives sure knew a lot of tricks. And some of those men were the strongest I have ever met. I remember particularly one huge fellow who saved my life as casually as you please. He used jiu-jitsu, I think.

Our little Hottentot and Tom an ox driver, an escort of natives, and myself had set out to recapture our wagons from the Mashona. We had been traveling about three weeks through the hardest kind of country imaginable, climbing mountains three thousand feet high, dropping down into valleys and fording rivers so deep we had to swim.

We were getting pretty tired one afternoon when we came upon a swift little stream, not very wide, about waist high, but rushing down the mountainside in a mighty big hurry.

There was nothing to hold on to, and we were loaded down with packs and rifles. If you lost your footing, you'd be shooting the rapids with nothing but a gun-butt for a paddle and a fifty-pound pack for a life-preserver.

I hoisted my rifle over my head and started across, a native just behind me. I had about five yards to go when I felt my feet going out from under me. I began to thrash around and yell for help when all of a sudden I was catapulted through the air and landed with a splash in the shallow water. With a twist of the wrist, the native behind had flipped me up on the bank, fifty-pound pack and all!

I turned around just in time to see Cape Corps, our native ox driver, slip in the same spot. He tossed his rifle to a native and tried to swim. The current got him and began to sweep him downstream. I had given him up for lost when another native dived in, grabbed him, and tossed him up on the bank.

I'll never know how they did it. . . .


We Sadeleers have always had thick skulls. Have had for generations. Otherwise my missionary career would have ended in 1883 on my way down to Grahamstown for supplies.

The Superior, Father Depelchin, had a horse named Dandy who hadn't done a thing to earn his keep for months. Dandy was as frisky as a young pup greeting you in the morning. He seized upon the slightest noise to make a big fuss—shying and snorting around as if it were a thunderclap. Even the jolting of the cart over the rocks as we rolled along put him into a froth. To calm him I tied a short length to his bridle and led him behind the wagon.

After an hour of walking, the sun started trickles of sweat running down my back. I thought I might as well ride him. I jumped on his back. Like a fool, when I found the strap too short to reach I took it out of his mouth and was just tying it around his neck when he took off.

Did you ever ride bareback on a bridleless horse? Pulling on the rope around his neck was like stoking a runaway train down a winding mountain track. The more I pulled, the more steam he got up. I saw I had to jump off at the softest siding I could find. Picking a clump of brush I jumped. Only trouble was that I was afraid to lose the horse. So I kept hold of the rope.

The next thing I know I'm getting a hind hoof in the chest. Still I clung to the rope. He spun around and kicked me in the back of the head. The last thing I heard was a native shouting, "The white man is dead." Then I blacked out.

When I came to, I was lying on my back with someone putting cold packs on my head and with a terrific pain in back of my skull. Like somebody was jabbing ice picks into my scalp. But they got the blood stopped and the pain settled down to a dull ache.

Pulling myself up, I walked over to the wagon. Should have taken their advice. I keeled over after five steps. They called a doctor who sewed up my fractured skull and told me to rest till it healed. So they pitched camp right there.

One good thing, the horse didn't get away. They went right up to the quivering animal and put a strap in his mouth again before he knew it.

In less than two weeks the wound had healed and I felt strong enough to get up. Perhaps if they hadn't lost half the oxen, I might have stayed up. But forty oxen were too many to let wander away. With a prayer to St. Anthony I set out and three hours later with the help of a friendly neighbor found all of them in a jungle thicket.

That the sudden demand on my strength was too much, I discovered as I lay down after the first stage of the journey. Later when I tried to get up, everything swam before my eyes. I cried out for help, even as I was spinning away into darkness.

I remember nothing till I woke up in a clean white hospital bed. They told me after a while that I had been unconscious two weeks. I thought I was going to die, and in my few lucid intervals during the next two weeks I was filled with joy.

What had I to fear? The Holy Father himself had promised me and all of us pioneers a plenary indulgence at the hour of death if we died on the mission. Besides I had a little prayer that I kept repeating over and over again— "My Lord and my God, henceforward I accept with complete resignation whatever death Thou shalt send me, with all its pains and sufferings." But He didn't take me up on it that time.

The concussion and brain-fever left me one day, weak and exhausted, but happy I had been spared to work a few more years on the mission. Then the doctor just about broke my heart. He insisted with my Superior that I would never live unless I returned to Europe. . . .

I'll never forget the morning Father Kroot, Lord have mercy on him, came in with the bad news. I was sitting up at the time saying my rosary to divert myself from my rising impatience at the forced inactivity of bed. I was in a fever of excitement that he might tell me I could get out of bed, but he went on laughing and chatting about news of the various stations for a while. Finally he came to the point. "Brother," he said, "the doctor says you will never be well unless you return to Belgium. This mission life is too hard for a weak man, and whether you know it or not, you *are* a weak man."

I was thunderstruck, so surprised I could only listen as he went on telling me the details of the doctor's report. At length he paused and I opened my mouth to reply. No sound came for a moment. Then "Fa-Father," I stammered, "before you send me home will you give me a few hours to think it over?"

"Certainly, Brother, you pray over it and I'll be back this afternoon."

That afternoon I had my answer. "If you order me to go, Father," I told him, "I'll set out here and now, but without that order I'll not leave my mission."

With a sigh of relief I heard him reply:

"I've been praying over the matter myself, Brother, and I won't ask you to leave for a while yet. We'll let God decide if He wants you to continue on here. But if you aren't your old self in a month or two, I'll have no choice but to send you home."

Everyone including myself was astonished at my speedy recovery after that. The doctor let me leave the hospital soon afterwards. Even Father Kroot was convinced when out of the corner of my eye I caught him watching me dig in a dried-up river bed for water on our way across Kalahari.

God has been so good to me. . . .

Recently I heard that somewhere doctors are advising shell-shocked soldiers to get a little farm somewhere and raise some chickens and vegetables. Seems to be a good cure for war jitters. I can testify that there's nothing better for jangled nerves than raising ostriches.

By the time I had been on the mission for five or six years, the hard work and the constant attacks of malaria had undermined my strength considerably. I suffered from fits of depression—the others suffered from my petty fault-finding. They sent me to Dunbrody in the Cape Colony where there was a farm attached to our house of studies. My mother saved a letter I wrote about this time describing the birds. It shows how much the ostrich cure was helping me.

(He encloses the following letter).

Our ostriches (we have about a hundred) are doing well. They are fierce animals. When they come out of an egg, they are as big as a six-months' old chicken; when they are fully grown, they may weigh as much as four hundred pounds or more. They have queer habits; for the first four years they do not mate. After that, the rule is: one husband, one wife. When the hen has nearly finished laying her eggs, she begins to brood just as other birds.

Their nest is very simple: sometimes behind a bush, mostly in an open spot. They gather a little sand with their wings to build up the walls and then their nest is ready.

As soon as the young are hatched, they walk about with their mother and pick up grass and leaves. But after one day we take the young away and put them in a yard, so that they do not know their parents. We do this in order to tame them.

When they are eight or nine months old, I feed them out of my hand with Spanish wheat; they love it. In that way they get to know me. As soon as I enter the yard, they run after me and peck at my buttons, my watch-chain and everything that shines. Up to their second year, they are innocent; after that they change—at least the males do; I must say nothing against the females; they remain good.

But you have to be careful with adult males. Shy as they are in the wilds, they become daring when they have been brought up among men. An ostrich who is in ill-humor is not an easy thing to cope with. It comes charging along at you, its tail in the air and its mouth open, and jumps on you so violently that it can break your arms and legs. I have had to fight with these fellows more than once.

One of them was a certain "Baas Stroogoed," a splendid ostrich which I liked very much. Baas Stroogoed rather fancied himself. Whenever we crossed the camp he stepped behind us with an air of saying, "Now then, get a move on!"

One day, when I was later than usual because of business at home, I was going through the camp with my little bag containing my dinner and a tin of water in my left hand, a small axe and thorny stick in my right to ward off ostriches. Baas Stroogoed went for me. He looked at me as if to say, "Where have you been so late?" I could see that he was not in a very good temper, so I kept an eye on him. . . . In an open spot he began to spit. I prepared to defend myself, but at the same time tumbled over a stump. He was on me like a flash, one leg on my chest and one on my arms. He had no doubt that I was in his power.

With all my strength I freed first my chest, then my arms and got hold of him with both my hands. I wanted to bring him to the ground but could not, so I let him go—and off he flew as quickly as his legs could carry him. I had probably pinched too hard. . . .

Now, what is the use of these birds? Twice a year we cut off the plumes of the males, which are sold for a good price. They are sometimes seen by you on ladies' hats. The finest of them cost about twenty francs each. The males give us on an average about one hundred francs a year.

To cut the plumes isn't as easy as with a pigeon. We first have to chase them into a cage, erected in the corner of the camp. In this cage, which is about seven feet high and four feet broad, they stand like a horse in a stall.

Even then it is a dangerous task. Almost every year we hear of accidents to Boers whose stomachs are ripped open by the ostriches. They have not yet had the chance of doing the same to me.

I will tell you the rest about my ostriches later, if not in this life, then in heaven; we have all eternity there to do it.

In 1891 I had been on the mission just twelve years. I was a little the worse for wear, gray as a pigeon with practically no teeth. Didn't think I could live out the year. At forty-seven, my father and mother were still living. I expected to wait for them in heaven.

Many things had happened in the last few years. The house of studies at Dunbrody where they had the ostrich farm had been broken up and the students sent to Europe to continue their studies. In 1889 a diphtheria epidemic had forced us to transfer St. Aidan's College in Grahamstown to the last mentioned Dunbrody. For six months I had nursed the sick boys.

By the time we had moved back to Grahamstown, I was in a bad way again. Moody and depressed and cranky, all my old pep gone. But there was a new wrinkle this time.

I began to be troubled by a fear of dying without seeing my parents and relatives. I remember digging out of my battered trunk every picture of them I could find, arranging them on my desk and brooding over the sad plight of a missionary a thousand miles from home. When an uncle died my folks received a letter which read in part, "I have put up the family photo in my room. At least in this way I can see you again. God's will be done. I am beginning to think of my grave too. Every day I draw nearer to it, and in Africa a man doesn't last long." After so many happy years, there I was pining like a boy away from home for the first time.

My father died, a good Catholic to the end, in January 1891. Father Provincial sent word that I was to come home soon afterward.

I can recall sitting in a deck-chair on the steamer to Belgium looking back over my life. As a missionary I was a failure.

At the end of 1885 they had withdrawn me to the peace and security of Grahamstown. The native uprising in 1890 had forced us to close the Zambesi Mission. The Fathers and Brothers returned to Kimberley in the south to wait for peace. Compared to the vast population, the conversions up to that time had been practically nothing.

I was returning again to a college, this time in Belgium, broken in soul and body. I had sweated and slaved for nothing. What good now were the teeth-rattling wagon miles under sweltering sun and soaking rain, hours of snaking out logs and splitting stakes, grimy days of slashing brush and blasting stumps, months tending goats and oxen on a lonely mission outpost, drudging years of domestic chores at Dunbrody? As far as converts went, twelve years poured down a rathole. I began to see why St. Joseph was a saint.

In July I was in the arms of my dear old mother in Lede. Hand in hand we went out to look at dad's grave. I offered the sacrifice of not seeing him a last time for converts on the Zambesi and everywhere.

My native air did wonders for me. As my health and strength returned, a great peace began to flood my soul. My fears were gone and once more I was my old self. . . .

Two years passed. The call went out for volunteers to pioneer the new Congo mission. Another vast field, 900,000 square miles of darkest Africa was to be opened up to the light of Christ's Church.

I thought it over. I couldn't hide from myself that I had left my heart on the mission. The fare in Belgium was too good, the bed too soft, the delights too many.

But I had my dear old mother to think of. Soon God would call her to her deathbed. I wanted to be by her side, as I had not been when dad died. Then, too, there was my own soul to think of.

The closest thing to fear I have ever known, if such it should be called, is to be left alone at a mission station, without a priest. It had happened to me more than once. I had even spent six months alone at Panda-me-Tenga deprived of Mass and Holy Communion.

As I told a Father, a close friend of mine at that time, "If Father Provincial speaks or only gives a sign of his will, I am ready. But I do not ask it myself. To live for months without priest or sacraments, in those constant dangers of a complete loneliness in pagan surroundings, I dare not meet it of my own accord."

My perplexity did not last long. That's one of the most consoling things I have found in religious life, that God makes difficult decisions for you through Superiors. From the moment they speak all you have to do is say "Yes," and God's got to see the job through.

Well, they decided to send me back to Africa again—to a new mission—the Congo. Didn't know it then but I was to spend another thirteen years as an active missionary.

We headed into the interior of the Congo country from Matadi on June 12, 1892. . . .

(The last words Brother wrote are these:)

Though danger of death on the mission taught me how to pray, I haven't prayed very much. I am trying to make up for that in my old age. Work was my life, because when I worked hard I was happy at the thought that I did not do it for money but for the greater glory of Him who supports me and gives me health. . . .

(At this point in his narrative occurs a notation in a strange hand):

"Brother Sadeleer is now totally blind, February, 1920."

"I, for my part," wrote Father Croonenberghs of their apparent failure, "thank God with all my heart for having called me to share in the holy labors of the South African apostolate. We cannot solve the mysteries of Divine Providence. Perhaps our work will remain fruitless for a long time; perhaps in the exercise of our ministry we shall fall victims to this murderous climate or to the sword of the persecutor, what does it matter? The Church of the Blacks will one day rise up from the earth in which our bodies will be laid. Others will come after us to build the Church, and after them yet others to set the Cross upon the steeple. . . ."

His vision of the Church of the Negroes has been fantastically realized. The Belgian Congo in 1900 had 11,000 Catholics. Today, fifty years later, there are 3.5 million native Catholics and a million catechumens.

In 1900 there were about a thousand Catholics in the Zambesi Mission. Now there are over 100,000.[1]

[1] In continental Africa in 1906 there were 360,000 Catholics. By 1949 the figure had jumped to 11,000,000 native Catholics and 2,000,000 catechumens on the missions alone. Almost a third of the native population of the Belgian Congo are Catholic, while one out of twenty-five is Catholic in the Zambesi. The latter mission has been retarded by war, famine, polygamy, etc.

# Known But to God

BY FRANK B. COSTELLO, S.J.

*Brother Joseph Mobberly, S.J. (1779–1827)*

S T. INIGOES lay unsuspecting in the fall sunlight. A British sloop glided out of the Patuxent into Chesapeake Bay in the early hours of October 31, 1814. Cruising cautiously south, the ship rounded Point Lookout into the Potomac and, hugging the pinked shore line, anchored in late afternoon opposite the Jesuit mission of St. Inigoes in St. Mary's County, Maryland. St. Inigoes was ripe for a raid. It was to be a Hallowe'en raid of revenge and a scavenger hunt for food.

All summer and during the early fall months, British sloops had terrified Americans in the Chesapeake area. During August, His Majesty's forces had marched on Washington, burned the White House and the Capitol and forced President and Mrs. Madison to race for their lives into the woods of Virginia. All these forays left St. Inigoes unmolested. Now on this last day of October, the mission, like a rich hive dripping with honey, was waiting to be plundered.

The War of 1812 was particularly hard on Jesuit houses in Maryland. The novitiate was opened that year at St. Inigoes. Rumors of war disturbed the Jesuit headquarters at Georgetown and rumblings of war so upset the routine at the novitiate that the little band of novices was finally moved. But someone had to be left at St. Inigoes to take charge of the farm and see to it that supplies did not fall into the hands of the enemy. A young American lay brother, hardly more than a novice himself, was chosen to hold this post against the British. His name, Joseph P. Mobberly.

Brother Mobberly's success in holding St. Inigoes must have exasperated the British commanders. The frequent raids on the neighboring farms always gave him warning that the English were moving his way. At the first alarm he would load his ox carts, hustle his steers and sheep, and having helped the Negroes to move into the woods, he would cache his barrels of pork and herring, the hams and shoulders, flour, sugar and beef in the cellars of distant neighbors. The steers and sheep were sent to the safest Jesuit farms. Time and again he outmaneuvered the raiders, always escaping just before they descended. They would arrive to find a deserted farm. Now in the closing weeks of the war, a surprise attack was planned and Hallowe'en chosen as the day. St. Inigoes was overdue for a raid. This time they would catch the Brother unprepared and capture one of the greater prizes of the war.

Brother Mobberly was not expecting visitors that day. It was just getting dusk as he finished the chores at the barn and started to the house for supper. Then he noticed the barge rounding the point and heading for the mission landing. They were making slow progress against the ebb tide but there was no doubt of their intentions. He had no time to hide the stores or cattle. The first thing to do was to order the Negroes into the woods. The terror in their faces as he hurried from shack to shack mirrored the fear in his own heart. He ran for the house and burst in on his superior, Father Rantzau. Maximilian Rantzau, a former German Augustinian, was a victim of the French Revolution. He was admitted as a Jesuit in America and assigned to St. Inigoes as a sort of chaplain for Brother Mobberly. He looked up annoyed that Brother should break into his room without knocking.

"Father, the British are at our landing. You'd better come down."

Without moving his finger from his Breviary, Father Rantzau icily informed Brother that he was not going down to the landing. He resumed the reading of his Office saying rather sharply that he had nothing to fear from the British. But by that time, Brother Mobberly was out of the room and down the hall. An American, at least, knew better than to say he had nothing to fear from the British. He stopped short at a window, turned and stuffed his watch and the currency of the house under the decayed sill.

Racing for the front door he was out on the path and down to the river bank by the time the barge was grounded on the tide flats. They did not go around to the landing, after all. The raiders were climbing down the side of the barge onto the oozy mud. Splashing through the little puddles and stumbling over barnacled rocks they ran towards Brother standing in fear on the bank. The

First Lieutenant, riding on the shoulders of a burly seaman, landed his immaculate boots on the grass in front of Brother. With an eye of contempt for the latter's farm clothes he snapped:

"We're here to burn this place down. You Americans have been burning some houses in Canada and I understand that the priests here have been telling the militia to fire on our men along the shore."

There was no denying that this was a raid of retaliation. Swallowing quickly, Brother Mobberly dared to correct him:

"We're hardly accountable here, Sir, for what's been done in Canada. And as for the priests urging the militia to fire on your men, I fear that you have been misinformed. We're religious men and have nothing to do with the conduct of the war. This is church property," he added with quiet dignity, "and it is appropriated for the use of the Church. I beg you to spare it."

At the word "Church" the officers's tone and manner changed. He took another look at this young American in farm clothes. There was a commanding calm in his bearing, and determination in the tone of his voice. Maybe this was one of the priests. At any rate he would not burn a church. With a nod to the men, the officer moved towards the house. That was the signal the sailors had been waiting for. They sprinted across the lawn, jumped onto the porch and disappeared into the house. There was no mistaking their intent. Brother Mobberly's first thought was for timid Father Rantzau who had nothing to fear from the British.

"Don't let them hurt the old priest," he pleaded.

The Lieutenant promised to protect Father Rantzau and asked to be taken to his room. Brother later wrote an account of this in his Diary:

"I took him to Father Rantzau's room and while we were talking, I heard a great noise in the chapel. I ran into the hall and saw the chapel door was open. I saw four or five ruffians carrying the Blessed Sacrament, the chalice, sacred vestments and linen. I ran to the officer and begged him to interfere. I protested that what we held most sacred, the adorable Sacrament of the altar, had been taken away and I begged him to restore it. I entreated him over and over again to protect church property. He promised he would and we ran out to the barge together.

"As we were going I said: 'Here, Sir, they are handing the chalice to a bargeman. Do have it restored.' He said he would and since they knew that he saw it, they gave it up. I received it from the hands of a villain. I then entreated him to restore the ciborium. 'Why,' said he, 'what sort of a thing is it?' I described it for he had not seen it. The men declared they had it not and I declared that they had taken it away. Seeing that I could not prevail I turned again to the house to get Father Rantzau.

"To the officer coming with me I protested: 'What an indignity to the Church!' After a short pause he replied: 'Sir, I did not come here to plunder—I came for stock but I cannot command these men—they are nothing but real ruffians.' I begged Father Rantzau to interfere. He did so, but in vain. Father Rantzau told me later that he was almost out of himself with fright and that he never expected such an attack.

"I again begged for the ciborium. The officer stormed and swore that everything would be thrown on shore again if they didn't restore the ciborium. Meanwhile the officer had some of the vestments and two beds brought back. I insisted on getting the ciborium but to no purpose. The sailors united in saying that they had seen no such thing and told the officer that my intention was to detain them longer in order that our militia might come up and fire on them. The officer, pretending to be alarmed, ordered a sailor to take him to the barge.

"Night was coming on. One of the other officers, having no one to carry him out, was getting ready to wade when I accosted him: 'Do you know Sir, what a crime it is to rob a church?' The officer holding a boot in one hand looked up at me: 'Don't talk to me about robbing churches. I've seen many a church robbed in Spain.' By this time the First Lieutenant was at the barge. I shouted to him to give it back. He promised he would, seated himself in the barge and ordered his men to move off without taking any more notice of us.

They had taken about ten minutes to complete their sacrilegious task."

Brother Mobberly stood on the bank, watched the barge pushed into the ebb tide, twist sharply around and right itself downstream. He hoped that even then they might turn around and restore the Blessed Sacrament. Ironically, he remembered, after all his previous precautions, they hadn't touched the food stores this time. He would gladly have emptied the cellars for them if they only had left him his God.

Minutes later he caught himself in these reflections, turned towards the house and began to pick up mechanically the debris in the path. They had dropped a shoe here. A purificator was still clinging to the hedge. By the time he reached the porch his arms were loaded.

That hour of horror had aged him; he actually seemed years older that night. But his work for the day was not yet over. He had to quiet the whimperings of the terrorized old priest. A Negress with two of her children had been captured and taken screaming to the barge. They later made their escape but their screams still echoed in his ears. The panic-stricken Negroes had to be calmed. Then, an ominous silence settled over the mission. St. Inigoes was like a captured city, sacked, pillaged and plundered. Only God had been taken, but to them, of course, that was Everything.

He was just finishing his survey of the damage of the first floor when he came to the chapel hall. The door still hung open. The sand-tracked floor gleamed in the moonlight. He entered the wild disorder of the chapel and instinctively glanced towards the tabernacle. The stripped altar had the desolate look of Good Friday. Around the room, chairs and prie-dieus were thrown about in all directions. The drawers of the vesting case were open and rifled linens still hung over the sides. Blank squares stared back at him where the pictures of Francis Xavier and King David had been. Where the crucifix had hung, a cross in white was outlined on the wall. As he moved to the window there was a harsh grinding underfoot. Bending down he carefully picked up pieces of broken glass.

Turning his hand to the lighted window he found a cruet handle in a setting of glittering glass. Methodically he searched the floor for the remaining pieces and placed them on a chair. When he straightened up, his body blocked the moon-brightened window.

Only then did he catch sight of the sanctuary lamp still flickering in the corner. There in the darkness cast by his shadow, he saw the red light dimly indicating the presence of the Blessed Sacrament. The dancing flame mocked him there in the deserted chapel. It shouldn't be here, he told himself. Where should it be? Perhaps by the side of a sailor's dirty sea chest in the forecastle of His Majesty's sloop of war. Perhaps it should be standing watch at a first-mate's pillow. Perhaps this tiny red glow should follow his mind as, Magdalen-like, it roved the coves and inlets of the Chesapeake, searching for his kidnapped God: *"Because they have taken away my Lord, and I know not where they have laid him."*

Still watching the flame he sat down on one of the chairs in the littered chapel and allowed the flickering shadows to fascinate his tired eyes. In the phantom light, shapes of yesterday hovered. Images of his early years began to tease his memory. He was thinking of home when he fell asleep.

They told him that he was born in the country of Maryland, January 12, 1779. Maryland at that time was one of the independent nations of the world. A voluntary orphan from her mother England, she had not yet joined her sister states in the temporary foster-home of the Confederation until the new family of the United States was formed. Somewhere in that country of Maryland, Joe Mobberly was born at the beginning of 1779.

Of his early home life nothing is known. His parents, problems and pursuits are hidden in the records of unknown history. He was of the generation that, seeded in the Revolution, blossomed forth in the Federal era of the country's history. When he was eight, the Philadelphia Convention met in 1787. At ten he reached citizen's stature for that year the new government of the United States was born.

The United States and Georgetown University had the same year, 1789, stamped on their seals. The year that saw George Washington innaugurated as first President witnessed the founding of Georgetown College by Bishop John Carroll of Baltimore. Joe Mobberly was one of its early students for his name appears on the college registers from 1798 to 1802.

He seems to have completed the ordinary college course of his day without distinction. He acquired a good English style and enough Latin to be able to write a long letter to the Jesuit General in Rome in later years. Perhaps the greatest formative influence in his college years was contact with the pioneers of the American hierarchy. Archbishops Carroll, Neale and Marechal of Baltimore, Bishop Fenwick of Boston and Bishop Dubourg of New Orleans were all associated with Georgetown in some capacity or other during Joe Mobberly's student days. It was Father Dubourg, the Rector of the College, who received him into the Sodality of the Blessed Virgin Mary as a climax of his college career.

The year after his graduation he asked to join the Society of Jesus. The fire of Jesuit life had been smothered in 1773. Not entirely extinguished, a little flame still burned in the White Russian dominions of Catherine II. In 1805, with papal permission ex-Jesuits in America reached their taper across the world and lighted the new fire of Jesuit activity in the United States from the embers of the old Society still smoldering in White Russia. When, nine years later, Pius VII restored the Jesuits everywhere again, the followers of Ignatius in this country were fairly well organized. Joe Mobberly seems to have applied to join this group as a priest but finally entered as a brother on October 10, 1807, and pronounced his first vows two years later.

He was assigned to St. Inigoes and spent most of his early years there, with the exception of twelve months in New York teaching reading and writing to one hundred and fifty boys in the grammar school there.

The Catalog of the American Mission of the Jesuits paints a neat picture of Brother Mobberly at this time. This Catalog is published in Jesuit Provinces every year as a sort of directory listing the houses in the area and the members of the various communities. After each Jesuit's name is a description of his assigned jobs. If a brother, for instance, is cook, sacristan and infirmarian, he is credited as such in the catalog. For St. Inigoes in trenchantly terse Latin, is the simple entry: *Josephus Mobberly . . . Ad omnia.* That's what he was doing, everything, on that last day of October, 1814, when the British came.

Father Rantzau, cold and tired from a sleepless night, woke Brother Mobberly in the chapel next morning and asked him to start a fire and see about getting breakfast. After breakfast he had to send a report to his superior, Father Grassi, and write Georgetown for supplies. Then there was nothing to do but wait for the supplies to arrive; nothing to do but keep the farm running, and keep the Negroes happy. Waiting would be a busy time.

Two weeks worried by. There were daily rumors of increasing raider attacks. The British, if people could be believed, were everywhere. Brother records in his Diary: "Our distress is so deeply felt here that we can scarcely do anything but keep guard. The alarm seems too great for the work of the farm to continue." The war of nerves went on, however, with little relief in sight but with no return of the enemy. Until one day—

But let Brother Mobberly finish the narrative: "On the 18th of November I went to the slave quarters at dawn of day. I saw something like a small sail stretch over towards the house. I soon discovered it to be a white flag; and then I saw the barge; my heart leaped for joy; I ran for the house—nay, I rather flew. When I arrived, they were in the act of throwing the beds up on the garden bank. The same officer that robbed us met me and requested me to walk with him into the garden. He then began to express his extreme regret that he ever saw the house.

"A rising tear made him pause for a moment. Then in broken accents he exclaimed: 'O, why did I ever come to this house! In doing so I was truly unfortunate. I call God to witness that I am innocent of this crime. You know, Sir, how much I endeavored at your request to command my men; but they would not obey. O, how I extremely regret having come to this house! Sir, I am to be broken for this affair—court martial. In a few days I expect to be sent to England.'

"We then walked into the house, where many articles had already been deposited from the barge. He presented the ciborium at the sight of which I cannot describe my feelings—the office of a priest was to be performed but the priest was not at home. With humble confusion mingled with emotions of joy I received the sacred treasure into my trembling hands, turned my back on the officer, fell upon my knees and adored the Author of Life.

"I then carried it to the chapel, opened it and saw one small pix. I concluded the Blessed Sacrament was there. Father Rantzau on his return found four sacred hosts. After placing it in the tabernacle I returned to the officer who observed that though an enemy from necessity and not bound to generous acts, he still desired to prove to me the generosity of a British officer. He then laid on the table $113 to pay damages and told me that his name was William Hancock; his residence, Lower Clopton, England; that if I should ever want anything from England to write to him and that he should always be glad to serve me. I thanked him and we parted."

Brother Mobberly did not wait to watch them leave this time but hurried again to the chapel and knelt in quiet adoration for a while. Then he got up, genuflected and went out. The morning chores at the barn still had to be done. He began to whistle as he hurried down the path.

For every day of acclaim in a hero's life, there are years that are lived in obscurity. We hear briefly of Nathan Hale, Colin Kelly or Commander Shea. Their moment of heroic effort came and they achieved renown. We know them in that fleeting moment. Of their lives up to that time we hear very little. What we do know is that they found fame in the line of duty. Poets are born but heroes are made. And strangely enough it is duty that makes men heroes.

Congressional medals are awarded for heroism "beyond the call of duty." What appears to others to be beyond the call of duty seemed to the hero to be just his job. Perhaps that explains his abashed smile and embarrassed handshake in the President's Office.

If heroism is a matter of a moment, greatness is lifelong. The humdrum task of yesterday becomes the epic achievement of to-day. A chance occurrence spotlights greatness. It can be almost anything. If this is true of life in general, religious life is no exception. For Brother Mobberly November 18th began like any other day. Father Rantzau happened to be gone. Brother Mobberly, as so often before, was left in charge of everything. When the Blessed Sacrament was returned, it was just part of his job to receive it in the name of the whole Church. It was his duty to kneel and adore the desecrated God he held in his hands. His lifelong greatness was summed up in that moment. Hours of menial tasks, days of domestic drudgery, years of Eucharistic adoration, find their consummation here. What looks like a chance occurrence turns out to be a searchlight from eternity revealing his greatness.

There are people who like to specialize in being ordinary. Just as there are Air force men who prefer a mechanic's suit to pilot's wings, Navy men who would rather man a galley than a six-inch gun, so there are religious men who prefer the retirement of the sacristy to the renown of the pulpit. They seem to know that *any* job done often enough becomes monotonous. By choosing the ordinary they protect themselves from the boredom of the extraordinary.

One writer called it the Seabee instinct. The Seabee is described as a man who specializes in doing everything. Before the War in the Pacific was won, someone had to build island airstrips, blast navy bases and move mountains of lava. Before there was peace again in the Pacific, someone had to build accommodations for men by the millions. Whether it was bulldozers or brass buttons, K-rations or quonset huts, wrenches or refrigerators, someone had to get it there, and that someone was the Seabee.

There are Seabees in religion too. Before the Church Militant can make a beach-head on an African shore, the brothers have to staff training camps for cadet priests. Fundamental as it seems, before a priest can pour baptismal water on the heads of heathen, someone has to boil water for his soup. The brother is the high priest of the fundamental.

Many people wonder why energetic young Americans become brothers. They might just as well ask why they volunteer for the Seabees. Brothers realize that for every dreamer there must be a hundred practical men to make that dream come true. The grand strategy of Christ for the conquest of the world needs the hands of Christ to make it real. Christ's Seabees prefer to fight that way and, like good Seabees, prefer to be unknown.

One final word about Brother Mobberly. He faded into the mists from which he stepped on that autumn afternoon. Age found him on his way back to the city, leaving his steers and farm clothes behind. They needed a teacher at Georgetown so he took a class and there finished his years, rounding out that *ad omnia* that so aptly describes his Jesuit life. On a late September day Brother died and they buried him on the college campus overlooking the Potomac. He lies there today under a simple headstone, gray from the weather, that says in effect: There was born a man named Joseph Mobberly, he became a Jesuit and after twenty years of service, died at Georgetown on September 30, 1827.

Across the same Potomac in the wooded hills of Virginia is another grave topped by a brilliant block of marble. To this grave they come by the millions to stand there in the silence, the deafening silence, watch the sentry pace, one, two, three, and think how this nameless American lying there symbolizes all their common aspirations. Perhaps no hero in our history has received such revering honors. Yet no one knows where he came from—maybe a town on the Oregon coast or the prairies of North Dakota or from a tenant farmer's shack in central Georgia. No one knows when he was born, who his friends were, what tunes he used to whistle on his way to school. No one knows what dreams he had, what prospects for the future. No one knows even how he died. No one knows but God.

That is what it says there on the Tomb of the Unknown Soldier: *Here rests in honored glory an American soldier known but to God.* We remain wordless before heroic self-effacement. Reverent silence is our most eloquent tribute for unknown heroes like a Mobberly at Georgetown or that nameless American at Arlington. They have given new stature to mankind and make us glad to share a common dignity. They are like monumental types caught suddenly at their job by the searchlight of eternity and reveal to us in a moment life-long courage and love. Then, just as suddenly they step back into the long line of the forgotten, the unnoticed, known but to God.

# Better a Day

BY E. R. ZIMMERS, S.J.

*Brother Patrick Harrick, S.J. (1839–1923)*

HIGH ATOP A HILL in the geographical center of "the city," (as San Francisco is commonly known in the west) stands the massive, million-dollar church of St. Ignatius. Its tall spires look down on miles and miles of jam-packed, white houses, and past them, in a wide sweep, the Pacific Ocean, the Golden Gate, Alcatraz Island, and the vast harbor of San Francisco.

The church, built for the fourth time in 1915, is as much a symbol of western courage and pioneer achievement as are the huge bridges spanning the bay; it is more an image of San Francisco itself than are the cable cars, Chinatown, and Nob Hill. Through its doors and into its pews have poured, Sunday after Sunday, for the past hundred years, a vast proportion of the city's Catholic population, one of the largest in the west.

Its tradition of famous pulpit orators, its kindly, gentle confessors, its friendly brothers have stamped the city's catholicity with the mark of St. Ignatius.

The university and prep school that stand in the shadow of its towers have been graduating San Franciscans since 1855, and these alumni now fill the law offices, the judges' benches, the business houses of the bay area. A host of priests and doctors, architects, newspaper men, scientists, and even a few San Quentin prisoners, have been St. Ignatius or U.S.F. graduates; they form a band of alumni as loyal as those found anywhere in the world.

Once the church was a wooden shack down on the sand-dunes of Market Street. There was no road to its front door, and every time the fathers and brothers dug one, the winds filled it in in a week. The walls had to be held together by two iron braces, and the school building defied heating. But the personal devotion and unselfishness of its teachers was sufficient endowment, and slowly the church and college established itself. The city grew its cobblestones and wooden sidewalks, stuck its docks, like fingers, into the sea, and raised its taxes to staggering heights.

Forced, by 1880, to move southward, the fathers chose a new

site near the present civic center, and there built the most beautiful and expensive church on the west coast. It was ornate in the best rococo style, and people jammed it to capacity (2400) every Sunday.

Already over their heads in debt, they spent another million building a college and high school, which boasted such advantages as "the first electric lights in the West," and the "largest inside pool in San Francisco." Four months after the final building was completed, and three months after Fr. Riordan signed his name to the last page of his book on the "First Half-Century of Church and College," the whole establishment collapsed, and burned to rubble, in the earthquake of 1906.

Though the insurance companies with whom they were insured refused to pay, the fathers and brothers managed to build a cheap wooden structure about a mile west of the ruins, and this became known as the "Shirt Factory." Here they taught and preached and ministered to the poor, and bit by bit gathered the funds to build a new church, then a faculty building and university, and finally in 1928 a new high school.

Now at mid-century, as in a flash of sudden symbol, the silver towers and dome of a greater St. Ignatius rise from a hill that was once a Masonic cemetery.

The long work of development is almost finished, and Catholic San Franciscans are proud of their school as they are proud of their city, for the two seem almost identified in their minds. When the city was small and wooden, their school was a crude board building. When the city grew, so did the church. When the city crashed to the ground, so did St. Ignatius. And so did it rise from its ruins, as the city rose, to a new and promising future.

One hundred years ago, the Jesuit fathers and brothers first came to San Francisco, then a wild, gold-rush, shanty town. And now a big celebration of parades and banquets, oratory and dignified congratulation will mark the event. But as the orators look back over the hundred years, they will find that the past is not pretty, except in the man-hours of sacrifice and drudgery of the fathers in class, pulpit, and confessional, and of the brothers in daily, quiet service.

They will try to single out, in that century of great expectations and tragic disappointments, the man that seems to symbolize for people the constant, hidden service of the church and college. It will be no easy task. The work done for souls has been a complex work, and no one man has participated in all of it.

But in the eyes of the poor especially, and to the hundreds of daily worshippers, St. Ignatius will find that the most famed character of its hundred years existence is an ex-gold-miner, who for fifty years was a door porter and church custodian, a gracious, hardworking brother, named Patrick Harrick.

His life as a religious ran parallel with the history of St. Ignatius, almost from the beginning. He shared in its success, he symbolized its charity, he helped shoulder its disasters. San Francisco's Archbishop Hanna once asked a Confirmation class at Presentation convent, "Who is the visible head of the Church?" and a child answered, without a moment's hesitation, "Brother Harrick is the visible head of the church." On a side altar in St. Ignatius is a bronze plaque in his honor, and still, twenty-six years after his death, people say of him with respect and conviction, "He *was* St. Ignatius!"

He was born in a little village of County Cavan, Ireland, nine years before the great famine of '48. His mother, a gentle, sparkling-eyed widow, was the inspiration of his life. To provide for her, when he was nineteen, he went off to America and the stone dwellings of New England. His first job was as coachman to the governor of Rhode Island. But while riding atop the governor's coach, he caught the strange plague that had been sweeping the Eastern seaboard. It was called "gold fever" and Pat Harrick got it as badly as anyone. He had made some friends in the sedate surroundings of Rhode Island, and soon joined these friends in St. Louis where he trudged off to California in a covered wagon caravan.

He came to California because he wanted to make a fortune fast. "I wanted to be a millionaire within a year," he said. He was a sharp-eyed, pink-cheeked, black-topped youth with twenty dollars in his pocket. During the long, dreary trek from Fort Laramie along the Humboldt River through Carson sink and up Carson's pass into Eldorado, Harrick's golden dream-bubble grew bigger and shinier with every step. He looked with amusement at the mud streets of Placerville, watched the fist fights and brawls in the saloons, and tried to look like a tough prospector who knew what he was doing. The real miners and desert rats were too busy buying provisions, quarreling about claims, and drinking themselves silly to pay any attention to his airs, but because he was shrewd and willing to learn he picked up many a nugget of information.

With his friends he panned the innumerable streams and rivulets of the American River's three forks. The bubble lost some of its sheen when he found that even with good luck and back-breaking work he could barely meet expenses; it burst completely at the end of the first year when he found himself three hundred dollars in debt and no bonanza. But in bursting, it splattered his soul with a residue of shiny matter that colored all his first seven years in the far west.

He searched for gold near Marysville, moved along the flank of the Sierra Nevada, past spots like Brandy Gulch and Poker Flat, trying every unclaimed gully and sandbar from Pleasant Valley to Pulga Pass, but never with much success. He often asked himself whether it was worth all the work, and one day when offered a job as a baggageman and guard on a stagecoach to Montana, he snatched at the chance.

On his first trip he met an old sour-dough who filled his ears with talk of a new strike at Hell's Gate in Missoula County. When they reached Montana, Harrick left the stagecoach and set out with his grizzled friend for the gold fields. Together they worked mines from Hell's Gate, through Bitter Rock, Jocko, the Big Blackfoot Valleys, up the Wind River country to the Gate of the Mountains, a few miles from Helena.[1] He learned the secrets of the "Long Tom," a sluicing machine, and became an expert at "pan-

[1] "Last Chance Gulch." Gold was discovered there July 15, 1864.

ning" and "cradle" mining. At first in Gold Creek and later in Grasshopper Valley he found rich deposits in the gravels of creeks, bars and gulches, making sometimes fifty dollars a day in gold dust.

It seemed like a lot of money, but in the towns that sprang up like magic wherever the miners made a strike, the money didn't go far. Provisions were exorbitant, and Harrick, like most miners, liked to gamble. On Saturday night the men would crowd around the crude faro tables and shoot the works. A whole month's diggings could be lost in a few hours of cards and drinks. Harrick loved poker, especially for high stakes—the old timers nicknamed him "Kid" and took his money as fast as he made it. But he was vivacious and resilient; he tried to be a good loser. When his money was gone, if his head was still clear, he stood around and watched the others, learning to tell a bluff from the real thing. He drank whiskey and the vile gin drinks "that could corrode the pipes of a boiler," but when he did his conscience bothered him. He knew his mother wouldn't have liked his carryings-on and he felt ashamed. Resolved to stop drinking and card playing, he sent home to Ireland a packet of five week's diggings, nearly a thousand dollars.

When the gold in Grasshopper Valley began to peter out, he started southward toward Livingston, becoming more conscious every day of his rough, hard-drinking, godless environment. He had met a priest only once since leaving California, a Father Cataldo, who heard his confession and then rode off to his Indians. Kid Harrick met hundreds of fallen-away Catholics, whose faith was buried under heaps of gold ore. He prayed hard to keep his religion; he was determined not to be a cast-off Catholic.

As part of the plan he made trips to St. Mary's mission in Montana,[2] a mission compound run by some very wise and famous Jesuits of that day, among them Anthony Ravalli, the pastor, and lean, old Vincent Magri, a skilled mechanic who operated the saw and flour mills. Harrick liked Father Ravalli, a gentle, affectionate man with snowy white hair, but became fast friends with Brother Magri

---

[2] Near present day Stephenville, not far below Missoula.

who used to argue with him about the vanity of always seeking for gold. "It's a-crazy. Lookit me. I'm a-happy. I no gotta dollar. *Money* . . . she's a-justa trouble."

But Kid Harrick liked that kind of trouble. The sacks of heavy ore he emptied onto the assayer's scales at the end of each week at first balanced off and then completely outweighed any arguments of the old Brother. So he kept up his wandering life through the gold fields of Idaho and Montana, and in 1863, near Virginia City, he struck a rich pocket of ore, which promised to yield hundreds of thousands of dollars. The gateways of promise were swinging open to the immigrant boy.

In the first flush of success, he paid off his debts and slid back into the old gambling routine. But as he made more and more money—two to three thousand dollars in a single day—the weight of the gold began to burden his spirit. An unaccountable emptiness and desolation crept over him. He sent home substantial sums to his mother,[3] but this only increased his loneliness. The infamous gang of robbers under Sheriff Plummer, was in power at the time, and the Kid took to wearing pistols for protection. He became uneasy about his gold, began to suspect his friends of thieving. He found himself becoming surly and bad-tempered; an avaricious greed took hold of him, and in his saner moments he began to suspect that he was losing his soul. "If a man gain all the gold in the world," old Brother Magri[4] had said to him once, "what is that, if he loses his soul?"

One night he was heading for the bright lights of a bare Montana saloon for a game of faro. He arrived just as a miner ran out, screaming, and behind him his half-crazed partner, with a pistol, bent on killing him. Cornered by the horses and wagons hitched in front of the saloon, the first man swung to face his assailant, and

[3] His mother used the money to educate his two brothers in the priesthood. Both of these brothers later came to America, and spent years of priestly ministry in the State of New York.

[4] It is reported that an old Indian fishing at Flat Head Lake, Montana, suddenly saw Brother Magri riding through the skies in a beautiful chariot the very hour that Brother died some four hundred miles away.

in terror begged for mercy. With a sneering curse, the other fired into his face, and pumped two more shots into the fallen body before he snatched one of the horses and raced out of town. The sheriff's posse caught him before midnight, and after a speedy trial, hanged him for murder the next morning.

But the slain man had fallen so close to where Harrick was standing that some of his blood splattered on his boots. Those blood drops completed Harrick's disillusionment: all the gold in Montana was not worth a man's soul.

So after nine years of prospecting in California, Idaho, and Montana, he gave away his mining claims which were worth potential millions, took a stage to San Francisco, and there joined the Jesuits.

He attended the school for recruits at Santa Clara, and the first afternoon there, as a simple act of piety, he put on the finger of our Lady's statue his last possession, a large ring of emerald stone inlaid on a golden harp.[5]

He made the grade in 1869, was assigned to a porter's job at St. Ignatius in San Francisco, and for the next fifty-four years wore the uniform of the Society of Jesus. He learned many things: that God's grace is all-powerful, and that the world's outlook on things is generally wrong. He found out that poverty was richer than riches, contempt for Christ's sake more honorable than honor, and that hard work for the cause of the Lord is the most satisfying labor on earth. Day after day, he dusted the grimy pews of the little church on Market Street, and found himself strangely content in the Presence of his Master. "Better is one day," he kept saying to himself, "better one day in the Courts of the Lord than a thousand anywhere else."

At first he was general handyman and jack-of-all-trades. When the school building leaked, he climbed on the roof to nail up new shingles; when windows broke, he put in new panes or pasted the pieces together with strips of brown paper; when visitors had

[5] This ring, and other votive-offering jewelry like it, was later stolen and taken to Belgium where the thieves were caught, but the ring never got back to America.

trunks for the express office, he hoisted them on his shoulders, and though it looked incongruous, these heavy trunks on such a small man, he just laughed at the idea of hiring a wagon.

But for forty years his main work was at the entrance of the faculty house, acting as a go-between or messenger, a sort of buffer-state between people and priests. When someone wanted a father for confession or consultation, Brother Harrick went in search of him. In the days before telephones, his job was vital to the success-ful running of a Jesuit community. He took all the messages, sorted and distributed the mail, and in the course of the day passed out hundreds of dimes and meal-tickets to the beggars and unemployed that lined up at the door. He became very clever at handling poor people, some of whom were derelicts he had known from his min-ing days. He called each by his first name when he knew what it was; when he didn't, he made one up. People enjoyed talking to him—his brogue was thick as soup—and would take advice or kid-ding from him as they would from no one else.

On Sundays and holy days, he was usher in the church, and soon developed a knack of moving people in from the end of the pews to the middle without making them peeved or huffy. For a man of as slight a build as Brother Harrick's, this was sometimes an ac-complishment worth coming miles to see. He simply put his hands on the shoulders of some end-seater and pushed.

Though the magnificent St. Ignatius at Hayes and Van Ness had front pews with plush-covered kneelers theoretically reserved for wealthy patrons and benefactors, Harrick never minded installing the untitled proletariat in these front seats. When a reporter from the *San Francisco Examiner* wrote a series of articles on the treat-ment he had received at the various community churches he had visited in the disguise of a down-and-out bum, St. Ignatius got first place on his honor roll: at the 10:30 Mass Brother Harrick had courteously escorted him to a box seat right up in front.

Every morning from 5:30 to 8:00, he served Masses in the church, shuffling about the altar with a strange flat-footed walk. He said his flat feet came from walking across the country; his arches gave out about the middle of Kansas.

Bit by bit he became identified with St. Ignatius church and residence. Except for the two hours between 9:30 and 11:30 A.M. when his duties required him to roam the city buying food and clothing for the community, he was almost continually on hand at the main entrance.

The business people he dealt with, the ladies who gave him money for the poor, the boys from the college who came over to argue themselves out of trouble with their professors, all knew Brother well and were glad to talk to him. He mended their broken rosaries and in his lifetime distributed thousands of others to his friends.

His career as a religious lay-brother was almost the antithesis of that as an itinerant gold-miner. "Kid" Harrick, the ambitious, tireless, greedy little miner had been in the game for himself alone, anxious to amass a fortune as quickly as possible and ready to go through any amount of danger and dreariness to get it. But at fifty-three, Brother Harrick was a calm, generous, and prayerful man; when he spoke, a quiet peace of soul shone from his eyes, and it is remarkable how many men he drew back to God by his endeavors.

A natural contemplative, he loved to talk quietly, interiorly, with Jesus and Mary. The hours, one by one, he lifted to God, as a prayer for souls—for drunkards, and tramps, and poor sinners, especially. He had an Irish gift for theology, a Catholic instinct that knew the right proportion in things. He loved to talk to the altar boys about our Lord and once when a fearful storm was raging outside and they were huddled together in the furnace room he spoke so beautifully of His Passion and death that the old men who are still left of the group can remember it vividly.

Each evening he accompanied his good friend Father Prelato to the County hospital, and while the priest heard confessions or administered the last Sacraments, Brother Harrick visited the wards and almost every night found one or more to prepare for the Sacrament of penance. "I just don't like to think of anyone dying without a priest," he said.

He refused to indulge in dramatics even when the situation was thoroughly theatrical. When the workers raised an awful fuss because they rashly supposed the bricks for the new St. Ignatius church were to be made by the Chinese who would work for much less than living wages, Brother Harrick bore the brunt of their noisy and obscene remarks. They formed groups in the streets and shouted insults at him as he went on his errands for the community. His ears burned but he kept his temper. By the time the misunderstanding subsided his patient mildness and quiet good humor had won him hundreds of new friends. In the novitiate he had prayed for contempt, calumny, and injuries in order to follow more closely the footsteps of His Master, but had never really expected his prayer to be answered.

And as the years passed by, he found that the secret of peace, and the balm of his native restlessness, was a firm adherence to God's Will. When the fire and earthquake came in 1906 to overwhelm the work of years, he quietly accepted it as from the hands of God, and offered himself for the new labors in store.

The cataclysmic hammer blows of that April earthquake smashed the streets, broke open water mains, twisted car tracks and steel poles into fantastic shapes, dumped huge masses of débris into the roads, and sent the populace running in panic from the falling buildings. The second quake, hours later, added to the terror and consternation and the number of people killed mounted from three to five hundred.

In one of the broken homes a fire started and soon a wall of flames, eighty feet high, whipped to fury by a westerly wind, swept across the defenseless ruins. The fire engines were useless without water and freedom of movement, and the inferno raged unimpeded towards St. Ignatius. Martial law was unofficially declared, and a great path was dynamited through the city in an attempt to halt the flames. The church and college could not be saved, and soon huge piles of smoldering bricks and two or three walls, like Roman ruins, were all that remained to show for fifty years of labor and sacrifice.

The Holy Family sisters, who lived further out in the city, assigned the main floor of their motherhouse to the Jesuits during the crisis. But even this sturdy structure was so ravaged by the terrible earth-shaking that Brother Harrick had to set up a kitchen in the street and help do the cooking. He hung up a sign naming it "Outside Inn," and dished out broth and bread to as many, besides the community, as their meagre resources could provide for.

The fire raged for four days, during which the fathers, brothers, and nuns did heroic work tending the wounded and dying at emergency hospitals in the Pavilion, Golden Gate Park, and the old Ingleside racetrack. When it was over, Brother Harrick and Father Prelato climbed to the top of Nob Hill to look at the devastated city. On the top an ornate wooden archway stood by itself, untouched by fire. At its base bloomed a perfect white Easter lily.

The brother and priest looked through the arch on almost unbelievable desolation spread below them in smoking confusion, but the lily was to them, as to thousands of other penniless men, a sign and symbol of hope and future glory.[6]

For the next ten years, Harrick took up his duties as porter, first at the residence Mrs. Welsh gave the Jesuits until they should reestablish themselves, and later at the "Shirt Factory" school on Hayes and Shrader. In 1915 the new Hilltop church was completed at the cost of a half-million dollars, and Brothers Harrick and Piccolo, a young recruit, went to live in makeshift rooms in the cold sacristy to be on guard against burglars.

The new St. Ignatius was built on the same spacious lines as the old had been: a cavernous, white-pillared nave and domed sanctuary, with a galaxy of odd-shaped rooms tucked here and there in the structure. Like many another San Franciscan, Harrick loved the building. It sat amid the empty Masonic tombs and mausoleums just above the Golden Gate Panhandle, where thousands had camped out in army tents during the summer following the quake.

One night a thief got in, and attempted to steal the heavy silver

[6] The archway became a city shrine, was removed in 1907 to Portola Lake in Golden Gate Park where it stands today.

candlesticks, but the brothers heard him and gave immediate chase. While Brother Piccolo headed him for the sacristy where they thought he couldn't escape, Harrick, now an old man, hurried to bar the door the thief had entered. In the huge sacristy they almost cornered him, but he climbed to a tall window, crashed through to the pavement twelve feet below, and escaped in the night.

But Brother Harrick did not stay on the hilltop long, for the cold made life there unbearable. He got arthritis so badly he could barely move his knees. So until the faculty house was finished in 1920, he lived in the "Shirt Factory" with the other Jesuits.

His hair which had turned snowy white by 1880, had long since gone, except for a fringe that showed around the pummeled skull cap he constantly wore.

But even as an old man he had little time to relax: twelve hours a day, seven days a week, he was at his post taking messages, ringing for fathers, directing salesmen to the proper authority, making contacts for the unemployed, escorting visiting priests to their rooms, answering an untold number of times, "Masses tomorrow are at 5:00, 6:00, 6:30 and every half hour till 12:15." No one who is still alive has ever seen him lose his patience, or be ungracious to any caller.

Sometimes he would find a few moments to read some pages of his favorite biography: the life of St. Alphonsus Rodriguez. "It's fascinating," he said. "He was doorman almost as long as I was." But most of his time between calls he spent saying his beads, or sweeping the front stairs.

On his golden jubilee in the Society, he learned that the house was in dire financial straits. Going into the office he asked the procurator for a large money bag, and with this gripped open in front of him, he clumped about the city stopping before each friend and business acquaintance to tell his story in his shrewd and friendly way, and to jiggle the money bag as he did the collection basket on Sundays when he thought the offering should have been larger. Dimes, quarters, dollars, $50-checks, dropped into the bag, and when he clambered off the No. 5 car in front of St. Ignatius in time for his jubilee dinner, there was $3000 in cold cash in the bag he still held open in front of him.

As a lay brother at St. Ignatius, Pat Harrick shared in the running of a community which is, like any Jesuit house, as helplessly dependent on its religious brothers as an incubator baby. In a single day it requires the complete attention of dedicated, dependable, and wholly humble men who, besides serving Masses and saying their prayers, roar about town on motorcycles to shop at twenty or thirty stores, keep in repair a fleet of cars and a half-dozen furnace rooms, tend the gardens and greenhouses, do the bookkeeping, clean the church and service its altars, supervise the upkeep of the school buildings, marshal the kitchen help and supply the food for faculty and students, act as infirmarians, book-binders, mechanics, carpenters, plumbers, night-watchmen, chauffeurs, and black-smiths. They must expect little thanks in this life for these labors, unless they do them for fifty years and someone then remembers to have a jubilee dinner in their honor.

One Sunday morning in summer, 1923, Brother Harrick's life came to a peaceful close. Not previously ill, he had said evening prayers with the community and had gone to bed as usual. At five he was up, with a strong, crashing pain over his heart. He received the last Sacraments calm and unperturbed, and in a few minutes (at 6:20) was dead.

To irreligious critics, his long years were a loss, a waste, "too bad," a psychopathic attempt to run from life, to hide from the hard reality of a cold world.

But to Harrick, his fifty-four years at St. Ignatius were more than surface comings and goings. His life of insignificant details was threaded with spiritual gold, of a costlier, dearer kind than can be found in Montana hills or gullies.

The prayers he said were emerald rings, the rosaries he mended diadems of jewels, the meal-tickets he gave out carved on beaten, gleaming silver. The pews as he dusted and the steps as he swept glistened in God's eyes like burnished gold in the afternoon sun.

Were the monotony and weary hours worth while? To Pat

Harrick, and to thousands of his fellow religious, the mere question was a blasphemy.

To him, each hour of his career seemed so crowded with spiritual conquest he would not have exchanged a minute for anything this side of heaven.

The Archbishop of San Francisco ordered a Solemn Mass sung for the repose of his soul. More than two thousand people, priests, and religious, packed the church for his funeral and, hours later, he was buried at Santa Clara, a rich man. He was one of the few who took his riches with him.

# "Wherever Thou Goest"

BY EDWARD V. WARREN, S.J.

*Brother William Saultemouche, S.J.* (*1557–1593*)

Declared Blessed  1926

ONE OF THE bothersome regulations at the stormy Jesuit boarding-school in Pont-à-Mousson was that none of the students could go into town without permission from the Father Prefect. The regulation was not always kept. One day, for instance, a young German nobleman living there received a call to the parlor. A law student from town had come to see him. When their visit was over, this student wanted to take him off for a trip to town—without permission.

But no such luck. The alert doorkeeper, a young Jesuit Coadjutor Brother, had been keeping his eye on them. Coming into the hallway just in time, he threw something of a block on the German boarding student, then as soon as the visitor had stepped out the front door, he shut it tight, and turning around sent the would-be traveler back to his books.

The young man outside stood scarlet-faced at what he considered a personal insult. Crouching against the boarding-house wall, he lay in wait until the doorkeeper next had to open it. At that moment he sprang upon him, dragged him out into the middle of the street, punched him with both fists, knocked him to the ground, kicked him, and hammered him with the pommel of his sword.

"You insolent black devil! Who do you think you're throwing out of this place?"

Not a sound from the Brother, who put up no resistance. Instead, the beating over, he staggered back to his feet, involuntarily rubbing his deep bruises and wiping away the blood from his face. Then he said quietly, "I am very sorry, sir. I had my orders and I was only carrying them out."

No, being doorkeeper at this Jesuit boarding school attached to the newly founded University of Pont-à-Mousson was not a mere matter of letting people in and out. For this school was not like Billom or Clermont in Paris, founded exclusively for a limited number of poor students. Pont-à-Mousson had been demanded by the parents of the sometimes spoiled darlings of the middle class and nobility. And since, in the early years of the Society of Jesus, the Jesuits had absolutely refused to take charge of boarding schools, this one was first run by laymen and diocesan priests. These men, however, somehow lacked the charism of quelling storms with a word, so that in 1578 the Jesuit Rector of the University was forced to send some of his men to help them keep discipline among the boarders. (One of the men he sent was a brilliant young Jesuit student of theology, James Sales.) But the Provincial of the Jesuits, objecting to this innovation, withdrew his Religious. Again the riotous boarders broke all bounds. This time the local Duke compelled the Jesuits to take charge once more. As a result, in 1580 the scarcely humdrum duty of doorkeeper was assigned to Brother William Saultemouche.

In manner and appearance, Brother hardly seemed the man for the job. Granted, he was already twenty-three, and in France young men mature early because responsibility and work are thrust upon them early. But this gentle soul, so kind and retiring, a simple man, lacking in formal education and in exterior polish—surely he was made only for insignificance, for the routine work which he could do reasonably well.

Besides, he had only recently arrived at Pont-à-Mousson, all fresh from a single year of novitiate. Even the customary six months of probation required of applicants for the Brothers' life had in his case been waived.

But the Fathers who had accepted him into the Society knew his worth; they knew that spiritually he was deep. For one thing, they were aware that in the Novitiate of Verdun, crowded as it was at that time with novices eager for self-denial and obedience, hard knocks as well as unforgettable inspiration abounded. Yielding to these influences, William learned the "folly of the Cross." He determined that he would never ladle out his love for his crucified Master; instead, the better to imitate Christ, he would willingly submit to and accept even the avoidable and "unnecessary" sufferings that came his way. To urge himself on he acquired the habit of repeating a kind of ejaculation-motto that came frequently to his lips: "Endure, flesh, endure." This motto stayed with him throughout the fourteen years of his Jesuit life. It turned out to be far more than pious words. It was his key to greatness.

The Jesuits had learned his merits also from his work as a servant at their College of Clermont in Paris, where he had applied for admission to the Order. One of the Fathers there he had taken as his confidant, revealing to him the purity of his young soul. This Jesuit, when speaking to others, did not hesitate to compare William to an angel, and to call him just that. Because the young man's gentleness, his perfect obedience, and his love for spiritual things were obvious to all who observed him, "angel" stuck. Even the official and laconic House Diary of the University of Pont-à-Mousson enshrines the epithet.

Besides working at Paris, William had worked for the Jesuits in their small college of Billom in southeastern France. At that time (around 1570), one of the eighteen free scholarship holders enrolled there was a boy called James Sales, whom twenty-three years later Brother Saultemouche would accompany on a never-to-be-forgotten journey.

Billom lay some sixty miles north of Saint-Germain-l'Herm, William's birthplace. In the latter town lived one Antonio Saltamochio, born perhaps in Italy, as his name would indicate. (In time Saltamochio was gallicized into Saultemouche, which is pronounced sote-*moosh.*) Storekeeper Antonio, quite unlike his Jesuit son, was a jolly, aggressive, vigorous soul. He was rarely home. While his French wife Marguerite minded both the store and the children, he was trudging from village to village in the neighborhood. And a welcome visitor he was, carrying his "store" about on his strong shoulders—a large pack of varied merchandise he had selected for the needs of all customers, including the littlest children.

William, it would seem, had never been destined for business. The closest he came was to spend a year as treasurer in the Trinity College at Lyons, in 1592. But at some time in his youth he had mastered the trade of shoemaking. Perhaps he practiced it while working at Billom, but during his Jesuit career he was almost always porter at the door.

Except for the account of his last days, scarcely more than a few incidents remain of his hidden and obscure life as a Brother. Yet they strikingly display his meekness, his ability to "take it" without complaining, out of love for the meek Christ.

The law-student's cudgeling we have already seen. At another time Brother Saultemouche fell sick at Lyons and had to stay in his room. Assigned to take care of him was a non-Jesuit servant. This scoundrel, knowing very well that the Brother never complained about things, took it upon himself to torment him in a hundred ways. Insipid meals poorly cooked and brought in late, nettling and unannounced intrusions, flashes of temper and scorn, long periods of neglect, flat disobedience—what did the fellow not think of to make the sick man not well but worse? Yet not a word from the patient man. Even should a visitor suspect, from obvious indications, that something was definitely lacking in the service, William would volunteer some extenuating circumstance, so that it would appear his "caretaker" had simply overlooked a detail.

Emboldened by this immunity, the tormentor went to the limits of ingenious malice. Still, nothing of all this would have been left to biographers, had not the same servant, overpowered by remorse, confessed everything a year later.

Again there was the time when a seemingly trivial incident took place, yet it indicated much. One day at the front door, an ex-novice, suitcase in hand, was bidding farewell to one of the Fathers of the house. The young man had just been dismissed for conduct unbecoming a religious. The priest, however, did not want to send him off wearing the disreputable hat he was holding. At the moment, Brother William was standing near the two. Noticing him, the Father reached over and took off the Brother's hat, handing him in return the crumpled specimen the boy had been wearing. The Brother resented it no more than would a statue.

(This sounds easy—until somebody tries it with *your* hat.)

The hat episode took place in the autumn of 1592 at Tournon, where Brother Saultemouche had just been sent to be doorkeeper. When he arrived, we are told, he was not put to work for several days. Most of this time he spent, not as natural inclination would recommend—resting up after the 48-mile walk down the Rhone Valley from Lyons, and getting settled in his new quarters. Instead, he was seen almost constantly on his knees before the Blessed Sacrament. To him, the Blessed Sacrament was the life of his life; under its appearances lay concealed the silent, all-powerful sancti-fier of men, Who on earth spent almost all His life in hidden suffering. God, it seems, was giving to William a special time in which to lay up treasures of strength for the days ahead.

From this time on, the life of Brother Saultemouche blends with that of Father James Sales; the two men became companions and close friends. They must be spoken of together.

"This year, Father Rector, we would like to have not just any one of your good Fathers for the Advent mission. The Protestant ministers around Aubenas are working harder now than at any time in the last five years since we took back the city. We need a real missionary who is a theologian too, a man who is fresh in Hebrew and Greek, and can handle the sophistries of the gentlemen from Geneva."

The Baron of Montreal, head of the city of Aubenas, was ad-dressing the Superior of the Jesuit College in Tournon.

"Very well, Your Excellency," replied Father Rossile. "Father Provincial is in the house now, making his visitation. I'm sure he'll send you the man you need."

Without delay, the Provincial Father Castori fixed his choice on a thirty-seven-year-old professor of theology then teaching at the college. For Father Castori was well acquainted with the priest, James Sales, and with his brilliant teaching career. Here was a man who at thirty-one had earned his Doctorate in Sacred Theology, had been on missions before, and had constantly manifested two great ambitions—to set men on fire with love for the Blessed Eucharist, and to die as a martyr. Father Sales' scholarly book and lectures on the Eucharist, his daily meditations on martyrdom, the fact that he wore a relic of Blessed Edmund Campion, English Jesuit martyr of 1581—these were only some indications of where his heart lay. It was little wonder, then, that when he learned of the Provincial's offering him the call to Aubenas he burst out with "Praised be God! You couldn't bring me more welcome news. Aubenas is just the place where I hope Heaven will give me the favor I've been begging for in my prayers a long time now."

Brother Saultemouche was assigned him as a companion. For this favor, too, Father Sales could only send up fervent thanks to God. Like all Jesuits who have had to endure the unglamorous homelessness of much traveling and living away from their community, he knew what a boon it would be to share the companionship of a "brother of like mind." (Those outside of religious life might find it hard to believe how close-knit becomes the bond of mutual esteem and brotherly affection between mature men who outwardly often appear utterly undemonstrative and independent.)

Father Sales and Brother Saultemouche, despite great differences in personality and talents, had much in common. Not only were they members of the same order of apostolic men. In age they were thirty-six and thirty-five respectively. Both had been born of poor parents, in towns close together in the same province, Auvergne. Both began living in Jesuit houses at an early age. Besides, they had been stationed, often at the same time, at the same colleges of Billom and of Clermont in Paris, at the Novitiate in Verdun, then at the Universities of Pont-à-Mousson and Tournon. More important, both men were consistently distinguished for their devotion to Christ in the Blessed Sacrament, and in their genuine desire to suffer for Him not just what they had to, but all they could. They were, in truth, "brothers of like mind."

Now only two months of Jesuit life together remained to them. For already Father Sales had an unmistakable premonition that the call to Aubenas had come as God's answer to his fifteen-year-long prayer for immolation. With this assurance in mind, when the two travelers were saying farewell at the front door of the Jesuit residence in Tournon, Father Sales smiled joyfully as he shook the hand of another Coadjutor, Jean Pavageau: "Good-by, Brother, and please pray for us; we are going to meet death."

Aubenas, however, only forty miles towards the south, lay utterly peaceful in December of 1592. The truce between the militant Calvinists and their Catholic opponents stood intact. Accordingly, one of the city's three regents, Charles Boyron, received the men of God with honor, lodged them in the house of a Judge Veyrenc who had recently died, and invited them to take their meals at his own home.

The four weeks of Advent preaching went smoothly. By his Masses, sermons, hearing of confessions, conferring of baptism, and personal visits to the homes of the townspeople, Father Sales stirred up the faith of the priestless Catholics. Huguenots who came to listen to him were astonished by the profound learning and power of his speech, and by his unvarying respect for their opinions. As for Brother William, his tasks were to tend the house, be the acolyte at the Father's Mass, act as the "Jesuit community" when the two recited Litanies together in the evening, and accompany the priest on his visits to the faithful and to prospective converts. But his most important function was to pray with his whole soul that the Catholics of Aubenas would open their hearts to receive the Christ Child in the way He deserved.

So successfully did the mission turn out that once Christmas was over, the Baron of Montreal petitioned Father Sales' Superior to let him stay until Easter. He stayed. Then lo! all but a handful of his congregation, who had become half-Protestantized anyway during the years when the city was under Calvinist domination, stopped coming. They had had enough religion until Eastertime. The two Jesuits, therefore, took to rousing up the Faith in the towns of the neighborhood—Largentière, Chassier, and especially Ruoms.

It happened at Ruoms that Father Sales was invited to debate publicly with a Protestant minister. This turned out to be no trifling event, particularly because his opponent was the well-known Pierre Labat, a kind of loud-mouthed individual (be it admitted) who went about defying all comers to debate on religion. Catholics and Huguenots, therefore, flocked to the great hall of the castle belonging to Madame de Chaussy. Father Sales was already there, and at his side sat the Baron of Montreal, ruler of Aubenas. The hour came; the hour passed; but no Labat. Catholics sat in silence while Calvinists fidgeted. At length, overcome with shame at the deliberate non-appearance of their champion, the Calvinists got up noiselessly and one after another slipped out of the hall.

This public humiliation, together with reports that the two Jesuits were increasingly successful in reviving Catholicism in the region around Aubenas, led to war. If, thanks to the truce between the Catholics and the innovators, priests could circulate freely, the Genevan reform was in danger. Aubenas had to be recaptured. So decided the ministers of the area, who consulted with Chambaud, Huguenot leader of the whole district of the Vivarais.

It is fitting to recall that in those times anti-Catholic opposition did not limit itself to debates and pamphleteering. Not a few Calvinists had been sword-point converts. Besides, one of the principal techniques in the spread of their ideas was the "purging" of priests and nuns, and the pillaging of churches and convents. To religious fanaticism was added political fanaticism when, around the middle of the sixteenth century, noblemen and two princes of the blood embraced the ideas that were pouring over the mountains from Geneva, the Rome of the Calvinists. As a result, in the thirty years before the events here described, eight religious wars had swept over France. Each of them ended in provisional treaties that did not last. Particularly at the end of the century, truces were readily scrapped and the massacring of priests and religious flared up anew. Betrayals, surprise attacks, mass murders, repeatedly blotched the annals of the period.

Accordingly, what followed at Aubenas was in tune with the times. Within two weeks after the Ruoms debate, the irate ministers and their regional chief, Chambaud, had organized a company of soldiers to retake Aubenas from the Catholics. Captain Sarjas would direct the attack. Cunningly enough, word was spread around that the Protestants were going to set upon the city of Arles.

Father Sales, however, guessed what was brewing and hurried back to Aubenas. There the good Baron scoffed at his fears. "My dear Father," he assured him with the air of a veteran campaigner soothing a pale and timid scholar, "the Calvinists are bound by a truce, just as we are. If they are stirring up trouble, it can't be against us."

They struck one hour before dawn. Unseen in the exceptionally black night of February 6, and unheard because of a strong, freezing north wind that howled through the city, fifteen of Sarjas' men scaled the wall with a ladder, then climbing down, ran here and there through the streets, blowing bugle blasts and shouting, "Kill! Kill!" These cries, repeated in various parts of the city, together with the shrieking of the trumpets of the sentinels, at last alerted on the wall, brought the utterly unprepared citizens leaping out of their beds, sure that the whole place was swarming with the enemy. In panic they rushed out of doors, stumbled through the streets and raced towards the Gate of the Grey friars (the Baron included). Chasing after them, the invaders found the Gate open, and sending two men outside, called in the hundred soldiers led by Sarjas.

The confused noise, followed by shouts and a general uproar, brought the two Jesuits in the Veyrenc home sharply awake. From the clamor, Father Sales knew what had happened. "Brother!" he cried out. "Brother Saultemouche! Quick, the Blessed Sacrament at Saint Anne's!"

To keep the Sacred Host from falling into the hands of the Mass-hating Calvinists, the two religious threw on their cassocks, rushed down the front steps, and fused with the darkness of the inky night. The street was reëchoing with the scurryings and screams of the panic-stricken inhabitants. Having groped their way inside the church, the Jesuits soon found the tabernacle. Then by the light of a single candle, Father Sales gave Communion to himself and to his faithful companion. It was to be their Viaticum. In their supremely fervent thanksgiving they prayed, "Life for life, O hidden God. Thou hast died willingly for us; we are ready to die for Thee. Be our unconquerable strength in the hours to come." Shortly afterwards they walked back in silence to their home, there to pray out the night.

About nine o'clock came a beating on the front door, and into the parlor strode Pierre Lantouzet and two other soldiers from Vals. (Shortly after dawn, the three Protestant ministers who had marched in with the invaders had prevailed upon Sarjas to send men after the Jesuits before they could take to their heels.) The armed trio found Sales and Saultemouche on their knees, praying to God.

Throttling the pair, the soldiers asked in scorn, "Who are you?"

"We are members of the Society of Jesus."

"Hand over your purse!"

"We have no money," answered Brother William.

"But we do," exclaimed the priest. "Here, take this handkerchief; it has some sous we brought from Tournon for our few expenses."

Furious at finding only thirty sous in all, the soldiers stormed around, cursing and threatening to torture the priest and slit his throat unless he handed over a greater sum in cash.

Calmly Father Sales explained, "If it's our money you want, we have no more, not even for a ransom. But if you want our lives, we are quite ready to give them up for God's honor and for his Church, with as many kinds of torture as you can think of."

At this, the soldiers lunged at him, struck him with their fists, and searched him insolently. Next they ransacked the rooms, cabinets, and drawers, and came away with an hourglass, a silver cross-reliquary, several Agnus Dei's and blessed beads, together with some books and writings that belonged to the priest.

Pushing the Jesuits out of the house, the three bandits hustled them down the street, all the while bawling out to the right and to the left, "Look, everybody, look here! We've caught the false prophets and the fakes!" When they arrived at headquarters, Captain Sarjas with a gesture of scorn waved away both his henchmen and their captives. "Take them to the ministers," he growled, "they'll know what's to be done with them."

The three martial ministers were enjoying a victory dinner at the house of Judge Louis de la Faye, who till that morning had been an undercover Calvinist. The judge had invited them to quarter themselves at his home and, to help in celebrating this glorious day, had called in the other leaders of the sect. One can imagine the profound satisfaction felt by this assembly when into their midst marched Under-Officer Lantouzet with the two chief prizes of the war.

During the rest of that morning, and all afternoon, and until the early evening—for seven consecutive hours—the victorious ministers engaged the captured theologian from Tournon in remorseless debate. What a prize it would be if the Genevans could "convert" the two Jesuits! They took additional spirit from the presence of a partisan crowd that had collected inside the house.

During all these exhausting hours, Brother Saultemouche stood by, suffering in silence and praying, as only a fervent Coadjutor can pray, that the God of truth would speak irresistibly through the mouth of His anointed priest.

The trio of Calvinists began the combat by at first engaging in would-be civil conversation. But with fiery Pierre Labat pressing the attack, and Father Sales calmly pointing out their fallacies, they soon slipped into wrangling argumentation. When their single opponent corrected their misquotations (he had a prodigious and accurate memory) and when he pricked their sophistries, they took refuge in venomous name-calling. For not only had they been frustrated in their scoffing at the Church's regulations about fast and abstinence. Attempting to defend John Calvin's degrading notion that man has no free will, they met with just as little success. Thus it was that they fell to attacking what really scandalized them most in the Church—the dogma of the Real Presence of Christ in the Blessed Sacrament.

"Bring me the Holy Books," Father Sales finally cried out; then turning to the bystanders he declared with daring forthrightness, "and I will show you how your ministers are deceiving you and leading you into hell."

No one dared bring him a copy of the Scriptures because he could use it too skillfully. But by his challenge he had cut his opponents to the quick. Stung and enraged, they shot at him a string of insults: "Impostor! Idolater! False prophet and worse than Antichrist!" Pierre Labat, who had been silent in a previous contest, thundered above the others: "Kill them!" he blurted, his face contorting with fury. "Kill the two of them! They are enough to infect the whole country."

The beleaguered defender of the Blessed Sacrament could only wait until his voice might once more be heard. "Allow me," he urged composedly, as he brought out a manuscript from his pocket, "allow me to give you a book which is completely my own work. In it you will find what the Church teaches about the Sacraments. Then you will see what it is I believe, because I composed it and declare it is mine."

The Reverend Railhet angrily snatched at the book, then in a body the three preachers stomped out of the arena, in high dudgeon at the theological thrashing to which they had just been subjected.

For twenty-four hours now, the only food which the two prisoners had eaten was the Sacred Host they had consumed in great haste before the dawn of that Saturday morning. Somehow that evening a small son of the Judge de la Faye had secretly slipped them a few morsels of dry bread. They would not eat again.

That night, the soldier who guarded them locked them up like beasts in a low, damp, freezing room. It was the depth of winter, when high-mountained Aubenas is always like a polar region. Shivering and famished, with scarcely enough vitality in them to cast a few petitions to God for strength to endure, the priest and the Brother waited out the torturing hours.

The reverend ministers, meanwhile, had been fortified by an

ample supper and a good night's rest. Moreover, they were bristling with new arguments and animated by theological horror at the "monstrous" propositions they had found in the Jesuit's manuscript. The next morning, they marched confidently back into battle. As for Father Sales, it must have been infused strength from the God of martyrs, together with the encouragement and prayers and example of Brother Saultemouche, that bolstered his forces. At first woefully white-faced, and nearly paralyzed by cold and hunger, somehow he revived wonderfully when once more forced into debate. There was a strong serenity in his manner as he answered objections lucidly and with precision.

"Bring me your own Bibles," he demanded at one point, stretching out his hand as if to receive them, "and by them I will prove everything I have said thus far."

Precisely what truth he was driving home is not recorded, but his opponents were extremely embarrassed by it. They could only stammer. Just at that moment, however, someone among the listeners-in (for a considerable number of Huguenots had again gathered for the contest) happily saved the day by crying out, "Time for church!" Labat and most of the assembly streamed out.

Labat needed no priming for a sermon that morning. With no contradictors to ruffle his eloquence, he unleashed molten blasts against the papistical doctrine of the Eucharist, against papistry in general, against Jesuits in particular because of their rabid defence of papistry, and above all (using the choicest portions of his late sixteenth-century vocabulary of zeal) against a certain Jesuit who was at that moment trying to corrupt all of Aubenas. As a kind of Exhibit A he brandished in the air Father Sales' manuscript on the Eucharist, flipping its pages forward and backward.

"Judgment and God's vengeance fall upon the man who wrote this thing!" Labat stormed. "He is an idolater, a false prophet who deserves the fate of false prophets. Did not Elias vow death to the prophets of Baal whom he proved guilty of fraud?"

The congregation had not been sufficiently prepared to accept this appeal for murder. Astonished rather than convinced, they began to disperse. Some of them went back to the la Faye home, where ministers Guerin and Railhet were still harassing their prisoner. Labat, flushed of face and sweating copiously after his Catalinian exertions, trod heavily down the pulpit steps. He felt angrily frustrated and humiliated because his murderous proposal had obviously not found support. No doubt his mind churned with the thought, "Where do these peasants keep their zeal for the things of God?"

But the keen-eared, prowling devil never leaves a willing co-worker without tools. Labat's gaze fell upon a small knot of men still talking in a corner of the church. It was Sarjas, with four or five of his myrmidons—the very man who had directed the capture of Aubenas! This compliant warrior, after only a few words from the minister, gave immediate orders to three of his men to go to the la Faye residence and there dispatch the Jesuits.

Strange to say, when the three soldiers got as far as the house, they were unnerved by their own humanity. Stopping, they looked at each other.

"I won't be the one to fire," one of them hesitatingly ventured.

"Nor I either," added a second.

The third man swore out loud, "The devil take me if I do any harm to those innocent men!"

They turned back and repeated their refusal to their captain. He cursed them all vehemently, but Minister Labat, realizing that the rebellion might be contagious, charged off towards the house, leading Sarjas and twenty of his men. Labat would direct operations himself.

Meanwhile, at the la Faye prison-court, someone had taken pity upon the visibly exhausted Jesuits, and had offered them some nourishment. But Father Sales refused; likewise the Coadjutor, whose words are recorded, "I shall never eat again."

In fact, just about that time, from down the street the two could catch the shouting of a mob that was following after Labat's squad of fast-marching gunmen. A few minutes later and, on an order from Labat, Sarjas and a handful of his men burst into the house.

Though Father Sales, on seeing him, greeted him courteously, Sarjas yanked him brutally by the arm.

"Follow me, you idolatrous pharisee, follow me!"

"Where do you want to take me?" the priest replied.

"Follow me, I tell you. You must die publicly."

"I am ready. Let us go, in the name of God." Then turning to his companion, the priest asked, "And you, dear Brother, what will become of you? Be of good heart. O how great we shall be in Heaven, little though we are on this earth, if we suffer something for God!"

The priest was sure that he alone was to be the victim of the Calvinists' hatred. Yet, in a last effort to make sure no harm would come to Brother Saltemouche, he turned to his guards and pleaded, "Kill me in the cruelest way, and I will submit willingly; but let this good Brother live. He is not a learned man and you have nothing to fear from him."

This was the moment, the opportunity for superhuman generosity for which Brother William Saultemouche had been preparing. As a religious he had lived like an angel, prayed with all his heart, had labored long years in silent obscurity for this. For this he had allowed himself to be literally kicked around. By thus submitting to voluntary "trial" martyrdoms he had heaped up in his soul immense reserves of compelling love and courage. Consequently, at this life-and-death moment all those graces burst in on him like a flood, sweeping away his natural timidity and fears.

"No!" he cried, stepping forward and protesting the priest's appeal for his safety. "No, Father, I will not leave you. I will die with you for the truth of the points you defended in debate."

One of the soldiers warned "the fool" to get back. Not he, but only the Father was to play a part in this tragedy.

With a kind of passionate solemnity, Brother Saultemouche fixed his eyes on the soldier and declared, "God preserve me from falling into this fault! I will never abandon the one to whom obedience has joined me as a companion, even though I have to die with him. I will follow him to the grave."

"Very well then," snapped the soldier heatedly. "If you want to die, you will die." And with a smashing fist to the Coadjutor's shoulder, he catapulted him forward.

Some mocked the Brother, others shoved him ahead as he squeezed his way through the crowd that jammed the room and the stairway. At length he forced his way through them, and found himself outside the house and at the side of Father Sales.

Labat was waiting for them in the street. With him were the two ministers from Meyras and Vals, and around them milled an excited crowd. An excellent setting for another debate with the accursed idolater! Now, thought Labat, he could capitalize on the starved Jesuit's feebleness and on the pressure of human respect in face of the crowd, but even more on the loaded muskets and the drawn swords and daggers that glinted in the afternoon sun. Assuming, therefore, the stature and righteous authority of a high priest before the Sanhedrim, the preacher called on Father Sales to renounce solemnly, here in the sight of the heavens and of men, all that he had spoken or written concerning the reality of the Body of Christ in the Sacrament of the Altar.

What followed was short but intense. The three ministers began firing questions at the priest, disjointed questions meant to overwhelm and confuse him, as much as to relieve their own overflowing hatred. The priest was divinely self-possessed in this final attack. His answers came back promptly, with ease, without perturbation. For his antagonists this was too much; the "idolatrous pharisee" not only did not abjure his belief in the Real Presence; he was making public fools of his accusers. Labat lost all control. "Kill him!" he shrieked. "Kill this man! He does not deserve to live. He is a pestilence." And making an about-face, he strode off, knowing Sarjas would do the rest.

At that, almost all the crowd fled from the scene, out of fear and pity at what was to take place. Even the band of Huguenot soldiers were affected by their human feelings. No one wanted to do the deed. Though ordered point blank by his captain, one of them retorted, "I'll have nothing to do with this. I'd rather be proved guilty of killing my father than bring the slightest harm to these men who never harmed anybody." The hot-blooded captain drew his sword and slashed him on the right shoulder.

Among the soldiery, however, were some of Sarjas' men, more compliant than the others. One of them, Vital Suchon, whom everybody called "the simple" because of his almost unwitting silliness, stepped forward, and motioning with his gun, told Father Sales to get back.

"I beg of you, friend," the priest pleaded, "give me a moment to commend myself to God and pray to Him for your sake." Then calling for the last time to the courageous Coadjutor, he suggested, "Brother, let us commend ourselves to God." With that he drew back to a spot about five steps from the gate of the la Faye residence. The Brother followed him and both fell to their knees. Suchon, as volunteer executioner, stepped around the pair and pointed his gun at the priest's shoulder. While Father Sales was invoking aloud his patron St. James, as well as St. Stephen the first martyr, and Jesus and Mary, Suchon fired. So close had he held the gun to the priest's shoulder that the cassock started to burn. Without delay the murderer leaped forward and plunged his dagger into the martyr's breast. Blood spurted to the ground. The sight of it, together with the gunshot, had by now let loose the killer instinct in those soldiers who a few moments before were horrified at the thought of murder. One of them, exasperated by the dying man's continued repetition of the names of Jesus and Mary, tried to silence him by stuffing into his mouth handfuls of mud and dung from the street. Another used the hilt of his sword to beat into bits the joined hands and crossed thumbs which the priest kept bringing to his lips as if they were a crucifix. Finally, one of the inhabitants of Aubenas aimed a long knife and gashed the priest's throat so viciously that two years later, when his body was disinterred, the mark could still be seen on his bones.

The Jesuit had not yet breathed his last when Brother Saulte-mouche thrust himself into the group of executioners standing around the bleeding body. Throwing himself onto his knees, he gathered into his arms the bleeding body of his friend. "O my Father," he sobbed aloud, "I swear that I will not desert you in death, just as I did not desert you in life."

An instant later and into his own breast burrowed the daggers of Suchon the Simple and Jacques Massis. With a mortal groan, Brother Saultemouche dropped his precious burden and extended his arms in the form of a cross. This great manifestation of faith, showing that he united his death explicitly with Christ's, infuriated the executioners, who rushed at him and wildly cut him down with their swords and broke his bones with two-handed blows from their steel-plated clubs.

At each deadly stroke, as eyewitnesses later testified, Brother Saultemouche exhorted himself to constancy by repeating in a loud voice the ejaculation he had learned at Verdun: "Endure, my flesh, endure a little longer." Six blows—ten—fifteen—sixteen—still another—and at the eighteenth the murderers stopped. There was no more blood in their victim. It all lay in a small red pool on the street, mingled with the priest's.

While these horrors were being consummated, one of the soldiers who witnessed the carnage was so overpowered by the unrestrained savagery that he rushed away from the place and into a nearby house, where he sobbed and cried.

Not so the others. Jeering and laughing and congratulating each other, they proceeded to strip the priest naked. On the Brother they left a shirt; it was too sticky with blood. Suchon, as chief executioner and therefore most deserving of the spoils, fumblingly put on the priest's cassock. Another valiant comedian picked up the priest's biretta, and after pinning to it a fox's tail, put it on a long stick. This would make a fine processional cross for the Catholic burial services they would now mockingly imitate. Coffins? No need. Instead, they tied a rope around the neck of each victim and dragged them along like dead dogs. As they paraded along, they derisively sang out a few off-tune snatches from the funeral chant—"Christ, hear us; Christ, graciously hear us." Having marched to their heart's content through the principal streets of

Aubenas, they ended at the spot where they had begun. The bodies they left lying in the gutter outside of a bakery shop. Captain Sarjas, first thundering out that anyone who valued his life would leave the corpses right there, dismissed his men.

For six days the remains of the martyrs lay exposed in the street. Dogs and birds of prey did not touch them, nor did anyone dare to take them away, for fear of Sarjas' order. At length, fearing that the Catholics might gather enough courage to steal them away by force and give them decent burial, the Calvinists decided to destroy them. They therefore tied ropes around their necks once more and dragged them to the city gate called Notre Dame, where stood the ruins of an abandoned church. The shell of this building, which was situated, it seems, below the level of the street, was at that time being used as a dump for garbage and butchers' offal. Into it the citizenry had the habit of throwing the rotting bodies of dead animals. Into this filth, accordingly, the Huguenots hurled the consecrated bodies of the men of God.

Yet neither the stench of the place nor fear of Huguenot reprisals could keep the Catholics away, since they realized that the Jesuits had undoubtedly been martyrs and most honorable servants of God. After a time, two courageous men came by lantern-light and stole away the bodies, burying them in an out-of-the-way corner of a deserted garden.

Naturally the men whose devilish hatred inspired them to defile so outrageously the corpses and memory of the Jesuits would not stop now. After a spirited general search, some soldiers from a garrison near the burial garden discovered the grave. On it they immediately built a latrine. The whole garrison used the place daily for two years.

But God also has *His* vengeance, a vengeance in which He loads with supreme honors those among His lovers who have been most disgustingly befouled by men. Thus at Aubenas influential Catholics had the garrison removed and the bodies disinterred. And only a short time after 1595 the relics of Father Sales and Brother Saultemouche were honorably escorted to their final resting place in the church of the Jesuit college at Avignon. At the door to meet them stood His Eminence, the Cardinal-Legate Francis Tarugio, while the population of the city crowded around. A few minutes later inside the church it was the Cardinal himself who intoned the Te Deum in thanksgiving for the finding and return of the Martyrs of the Blessed Sacrament.

Again, only ten years after their death, the martyrs were honored vicariously when a Jesuit college was founded in Aubenas itself. During that decade, so wonderfully had their blood revitalized the Catholic faith of the whole region that a long and solemn procession marched out to greet the Jesuit Fathers who were coming to organize the school. Fifteen thousand Catholics, including all the confraternities of penitents and all the pastors and parishioners from ten to twelve miles around, marched fearlessly in public that day. On the sidewalks gazing at all this display, stood the members of the Calvinist church, once lords of the city, now overmastered by a strange stupor.

A half century later and Aubenas, which had but shortly before been almost wholly Calvinist, had become almost entirely Catholic. Moreover, numbered among its new buildings was the convent of St. Claire, constructed and opened in 1647. It was built in the very garden, and its chapel was purposely placed over the very spot where for two years the bodies of the Jesuit martyrs had been buried and desecrated.

Finally, God with His long memory and invincible determination to honor those who have honored Him, brought it about that the merits and miracles of Father Sales and Brother Saultemouche should be proclaimed to the whole world. On June 6, 1926, surrounded by ceremonies of special lavishness and dignity, a great Solemn Mass was offered up in the spacious hall above the vestibule of the basilica of St. Peter's in Rome. Officiating as the celebrant was His Holiness, Pope Pius XI. During the Mass there was read out the pontifical brief that placed the two Martyrs of the Blessed Sacrament among the Blessed, men approved to be honored by the members of God's Church.

Hence it is that every year on the morning of February 7, in almost every nation throughout the world, 30,000 Jesuits kneel to offer and pray the Mass in honor of God, in honor of a brilliant young priest who loved Christ in the Blessed Sacrament, and in honor of their exalted Brother, William Saultemouche, doorkeeper, "angel," and martyr, a man seemingly born for oblivion, who nonetheless scaled heights of heroism that few men ever reach.

# The Glory and the Dream

BY CLINTON E. ALBERTSON, S.J.

*Brother Rene Goupil, S.J. (1607–1642)*

Declared a Saint   1930

Hidden somewhere in the cool shadows of a little wood in the northeast corner of New York state lie a split skull and some few other pitiful fragments of what was once a man. Of the many storied and tragic graves that doubtless lie hidden in those forests, one in particular contains these bones of a young French doctor. Iroquois Indians had hacked and crushed the bones while they were still covered with twitching flesh, dogs had gnawed them after the flesh was quiet, and one broken-hearted man had gathered them up in his broken hands and blessed them and washed them with his tears and scooped out a shallow hole in the earth to hide them in.

He had loved the young man that these bone-splinters had once been. He had loved him with that strange and adamantine love known only to brave men who have adventured to the gates of death together and have come back again; men who have gazed on the carefully guarded nakedness of each others' inmost souls as they stood unblushingly revealed for one blazing moment in the face of violent death. In an unspoken pledge of trust such men are bound to each other for life.

So now, the broken-fingered man would have shown some fitting sign of love for this hero friend of his—and of God's. But in the perilous haste of the moment he could do no more than hide the remains among the deep shadows of the trees. Some day he meant to return in peace and give Christian burial to these poor bones that had been his friend. But then of course, on that Spring day in 1642, he could not foresee that this was never to be. The filtering sun rays and cathedraled shadows of the forest were to guard this hidden grave for over three hundred years, and in all probability will guard it till the Judgment blast shall break open all the graves of the world. This friend with the broken heart was to return within several hundred yards of this lonely spot four years and many adventures later, only to meet violent Mohawk death before he could keep the tryst at the burial place in the wood.

But the trees and the seasons were kind. Three hundred and

seven autumns have spread a leafy shroud over those pieces of bone and have built over them a thick catafalque of twigs and branches. Even today, when loving friends would find that hasty grave to pay it the supreme honor that is now its due, the faithful forest still keeps its secret. It knows not how to distinguish between enemies and friends. It will take no chances with its treasure.

All the world knows that somewhere on the wooded slopes of that little ravine near the Mohawk River are hidden the earthly remains of Rene Goupil of the Society of Jesus, martyr of Jesus Christ and canonized saint of the Catholic Church. And the man with the mangled fingers, who took to heaven with him the secret of the grave, is another Jesuit Martyr, a priest, Isaac Jogues. On the same day in 1930 these comrades in arms and brothers in blood, one a coadjutor brother and the other a priest, were raised to the highest dignity of which human kind is capable.

The creek that cuts through the bottom of this treasured ravine is called Auries, and the near-by sight of the old Mohawk village of Ossernenon is now called Auriesville. The whole locality is dedicated as a great shrine with many chapels and monuments and the beautiful Church of Our Lady of Martyrs. This is the story of the man whose unknown grave those buildings are meant to honor.

### OLD FRANCE

As Jogues scooped into the dark earth that precious little pile of shattered bones he must have reflected, like another Hamlet with the skull of Yorick, on the brief but thrilling history that these bony fragments had had as a man. Jogues must have mused on the unpredictable designs of destiny. It had brought this young man from a dawning modern world to meet a lonely hero's death in the wilds of this primitive continent where the Prince of Darkness still led his savage armies.

None who know the boy Rene could possibly have guessed how and where the young man Rene was to meet his death. That much we can certainly say, though we know very little about the young Goupil. Providence is at times quite indifferent about seeing to the recording of the earthly career of some of its heroes, and Rene's case is certainly one in point. His youth and young manhood are for the most part as hidden to us as is his grave; the last three decisive years emerge more clearly from the shadows—and then those final terrible and magnificent months blaze out at us in sharp and throbbing detail.

It is as though it were Goupil's martyrdom alone that heaven would spotlight for posterity. It is there that God would place the purpose of Rene's career—with his life's blood to drive back the legions of Darkness from a new continent, by his death to consecrate a new portion of the globe to the Kingdom of Christ. The Old World gave him life and he sacrificed it for the New World.

He grew up in the old and beautiful little cathedral town of Angers—though now with a population of some 90,000, it would more properly be called a city—that rises on the banks of the Maine River a few miles above the point where the latter flows into the Loire. About seventy miles to the west the Loire meets the sea at St. Nazaire, a spot nightmarishly familiar to many an English and American bombardier who struggled to catch the Nazi submarine pens in his bomb sight. About two hundred miles to the northeast of Angers is Paris.

Looking back from the vantage point which time has given us we can peer down into history and see how from his very birth the strands of Rene's destiny were feeling out their invisible connections with men and distant places which were later to loom so large in his life. The year of Rene's birth, 1607, was the year, too, of Isaac Jogues' birth at historic Orleans, further up the Loire. Born at the same time in the same country, they would not meet till thirty-five years later, and then in a strange and distant world on the eve of a terrible adventure that was to bind them inseparably by the bond of shared suffering, and was to end in martyrdom for Goupil.

And the year after Rene's birth Quebec was founded by Champlain and some fur traders. The year-old baby in the Goupil home in Angers was one day to know intimately this little forest-girded settlement of New France across the ocean from Angers. He would win his spurs as a surgeon there, and from there he would set out on the river journey to his death.

As a boy in Angers, Rene lived like any other French boy in many a similar provincial town. Angers was quiet, unpretentious, impassive with the stolid dependability of a community that has long worked its life from the same soil. But Angers also possessed that indefinable dignity which is known to a place heavy with history and important in the chronicled happenings of its region. Much of France's colorful antiquity could be traced out by some future archeologist delving into the stratified remains of Angers.

Many a winter's evening, before a fire that invited storytelling, Rene's grandfather would unfold for the little boy the romance of Angers—how the old Gallic tribes had first settled it, and the clanking armor of Rome's legions had echoed in its streets; how it had been sacked in turn by the Normans, the Plantagenet English, and the French Huguenots; how the warlike Counts of Anjou had built the massive, many-towered castle that glowered protectingly over it, and from whose battlements a sentry commanded the sea of black slate roofs and the rolling farm and vineyard land beyond, green and gold at harvest time.

And Rene heard tales of great things that had so recently happened outside the boundaries of his own town. Through more than one night his dreams must have been filled with the fire and smoke and battle thunder of the great ships clashing in the terrible battle of Lepanto. And he must have quivered to stories of the cruel Queen Elizabeth (who died just four years before Rene was born) and her Catholic victims; and of how her clever English seamen had shattered "his most Catholic Majesty's" magnificent Armada, and how the battered remnants of that proud Spanish fleet had limped homeward down the near-by French coast after their tragic voyage around Ireland.

Many a terrible episode Rene must have heard from the countless battles and sieges and massacres that bloodied France—and especially his section of France—during the half-century of Huguenot and Catholic fighting that preceded his birth. Eight religious wars had snuffed out almost a million lives and wrecked two hundred and fifty villages. Rene grew up in a France that took its religion seriously. For a Frenchman to shed blood for his faith, Rene gathered, was quite a natural thing.

But there was also the unbloody glory of the faith to fill his childish mind and imagination. God and the saints and the whole bright world of the supernatural were very real to this boy who lived in a town that was so famous for the number of its churches and convents and abbeys, and especially its great cathedral of St. Maurice. As they wound their way up the uneven hills of the town, all the narrow, crooked streets of Angers seemed to point to the towering Plantagenet cathedral with its three towers.

Little Rene must often have gazed up in awe at the stone warriors who stood silent at the base of the middle tower, and many a fascinated glance he must have cast at the rich tapestries and rose windows as he knelt wonderingly in this tall house of God. Then there were the many stories and festivals of the saints, and the great Feast of God each year that brought the happy country folk swarming into the town for the gay and holy pageantry of the processions.

All in all, with that marvelous facility childhood has for accepting the unseen, whether it be fairies or angels, Rene must have very soon acquired the common and nonchalant Christian art of living in two worlds. With the years this faith was to grow and deepen until one day even the most terrible of agonies would not suffice to tear it from his soul. In this venerable old town with its wondrous cathedral and its twisted streets, two little feet took the first faltering steps that were finally to march with hero's pace through fire and death into the unseen world where is "the substance of things to be hoped for."

It may seem but a fine line, that which separates the dreamer from the man who hopes, but it is in reality a bottomless chasm.

The dream makes only the poet, hope makes the saint; they are not always the same, and France is famous for both. Now Rene was one of those who hope. The supernatural world of beautiful things he believed in was more than a dream. They were uncompromisingly and "prosaically" real; so real he pawned his life for them.

Of course, saint-to-be or not, little Rene did not spend all his days in the cathedral. There were the jobs to be done at home, and the games in the streets and in the fields down by the river bank, with maybe an occasional hike out to Angers' famous slate quarries. There were the long tiresome days in the classroom. But it was the steady, unnoticed atmosphere of his everyday life at home that left the greatest mark on Rene's character. Many years later he was to be known for an exquisite kindliness and courtesy and a delicate purity that would win the admiration of even the rough adventurers of New France.

You don't grow a personality like that overnight. A great love of God can come of a sudden, like a summer thunderstorm, but there is an instinctive, great-souled gentleness and reverence for human sensibilities that Providence seems to grow only within the warm walls of a Christian home. Rene had the great good fortune to form his childhood philosophy and theology of life against the supernatural background of a loving and living faith for which the old France of the cathedrals was not much longer to be famous.

It was a new world which the schoolbooks and lecture rooms later opened to Rene's vision. It was a world of rich promise in which human reason seemed to be on the verge of mastering all Nature's secrets. Descartes in France, stung by the mocking skepticism of Montaigne's brilliant essays, and Francis Bacon in England were pioneering new paths in the world of thought and opening giddy vistas of conquest. In the seventeenth century their bold visions and revolutionary methods caught the fancy; they enthralled spirits grown somewhat heady with the breath of adventure and they inspired minds to a new consciousness of liberty and power. Unfortunately these proud visions were to lure philosophers into a hopelessly landlocked kingdom of subjectivity where freedom from tradition and objectivity was exchanged for slavery and confusion.

But when Goupil was a student no *cul-de-sacs* were yet in view down the long inviting highways. In Italy, Torricelli plotted the secrets of the weather with his barometer. Kepler, in Germany, mastered the movements of the planets, and Napier, the Scotchman, advanced the science of mathematics with his logarithms. Gassendi, Huyghens, and Malpighi were shortly to become famous names in the new adventure story of science. The discoveries were splendid, but the idea spread that if the past had been surpassed it should also be suppressed.

In art and literature courses Goupil heard much of "modern" names like Murillo, Velasquez, Rubens, Van Dyck, Shakespeare, Milton, Jonson, Cervantes, Calderon, Lope de Vega, Corneille, Malherbe. Shakespeare and Cervantes died when Rene was nineteen, and the year he turned twenty-five saw the birth of Pascal and Molière.

But man's feet had become as impatient of confinement as his mind. The seventeenth century's "brave new world" must have no limits in spirit nor in space. Daring adventurers were opening new geographic frontiers to bring the marvels of man's new civilization to the "last continent." English voyagers settled at Jamestown the year Goupil was born, and the French founded Quebec the following year. Champlain dreamed of a joint advance by the French flag and the Cross into the new lands; but in Richelieu's dream, the Cross lagged sadly behind the flag. It was here that Richelieu's and Goupil's destinies converged.

Expansion into the northern forests of the New World was but part of Richelieu's ambitious design for France's future. Louis XIII's masterful minister, who took office when Goupil was twenty-seven, set out to plant the white banners of France in the place in the sun that Spain and Austria had so long held. His design was to be accomplished even at the cost of shattering the spiritual unity of Christendom. At home the Cardinal was relentless in his suppression of the Huguenot Calvinists, but beyond the boundaries of France, he watched Protestantism march into the capitals of Europe behind his French halberds. And even Paris was not long to be safe. From the time Goupil was eleven, till six years after his death, the Thirty Years War was to plague Europe with death and destruction and the bitter hatred of confused loyalties. The Christian unity of the West was lost forever in that bloody maelstrom of fire and smoke. Yet from the wreckage of the Old World, the Church, by means of men like Goupil, was to reach out and gather other larger worlds to herself and to Christ. "Attacked by robbers in a corner the Catholic Church defends herself with the universe."

What effect all of this worked in the young mind of Goupil we can imagine from the fact that after he finished school he went to Paris to become a Jesuit. From ancient Angers and the Catholic Middle Ages he stepped into the excited modern world at Paris. There converged all the colorful elements of this new world in the making. From there the King and his Minister controlled the complicated chequerboard pattern of policy which was building a French empire at so dear a cost to Europe and the Church. There about the University of Paris gathered the emancipators of knowledge, impatient to have the bright new world of science baptized by Reason and divorced from the shackles of Faith.

Discovery, conquest, and revolt were the watchwords of the day, and the wealthy Huguenot princes and merchants were quite pleased with the way things were shaping up. If all went well they would soon be free of both Pope and King. This same fever was burning in the veins of countless others of Europe's disgruntled minor princes, men whom the breath of the Protestant revolt had inflamed with a golden idea—to use religious freedom as a wedge for political and financial independence. How easily legitimate freedom and selfish pride become entangled in the labyrinth of our conscious motives.

But through the midst of the hubbub, Rene took his way to the buildings of the Company of Jesus' novitiate. The boy from the Provinces, from an old town still washed by the last lingering light of the medieval faith, stepped into the strange and cynical new world of Paris and cast in his lot with a body of men who were leading a gallant fight to keep the new world in the old faith—the old faith that had now been pruned of many of its disedifying encrustations at the Council of Trent.

"Jesuit" was already a word to conjure with. To their enemies these modern religious whose monastery was the world were sinister cloak-and-dagger figures, tools of foreign powers. To their friends they were new heroes with an air of holy gallantry. As missioners they adventured into such fabulous lands as the Congo, Tibet, Persia and India, and they dared their way into the Protestant citadels of Europe to bring hope to Catholic hearts. Edmund Campion and Robert Southwell, the courtly young men who had jested with death while they brought the Sacraments to Elizabeth's England, were already magic names. The gallant Frenchman, Père Henri Samier, specialized in trying to rescue captive princesses, like Mary Stuart.

The blackrobes' efficient schools dotted the map of Europe. Their list of graduates reads like an honor roll of seventeenth-century history: Emperor Ferdinand, Maximilian the Great, Generals Tilly and Wallenstein, Cardinal Richelieu, Descartes, Corneille, Molière, Bossuet. The Spanish soldier-mystic who founded their Order told his sons not to hang back and dream of the old days of musty copy rooms and illuminated manuscripts, but to go into the modern world and bend all things to Christ. The world was good and man's mind was good, but in the enthusiasm of his new conquests and his new liberty he must not be allowed to forget that it all must be orientated ultimately toward God—like a medieval cathedral. And the Church must be defended from heresy.

When Rene was a boy the French Jesuits were the Huguenots' special nightmare. These French Calvinists saw Jesuit confessors at the court of the King, they saw Jesuit chaplains in the King's armies, they saw Jesuit pupils, like Tilly and Wallenstein, leading the Catholic armies, they saw Jesuits in the most influential schools of France, they saw Jesuits everywhere and anywhere, and always between them and their goal—the destruction in France of the "foreign Church of Rome."

But one dark night in 1589 the Calvinists, to their extreme discomfort, failed to see the Jesuits. Paris was under siege by the Protestant armies. The King of Navarre, directing operations for the attackers, ordered a surprise assault against the walls in the middle of the night. The defenders, thinking the unusual blackness of the night would rule out any attack, had left the walls for bed. But at one place some sentries kept their post. They were Jesuit brothers who had been stationed on the walls by the public-spirited Father Minister of the College of Clermont.

And of course fate would have it that the unfortunate Protestants should happen to pick that part of the wall for their attack. The first skirmisher reached the parapet, pulled his scaling ladder up behind him, and placed it against the inside of the wall. He did not see the two startled sentries on either side of him, halberds in their inexperienced hands. As the soldier prepared to climb down into the city, a third Jesuit brother at the foot of the wall deftly removed the ladder. The startled Huguenot reached the ground of Paris much sooner than he had expected. In a rage he picked himself up and started out after the brother who was now making a religious withdrawal. But meantime the alarm was given, the garrison manned the battlements in time to repulse the attackers, and in tribute to the diligent sentries the Paris citizenry presented the College of Clermont with the scaling ladders Navarre's troops left behind them.

With reason, then, the Huguenots hated the Jesuits. And when we remember that Angers, Rene's home town, was within the orbit of Huguenot influence in south-eastern France, we can realize more clearly what must have been in the young man's mind when he went to Paris to be a Jesuit. A love of God he had of a surety, a strong and personal love that had grown with his maturing consciousness, but it was a love of God that impelled him to action— that sent him into the midst of the "modern" world where the Church of his God was in danger, where Christ called out to him that souls were most in need of being saved.

Rene loved, and his love called him to service. Just as Ignatius had elected to leave the monastery of Montserrat and go into the world to save the world, so Rene decided on the active apostolate in preference to a contemplative service in one of Angers' many abbeys. Perhaps in both cases it was an almost intuitive sensing of the fundamental import of the Incarnation and Redemption that gave direction to their spiritual aspirations. At any rate, like Ignatius a hundred years before him, Goupil went to Paris.

The novitiate there was new. It was the third to be opened in France, and Henry IV had signed the papers authorizing its foundation just before he died in 1610. Goupil was happy there. His natural graciousness and affability plus a desire to be of service, and his solid spirituality, rounded off the rough edges of novice life. He felt at home, he fitted into the spirit of the life, and in no time at all he began to feel that he had been a Jesuit for years. The *Spiritual Exercises* fanned the flame it found in this young soul. Christ, the loving yearning Christ of the Redemption, filled his heart until Rene found room there for nothing else.

Then, of a sudden, tragedy struck. His hearing had begun to fail, the effect of a boyhood illness. Soon his deafness became quite pronounced and Superiors decided that Rene would not be able to follow the many classes that he must hear during the long years before ordination. So, regretfully, expressing the sincere hope that Rene's deafness would be cured in time and that he might have another opportunity to become a Jesuit, the Novice Master said good-by to his promising young novice. Rene was broken-hearted. In the short months he had worn the black robe he had grown to love this *Compagnie de Jésus* with the passion of a strong heart whose young-man's love, so much deeper and starrier and less definable than the simple love of the boy of Angers, had till now not found a focus on anything short of God.

Goupil could not dream of anything else God could want him to do except serve Him in company with these men of Ignatius. But obviously there must be another road for him. Perhaps this was but to try him, and some day he would still be able to follow his heart's first adult desire. At any rate, Rene did not marry, and he did not enter another religious order or the secular clergy. Like a sensitive young man who had lost his first and only sweetheart in death, Rene never dreamed of looking for another to fill the vacancy in his heart. Perhaps if his hearing improved he could become a Jesuit brother—but a Jesuit it must be. Meantime, what was he to do?

The issue was not long in doubt. Nature and grace alike had conspired to fashion in him a heart that yearned to be of assistance to others, and it took very dull ears indeed not to hear the groans of Christ's sick poor lying in squalor in Paris' callously neglected back areas. Rene turned to medicine and began studying to be a doctor; special reading and private tutoring making up for the things he failed to hear in class.

Of course the boy from Angers was attracted by the romance that attached to the Jesuits of his day. No red-blooded, Catholic young man could have been impervious to the charm. And to qualify for sanctity one can hardly be noted for a lack of red blood. Man has a heart as well as a soul, and the Church is careful to appeal to the former with the grand pageantry and stirring poetry of her liturgy. Goupil, as a boy in Angers, had not displeased God when his heart had "leaped up" to behold the sunlight touching the great rose windows of the Cathedral and turning it into a massy translucent flame that diffused its soft radiance throughout the vaulted interior.

But it was clearly not principally the exterior glamour of the Jesuit life that had called Goupil to Paris. The absolutely God-centered character that he is soon to show us leaves us no room for doubt. Through the feverish complexity of the very human and ambitious strivings of his world, through all the cross-purposes of the proud visions of wealth and nationalism and intellectual prowess with which Goupil came intimately in contact during his medical studies at Paris, the soul of this young man remained fixed as straight and true at the God he loved as did the tall adoring towers of the old Cathedral above the winding twisting streets of Angers.

We shall see that if ever there was a life which showed the proud seventeenth century that all is vanity which is not orientated Godward like a medieval spire, and if ever there was a life that instinctively differentiated between reality and the dream, realism and romance, that life was Goupil's.

"Christianity is prose," as Kierkegaard so well puts it, "but it is precisely the poetry of eternity." It was the mistake of Goupil's "modern" France to begin to identify Christianity with the poetry of this life. The romantic allure of their new-found liberty and power beguiled them into confusing their God with the proud trappings of worldly pomp and glory. Goupil would show them that Christ's Christianity speaks prose on earth and is wary of the dream; it carries a very prosaic cross through the world, and looks forward to singing its poetry in heaven. Not that Christianity does not sing and dream on earth, but its songs and poems are always incomplete, are always only symbols. And they are joyous and beautiful precisely because they are symbols . . . signs and harbingers of reality, the beautiful Reality ahead.

No, Rene Goupil did not love the Society of Jesus just for the gallant chivalry of its exterior life. He loved it because of its intense devotion to the service of God. If he had merely ambitioned the outer romance of an adventurous career such as that of a Father Samier, then Rene would have looked elsewhere for that worldly satisfaction after he left the novitiate at Paris. In this vibrant, colorful city were gathered all the throbbing heart strings of the world of new empires. From the Paris of science and wit and wealth, the nerve center of the royal business of conquest and exploration, bright and noisy with swashbuckling cavaliers and their fashionably gowned ladies, a hundred avenues lay open to success. A quick mind and a daring hand were guarantees enough for an exciting future.

Instead, Rene devoted himself to the quite unglamorous task of learning to be a doctor. It was the very real ideal of serving the poor of Christ that he was aiming at. His aim was not very definite; it ambitioned service for all mankind. If he could not devote himself to saving the souls of the men and women Christ died for, then he would spend himself at least in saving their poor bodies. It was not to a comfortable and fashionable practice among the nobility that he looked forward.

His doctor's work would be hard, often unrewarding, unappetizing frequently and often unappreciated, but would he not be doing the very thing on which Christ had promised to base His reward when life was over? "Come, ye blessed of My Father . . . for I was sick and you visited me." A life of service it would be, not outwardly very grand but in reality how noble. "Christianity is prose . . . but it is precisely the poetry of eternity."

So Rene, hard of hearing but determined, plunged into his medical studies. Discouraging years of class lay ahead of him, and years of internship in hospitals where conditions would turn the stomach of many a modern doctor habituated to starched and antiseptic efficiency. St. Vincent de Paul was just then in the midst of his heroic labors to bring Christianity to the hospitals of France. But to Rene it was all beautiful because it meant serving the bodies and souls of the one God loved. In the "prosaic" repulsiveness of a Paris hospital there was the "poetry of eternity."

And then, perhaps he might still one day be a Jesuit and continue to serve but from a higher level of consecration. Though he may not have been aware of it, the ever-purposeful designs of Providence were working out in the evolutions of Rene's spiritual life as a strange parallel to the birth of that great vocation which had bloomed in the soul of Ignatius of Loyola. The wounded hero of Pamplona, knightly *caballero* of Charles V's conquest-minded Spain, burst into a flame of love for his new-found "Divine Majesty," but it was a love which pointed to nothing more definite than an ideal of service. Its spirit was distilled in the first germs of the meditations of the Kingdom of Christ and the Two Standards that came to Ignatius as he pondered over Ludolph's chivalric-tinted *Vita Christi* and the *Flos Sanctorum.* Of the Benedictine and

Dominican monks at Montserrat and Manresa, of the Holy Places at Jerusalem, of the scholars at Barcelona and Alcala and Salamance, the soldier-mystic sought a more definite and particularized orientation of this inspiration toward service.

It was not until years later that he fully realized how the mystic graces of Manresa had really meant to convey to him an ideal as wide and boundless as the Redemption itself. He was to serve God in the world, the *whole* world, and to apply the Blood of the Redemption to *all* souls, concentrating his energies whenever, and wherever, and however the concrete exigencies of any given historical situation should demand—to be determined by the bidding of the Supreme Vicar of this temporal part of Christ's Kingdom. And then Ignatius formed his Company accordingly.

Just so, one hundred years later, Rene Goupil was retracing the growth of Ignatius' spirit. His ideal was service of all Christ's souls, and he was not allowed to particularize or channel this service even within the limits of the Society of Jesus itself. His heart's desire was to be a Jesuit, and God answered by making him, in a sense, more Jesuit than a Jesuit. So we shall see that one of the charming mysteries of Rene's story is that though in the records of the Society his Jesuit life is measured by months, his actual life for years had traced out the letter and the spirit of the Jesuit vocation—more particularly, the vocation of a Jesuit coadjutor brother.

### NEW FRANCE

While Rene, in Richelieu's ambitious France, was busy poring over medical tomes by night and swabbing the wounds of Christ's Body by day, the storm-clouds of his destiny were gathering over the New France across the sea. At Henry IV's earnest request, Father General Aquaviva had sent the first Jesuits to the New World about the time that Rene was born. This first venture was wiped out by the British pirate, Argall, the same worthy who later abducted Pocahontas. In the sack of the little French outpost a coadjutor brother was killed, Gilbert Du Thet. Then Champlain invited in some Recollect Fathers to care for the French settlers along the St. Lawrence and to evangelize the Indians. But by 1624 the work had so increased that the Jesuits were asked in again to help.

Among the recruits from Europe this time came big Father John de Brebeuf. But again the English destroyed the work. David Kirk, a French Huguenot from Dieppe, appeared off Quebec one day with a war fleet under English authorization. The under-manned French settlement decided the wiser course was to capitu-late. So back again to Europe, under guard, went the blackrobes. In the meantime Richelieu had bluffed England into signing an agreement that restored Canada to France. The Cardinal then re-organized his famous Company of the One Hundred Associates, put the Jesuits in sole charge of spiritual ministrations, and launched a vigorous effort to colonize the St. Lawrence region.

So in 1632, while Rene was studying and working in the hos-pitals of Paris, the first permanent Jesuit outpost was set up at Quebec. Brebeuf returned the next year and Isaac Jogues arrived in 1636, bringing the total force of Jesuit priests and brothers in New France to twenty-eight. The Jesuits cared for the spiritual needs of the French settlers at Quebec and at the settlement of Three Rivers, eighty miles further up the St. Lawrence. But it was to the task of bringing the faith to the savages that they principally de-voted their energies.

There were three Indian nations living in the neighborhood of the St. Lawrence—the Algonquins immediately west of Three Rivers, the Hurons further west above Lake Ontario and to the east of Georgian Bay, and the Iroquois further south below Lake Ontario in what is now New York State. East of the Iroquois, be-tween the Hudson Valley and the seaboard, roamed more Algon-quins, James Fenimore Cooper's famous Mohicans. At the time, the main interest of the white colonists was in the beaver skins and other pelts which the Indians eagerly bartered for a few cheap trinkets but which commanded handsome sums on the European market. The French at Three Rivers traded with the near-by Algonquins and with the more distant Hurons who paddled down the waterways each summer with their furs.

The Jesuits had not had much luck at Christianizing the roving Algonquins, but their mission station of Sainte Marie in Huron land was a success. Conversions among the Hurons were thrillingly numerous. Jogues joined the little band of blackrobes. As there were some twenty thousand Hurons in all, the constant refrain of the *Jesuit Relations,* which the missionaries had been sending to France since 1632, was for more and more recruits.

These savages of the forest were much given to witchcraft, had some conception of an after-life and accordingly showed an astounding reverence for their dead, and feared and worshipped an impersonal higher force which manifested itself in the elements of nature. They had practically no conception of a personal God. But the Jesuits found an opening in their preoccupation with thoughts of an after-life. Death was ever before their eyes, death in war or by the many sicknesses to which their poor living conditions made them terribly susceptible. Such a frame of mind often proved good ground for the seed of instruction about hell, the eternal torture pyre, and heaven, the everlasting "happy hunting ground" for those who keep God's law in this life.

Baptisms at first were very few because the jealous witch doctors accused the priests of sorcery. But gradually the conversions increased, and in time there developed a small body of Christian Hurons whose happiness and inspiring nobility of soul impressed not only the blackrobes but the other Hurons. Native catechists multiplied and the hopes of the missionaries rode as high as the wild geese arrowing into the northern sky.

But there was one dark spot in the picture. The deadly enemy of the Hurons was the Iroquois tribe to the south. These latter, a much fiercer and more warlike people than the Hurons, were divided into the Five Nations, whose names have been immortalized in fiction: the Senecas, Cayugas, Onondagas, Oneidas, and the Mohawks. Each summed they crossed Lake Champlain, paddled up the

Richelieu River, and hid out along the St. Lawrence to waylay and massacre the Huron fur parties travelling down to Three Rivers. Now the Iroquois had become the wholesale fur dealers to the Dutch who had settled along Long Island Sound.

And the genial burghers furnished their redskin allies with a plentiful supply of arquebuses and encouraged them to make things uncomfortable for the French palefaces up North who were befriending the hated Hurons. This the Iroquois proceeded to do, following the ancient principle that my enemy's friends are my enemies. The Dutch also let the Iroquois in on the secret that the French blackrobes were devilish sorcerers. Thus, unconcernedly, was the stage set for what was in a few years to be the tragic finale to the Mission of Huronia. The Iroquois had been dreaded enough before, with their tomahawks and arrows, but now with guns in their cruel hands, the eventual extinction of the terrified Hurons was assured.

But in 1639 only the first mutterings of the distant storm could be heard among the silent green world of towering trees out at Sainte Marie, and at Three Rivers. No black clouds sailed the radiant blue ocean of sky over New France. The missionaries increased their stirring pleas for reinforcements. Along with thrilling accounts of the hazards of missionary life, learned observations on exploration, map-making, local geography, and native customs and languages, these appeals were included in the letters which the missionaries in the front lines sent back to their local superior at Quebec.

There they were transcribed, often with difficulty, since more than once a hard-pressed campaigner sent in his report written with charred wood on a piece of bark. The copied letters were relayed to the Jesuit Provincial at Paris, and there they were published and circulated throughout France. They were a sensation. Everybody read the *Jesuit Relations*, even the Huguenots. Their simple accounts of unbelievable heroism and of hardships that even the imagination could not have surpassed, and their unaffected revelation of a manly and most tender heart-warming love of God, implanted a divine and salutary discontent in the comfortable soul of many a reader.

Rene read these accounts. He had been reading them for years while he toiled among the sick at Paris. In a soul already afire with love, the *Relations* merely fanned the flames to an unbearable intensity. He was doing all he could for Christ at Paris, but here was a chance to do more. Here was an opportunity to help in the glorious venture to bring the Christ he was so madly in love with into the hearts of a forgotten people. Here was a chance for greater service. And he would be helping his beloved Jesuits.

It was with an eye to the possible opportunity of becoming a Jesuit brother and going to New France that Rene had picked his particular type of medical study and work in Paris. It was to minor surgery and simple therapeutics that he had devoted his energies. This was the type of medical skill that would be most valued in a Jesuit brother in New France, and it was the field that most immediately and universally answered to the need of the sick poor of Paris. Rene's driving motive-force was ever, at least subconsciously, the applying of the absolute and infinite Redemption to the contingent and finite needs of the given historical moment. Almost by divine instinct Rene was ontologically and militantly Christian, a selfless instrument by which Eternal Providence worked its designs in the world of time.

Father Le Jeune's letters of 1635 from New France had given Rene great hopes. "I had thought that miracles were necessary to convert these flying Savages; but I was mistaken, for the real miracles of New France are the following: To do them much good, and endure many pains; to complain to God alone; to judge oneself unworthy, and to feel one's uselessness. He who has these virtues will perform miracles greater than miracles, and will become a Saint. Indeed, it is harder to humiliate oneself deeply before God and men, and to annihilate oneself, than to raise the dead; for that needs only the word, if one has the gift of miracles, but to humiliate oneself as one ought to—truly, that requires a man's whole life.

"Here deep learning is not needed, but a profound humility, an unconquerable patience, and an Apostolic charity, to win these poor Savages, who in other respects have good common sense. And if we begin once to gain them the fruit will be incalculable."

Such news set Rene to trembling with eagerness. He had feared that perhaps only the learning and holiness of the religious state would be useful among the Indians. But here an opportunity lay open for the patience and kindness which even a layman like himself might exercise. True, he was sadly lacking in the requisite humility, but might he not risk it and trust to God's goodness to overlook his faults and accept his eager love and his desire to serve?

So at length Rene emerged from his studies and internship with the title of *chirurgien* and plunged with ever more zest into his work among the sick bodies of the poor. He was an excellent surgeon. His rather clumsy body seemed to have generously bartered all of its grace for the marvelous skillfulness of his fingers. The busy weeks and months went by. His doctor's obligations reached out across the humbler districts of Paris in an ever-widening skein of attachments. The work absorbed his every waking moment.

St. Vincent de Paul had few more zealous disciples in this urgent apostolate of Christian social work. Understandably, Rene found less and less opportunity to apply again at the Jesuit Provincial's residence. And, busy as he was about God's work, *ad majorem Dei gloriam,* he no longer felt quite that same aching need to channel his ideal into the formally Jesuit mold as had overwhelmed him the day he stumbled away from the novitiate, his dreams crashing about his ears. Soon it was 1639 and, though his hearing had improved, no chance had yet presented itself for another attempt at entering the Society.

Then Rene heard that the French Jesuits were anxious to receive *donnés* for the Canadian Mission. Though not really a Jesuit and not binding himself to the Society by vows either as a priest or brother, a *donné* was still very much a member of the family. He was a layman who consecrated his goods and his services to the

Society for life, and in return was received into the Jesuit residence to live. He shared in the Masses and prayers and spiritual ministries of the Jesuits, contributed positively to the overall success of the Society's work; he was cared for in body and soul in this life and the next.

Things in the forests of New France had taken a discomforting turn. The savage Iroquois, emboldened by their supply of Dutch firearms, had increased the tempo of their raids on the Hurons. The river roads between Huronia and Quebec were infested with lurking war-parties. Even the fortified Huron villages were threatened, and the French settlements were brought into danger. But it was the French blackrobes against whom the Iroquois seemed to be working up a particular spite. The Huguenot traders who touched at New Amsterdam and some of the Dutch settlers had sown their poisoned words well. To the enraged Iroquois it was the white-face sorcerers in the black gowns who began to assume all the responsibility for whatever little success the Hurons might have in a raid, and for every beaver skin from Iroquois territory which the Hurons managed to filch.

The Jesuit superior at Quebec, Father Vimont, became increasingly apprehensive for the safety of his men at their outposts in Huron land. Martyrdom was wonderful but a dead Jesuit could not instruct and baptize many Hurons, and a burned mission station could not be replaced at will. Could not able-bodied laymen who would not be prevented by any religious status from wielding arms in an emergency, be brought over to live and work with the Jesuit fathers and brothers? It was not to be thought that any amount of money in the skimpy Jesuit Mission fund would be sufficient to attract men to such a dangerous and materially thankless life, so they would have to be *donnés*. They would have to be men who had bound themselves to the Society for spiritual reasons.

It was very important, too, that some of them be skilled in medicine. Smallpox epidemics were running like wild fire through the filthy Huron villages. The Indian population was being decimated, and the poison had even spread down the riverways to

Three Rivers and Quebec. The priests would soon be doing nothing but burning corpses unless doctors were sent to the Mission.

This last was what Rene Goupil had been longing to hear. Doctors were needed with the Jesuits in Canada! Here was his chance for even greater service even than he was rendering in the hospitals of Paris. Other hands were readily available here. So, not even stopping to reflect that this time he was sacrificing the honor of being a Jesuit brother as before he had offered to God the holocaust of a priesthood which was never to be his, Rene eagerly applied again at the Provincial's residence in Paris. And again he was eagerly accepted but this time instead of another eventual disappointment, God had in store for him two grand honors and rewards each greater than the other.

At last, one spring day in 1639, when the wind stood fair from France, a little fleet set sail into the Channel off Dieppe, sails flapped for a moment tentatively, then bellied in the wind, and Rene Goupil, surgeon *donné* of the Company of Jesus, was following his dreams to the new world. As his wooden ship slowly slipped away from the continent, the sad angels of France must have brightened a little to see the splendor of that God-centered soul on board. At last that spark of the fading glory of France's medieval love was on its way to spread the flame to a fresh world. In a sense, the Cathedral of Angers was going to this new world. Old France was giving New France of its best.

But as Rene's ship dropped below the horizon the angels looked disconsolately back again to the land below them. They watched a man in a little room. He was reading a manuscript with deep concentration. He was reading of a strange God "with a newer face of doom," a God who did not wish all men to be saved. What he was reading would be published in a few months, and the book would be entitled *Augustinus*. Its author was Jansenius. The man who was reading would publish a similar book of his own in a few years. His name was Arnauld. But the man thought too much, and did not love enough. Rene Goupil, on the ship at sea, loved more than he thought and instinctively he was tracing out the *real* order of things as he set his face toward a strange land to help in the salvation of unknown men. He was to give his blood in the attempt, and all the ink Jansenius could spill would never blot out the argument of that blood.

Rene was at sea for two months. In those days your adventure did not await you at the end of your voyage, it came to meet you the day you left port. Storms, pirates, calms, all conspired to keep you from your destination. And if you were a Jesuit traveller in the seventeenth century the chances were very high that it would be pirates, Protestant pirates—politely called free-booters, sea-dogs, etc.—who would put a rude end to your sea voyage. Of the six hundred Jesuits sent to China in the century following the first entry in 1581, four hundred perished en route either by storm or at the hands of English and French Protestant rovers. So, even though he wore no black cassock, Rene did not look forward to the crossing with the same unconcern with which we would set off for a pleasant week on the *Queen Mary*.

Of all the passengers, he talked most with Guillaume Couture, another young *donné* from Rouen. In the easy comradeship of men dedicated to an identical noble purpose the two would talk by the hour, leaning on the gunwale and unconsciously searching the rolling horizon with their eyes at the point where New France would probably first appear. Guillaume was tall, and powerfully built; Rene was smaller and stockier, strong, but not at all what we would call athletic.

He would have been as enormously out of place on the brilliant ballroom floors of the Tuileries as in the fencing room of the royal musketeers. They laughingly agreed that if they ever ran up against any Iroquois in New France Guillaume would do the fighting and Rene would stand by and bandage him. Then, like men sailing to their first battle, their banter would remind them of the probable reality, and they would fall silent, staring out to sea and each thinking his own thoughts about what lay in store for him on the unseen shore ahead. But, as is always the case, their imaginings never quite hit upon what actually was to befall.

On calm nights, when all was still except the creaking of the rigging and the slap of the waves against the hull, Rene would steal up on deck and pray. It was easy to speak to God at sea, at night. The vast silent emptiness in which the ship was enfolded made it so easy to realize and feel that you and God were alone and very real to each other, and that that was all that really mattered after all.

But in the course of the last few years Rene had found himself praying almost continually, even when he was busy in the midst of a crowded hospital—not that he was always repeating formalized prayers, but more often than not he was silent, merely attending to the presence of God within his soul and relishing it. In the same way he had often sat of an evening before the fire at home with his mother at his side knitting and his father smoking, and none of them saying a word, but each just being glad, being glad to be there, each in the other's company.

Now on the ship Rene spoke to his God from the depths of his warm heart, thanked Him again and again for the great gift of this opportunity to serve Him where the need was greatest, and begged passionately that he might never be found wanting in his loyalty and duty to these blackgowned men to whom he had pledged his life—these men whom he had not been found worthy to join in complete and sacred fellowship. He had not been found worthy to be either a Jesuit priest of a Jesuit brother, but would God please grant him the grace to serve at least as a *donné*, to serve till death, whatever might come in the venture ahead? The angels must have wept at such sincere and tender humility, knowing as they did what God had in store for this man of the bashful heart.

Almost eight weeks out of France the little fleet ran into the milky fog that hung low over the sea off the Newfoundland banks. A few more expectant days and they turned into the expansive lower reaches of the St. Lawrence. Most of the vessels hove to off the trading village of Tadoussac, but Rene's ship sailed on up the St. Lawrence one hundred and twenty miles to pull into the wharf at Quebec.

He marvelled at the sheer expansiveness of this oceanlike river. Surely the Maine, on whose banks he had played as a boy, and even the Loire and the Seine were dwarfed by the wild giant. But the massive beetling rock of Quebec reminded Rene somewhat of the Angevin castle back at Angers, and as he made his way along the path to the newly begun upper city he thought he could detect the quaint confusion of an old French Provincial town recreated in the shacks and warehouses and log homes clustered below him at the face of the cliff.

Father Vimont, in the Superior's log hut atop the Rock, welcomed the new recruits warmly and sincerely to New France. Rene was set to work at the Hotel Dieu helping the Sisters get control of the smallpox epidemic.

As the busy months drew on, the epidemic slowly spent its force against the Rock. Meanwhile this gentle-mannered and amazingly selfless young surgeon was unconsciously endearing himself to Quebec even as, all unknowing, he was fast winning the Heart of God. The courtly old world graciousness of his manner was a refreshing balm to spirits somewhat parched by the crude roughness of this hard new life. And hearts which had begun to feel the infection of the animal licentiousness in which this savage world encompassed them were reinspired to the ideals of their faith by Rene's smiling purity of soul and the obvious warmth of his love of God. The sick and the Sisters idolized him. The Jesuits were more than glad to have such a comrade-in-arms, and Father Vimont thanked God every day for the ship which had brought to Quebec this saintly surgeon, *incomparable en son genre.*

Out in this fresh new world where all the sham of civilized sophistication was swallowed up by the demanding wilderness, Rene felt that he was closer to the heart of things. The fundamental values and relationships of life were outlined. God became more real and more important. He remembered now something one of the Jesuits in New France had written.

"Never have I understood in my life in France what it was to distrust self entirely and to trust in God alone; I say alone, and without the presence of any creature: *Major est Deus corde nostro*, 'God is greater than our hearts'; this is evident in New France, and it is an unutterable consolation that when we find nothing else we immediately encounter God, who communicates himself most richly to good hearts."

But then Rene was forgetting that even in the noisy and worldly glitter of Paris he had been as conscious of God's presence as he was now. Many a good man in Rene's France had been beguiled by the new vision of the glory of this world, and had imperceptably exchanged God for a dream. Rene was always remarkable for never getting his dreams mixed up. Shadow and substance, romance and reality, they were never confused in his loves.

Even as a small boy he instinctively differentiated between the fairies that were supposed to inhabit the wooded dell by the old bridge, and the God who, his mother said, lived above the clouds and to whom he prayed on his knees each night. It was to that God that he turned when he had something important to say, not to the "folk" in the forest. These were not real people, but God was. And among the many things in life that were really important God was the most important.

Rene was fast beginning to realize the deep truth of something that had struck him in one of the *Relations* Father LeJeune had sent back from the new world. "Three mighty thoughts console a good heart which is in the infinite forests of New France, or among the Hurons. The first is, 'I am in the place where God has sent me, where he has led me as if by the hand, where he is with me, and where I seek him alone.' The second is, in the words of David, 'according to the measure of the pain I endure for God, his Divine consolations rejoice my soul.' The third, that we never find crosses, nails, nor thorns, in the midst of which, if we look closely, we do not find Jesus Christ. Now, can a person go wrong when he is in the company of the Son of the living God? . . . Strange thing! the more crosses I see prepared for me there, the more my heart laughs and flies thither; for what happiness to see with these eyes nothing but savages, crosses, and Jesus Christ. . . .

"When I see myself surrounded by murderous waves, by infinite forests, and by a thousand dangers there comes to mind that precious saying of the martyred St. Ignace, *Nunc incipio esse Christi discipulus:* to-day I begin to be of the company of Jesus. For what avail so many exercises, so many fervent meditations, so many eager desires? All these are nothing but wind, if we do not put them into practice. So Old France is fitted to conceive noble desires, but the New is adapted to their execution; what one desires in Old France is what one does in the New."

But this did not mean that, for being supernaturally motivated, Rene's love was less personal or his service less warm-hearted. One of his more philosophic countrymen was later to rhapsodize about the "noble Savage," and Chateaubriand was to romanticize in exquisite poetic flights on the untarnished beauty of soul in these "unspoiled children of the forest"—but it was all Platonic musing by a warm fire. Neither of these speculating poets would have been so enraptured if confronted with one of the real and quite disillusioning sick pagans at Quebec.

Rousseau's enthusiasm would doubtless have died a quick death. Rene, however, always sensitive to the distinction between reality and romance, was never inconsistent in his Christianity. He loved men, not man. The supernatural orientation of his love did not result in that chilly impersonality which is doled out dutifully to its mere human recipients. Rene's God was a living Person Who in this world of the Redemption has willed to be loved warmly in the living personalities of quite human men and women. "Amen I say to you, as long as you did it to one of these my least brethren, you did it to Me."

Rene was a Christian after the Heart of Christ. The human personalness of his love stands, with St. Vincent de Paul's, as a beacon light pointing out the "prosaic" exigencies of Christianity to an era that was fast "poeticizing" its faith. The Age of Reason, neglecting the concrete and exacting realities that love knows, withdrew its Christianity into the more comfortable and ideal world of the mind.

But thought feeding on itself gives you at best only a dream—or perhaps a poem; and Christianity is neither, it is an adventure.

From Quebec Rene was sent to the new reduction of Sillery, a little further up the St. Lawrence, to fight the disease among the sick Algonquin families there. At Sillery, Rene's love was tested even further. More often than not it was a servant's rather than a surgeon's hands that were needed. The few Sisters who had come out from Quebec to help the handful of Jesuits had more than they could do tending the ailing Algonquins who crowded the small log hospital and filled the Indian cabins of the settlement. They had no one to take care of the thousand and one little menial, distasteful, and time-consuming tasks that go with any kind of hospital work. Rene did not wait to be asked. He had given his hand and his heart to Christ when Father Vimont had welcomed him to New France. He had put no restrictions on that dedication. His service was still as wide as the Redemption, so it easily included the little disagreeable jobs around the hospital. And, as at Quebec, by winning the heart of God, Rene soon won the hearts of men as well.

Even these gruff savages from the wilderness responded to Rene's perpetual cheerfulness and puzzling kindness. At first the reserved Algonquin braves had almost despised this white man with the gentle manners who seemed to enjoy doing the work of women and of slaves. He must have the heart of a squaw.

But to their astonishment they found that this soft-voiced pale-face had a heart of steel. And they were not wrong. A man does not launch his life onto a one-way adventure which runs high in risk but low in palpable returns and glamour unless there is more to his spirit than a schoolboy's uncertain desire to be agreeable. There was steel in Rene's gentle heart, as true and finely tempered as any in the blades that Louis XIII's Guardsmen were flashing in Richelieu's battles. The bold musketeers of Dumas' France paraded in a handsome world of ladies' smiles, and faced death on regimented battlefields with drums beating an anesthetizing battle-fever into their pulse. Rene courted a lonely, naked, despicable death where his only encouragement would be in the unseen grace of God.

One day some Algonquins dragged a wounded Iroquois into the clearing outside the stockade at Sillery and began torturing him to death to the accompaniment of a hellish pandemonium. In the fiendish yells could be heard the hate of immemorial enemies and the overdone bravado of men who in superior numbers have cornered an enemy whom they would not dare to face singly. This Mohawk warrior had been surprised and overpowered in some fracas down the St. Lawrence. The Algonquins thought the blackrobes would enjoy seeing them making mincemeat out of one of their mutual enemies.

One of the Jesuits came running from the log fort just as Rene stepped out of the hospital to investigate the uproar. The father called out to Rene to come and help him and then plunged into the midst of the screaming Algonquins. He began to berate them at the top of his voice. Standing over the bleeding Iroquois he shouted at the Algonquins to stand back. They had been slicing flesh from the captive's thighs and pulling out his fingernails. When Rene came up he almost swallowed his heart at the sight of the furious rage in the circle of blazing eyes. It reminded him of the time at home he had been bitten by a dog when he had playfully tried to grab away a bone it was gnawing on.

The blackrobe accused the tormentors furiously of being "squaw men." They insulted their French brothers if they thought the white men considered this a display of Christian courage. Rene expected tomahawks to fly any second. But the two men bent down, picked up the seemingly unconscious Iroquois, shouldered their way through the thunderstruck mob without a hand being laid upon them. Their very boldness carried off the action. This was coin the braves understood.

Yet on this lonely fringe of Richelieu's proud Empire, where Rene was humbly giving his all to turn a dream of worldly conquest into a supernatural actuality of won souls, Rene found himself almost overwhelmed by God's love. "It seems as if God shed the dew of his grace much more abundantly upon this New France than upon the Old, and that the internal consolations and the Divine infusions are much stronger here, and hearts more on fire. . . . But it belongs to God alone to choose those whom he will use, and whom he favors by taking them into New France, to make saints of them. St. Francis Xavier said that there was an Island in the Orient which was quite capable of making a person lose his sight, by crying from excessive joy of the heart; I know not if our New France resembles this Island, but we know from experience that, if any one here gives himself up in earnest to God, he runs the risk of losing his sight, his life, his all, and with great joy, by dint of hard work; it belongs only to those who are here and who enjoy God to speak from experience."

By the summer of 1642 a dreadful diversion to the monotonous life at Sillery was very much in prospect. Fear of the Iroquois hung as heavy over the St. Lawrence as did the oppressive summer heat. The Mohawks especially had swarmed up the Richelieu River and fanned out in murderous bands east and west from the point where the two rivers met. Three Rivers had heard the war whoop, and Frenchmen had been killed at the new settlement of Montreal. Of the few Huron flotillas that braved the journey down the Ottawa and the St. Lawrence few arrived unscathed at Three Rivers. It was very doubtful if any news would come down from the Huron missioners this summer.

Then one fine day a fleet of Huron canoes from Sainte Marie pulled up onto the beach at Three Rivers after a breathless thirty-five day race down the imperilled waterways. Though Rene Goupil certainly did not realize it at the time, God's last overwhelming gift of love for him rode into his life that day in those Indian canoes. The final scene in Rene's life was set. Father Jogues had come to ask Father Vimont for a surgeon to help among his smallpox stricken Hurons.

Rene was summoned to Quebec and he hurried down with a great joy dawning in his heart. He half expected what Father Vimont was going to request before the question was put to him. He was introduced to a small, wiry, leather-skinned blackrobe with burning eyes and a charming Old World smile. Father Isaac Jogues. Would Rene be willing to go back to Sainte Marie with Father Jogues and work among the Hurons? It was not a command—the risks were too great—it was only a proposal. Both the priests joined in pointing out and magnifying the terrible dangers of the return journey to Sainte Marie and the further dangers and hardships that awaited him when and if he should reach Huron land.

Rene respectfully cut them short with a sincere request to be accepted for the trip—come what might. Struggling with the joy that was bursting from his heart and confusing his words, Rene explained that it was to work among the Hurons that he had first come to New France. It was for this grace of serving and suffering for his Lord at the post of greatest need and greatest danger that he had been praying all the while he was at Quebec and Sillery. Rene was accepted, along with Guillaume Couture.

In the cool, gray, summer dawn of August the first, the heavily laden flotilla of twelve canoes paddled out into the St. Lawrence and headed upstream from the fort at Three Rivers. Of the forty persons in the band only four were Frenchmen. There were two Huron boys returning home after a winter at Father Brebeuf's school in Quebec; Theresa, a beautiful young Huron girl, the idol of the Ursuline nuns at Quebec; and most of the rest were Huron warriors, many of them Christians. The leader of the party was Eustace Ahatsistari, the most feared and respected of the Huron war chiefs. He was a Christian and Father Jogues' devoted friend.

Father Jogues had said Mass for the Christians in the party, and after a traditional war council on the beach among the warriors, the canoes had been carefully loaded and the little flotilla pushed away from the shore in the eerie half light. All that day, tense and watchful, they paddled westward along the thickly wooded north bank of Lake St. Peter, scanning the shoreline for the slightest suspicious sign. In the cool of the August evening they pulled into shore and bedded down on the turf for the night.

Despite his aching muscles Rene could not get to sleep for a while. He lay still with his eyes fixed on the sparkling wrinkled surface of the silent lake, and thanked God for His goodness. The graces his Lord was showering him with were out of all proportion to his merit, but of none was he more enormously unworthy than this last. To be actually on the way to the land of the Hurons with Father Jogues! It was as though every time he had dared to dream, his God had touched the fantasy with a magic wand and made it real. But actually it was because Rene dreamed not as dreamers dream, but as saints dream. He dreamed with his heart as well as with his fancy and so God answered his acceptance of grace by a further shower of grace.

And for Rene, the crowning joy of this treasury of happiness was that it was as a companion and helper to this Jesuit priest that he was setting out on his great venture of service. It was almost as if he were actually a Jesuit coadjutor brother. God was indeed very, very good to allow him to approach so close to the one dream which clearly was never to be his. And would it please God to give him the strength to offer his life without faltering if the murderous Iroquois should bar the way to Sainte Marie. He made the offering of his death now, willingly, gladly. Might God deign to be pleased with it. He had long since made the much harder offering, that of his life, by consecrating each moment of it to the service of his God. It was simple now to make the easier offering of his death.

The Indians were up with the dawn and after hurriedly gulping some corn mush pushed off again. The day was hot and bright but no one paid attention to its beauty. Forty pairs of eyes scanned every clump of bushes along the bank as the canoes slipped along in single file. Rene fell to studying the broad, bronzed backs in front of him. Even when travelling the savages maintained their solemn, impassive silence. They would have been just as silent if this scent of danger were not hovering in the air. The sun glinted off the greasy reds and blues and whites daubed in grotesque patterns over their sweaty bodies. The muscles of their long limbs stood out with the rhythmic strain of their paddling. Their stiff black hair was cropped short, and narrow furrows from the forehead to the nape of the neck had been shaved to the scalp, leaving a weird, regular pattern of black ridges of hair—like the tufts on a boar's head. Rene could understand why Champlain's men had named the Hurons after *la hure*.

With a sudden startled shock the long line stopped paddling. A brave up front had spotted Iroquois footprints in the soft clay at the water's edge. After a tense council of war on the beach Eustace decided that the signs did not point to a large enough body of the enemy to warrant turning back. The canoes nosed out into the current again. Nerves were as taut as bow strings now, while the long file slipped along.

A little way further on and the Islands of Lake St. Peter crowded over toward the north bank, narrowing the channel. Ambush was in the hot, heavy air. The canoes crept apprehensively by the danger point as their occupants scanned the small area of swampy marsh on their right. Clumps of reeds dotted this shallow stagnant water that lay between the channel and the shore. The half dozen canoes in the vanguard slid abreast of the swamp.

The nervous silence exploded. War whoops screamed out, and thirty hideously painted Iroquois burst from the cover of the reeds. Their muskets barked, bullets whistled and spat among the Huron canoes. After the first shock of surprise Eustace pointed his canoe toward the marsh and led the other five boats against the Iroquois. The remaining seven canoes twisted around and fled. The Huron battle-cry rang out and a shower of arrows flashed from the canoes of Eustace's band. Blood-curdling yells from both sides clashed in the torn air and beat in throbbing waves against the ear drums. The Iroquois splashed back to the firm ground and the Hurons leapt from the canoes and dashed after them. Tomahawks and knives glinted in the sun.

When Rene could get his heart out of his throat he grabbed his musket and clambered through the reeds and marsh water toward the mêlée. This was it. Now it was his job to fight, to protect Father Jogues. But how to do it? He felt like a man in a nightmare, leaden-footed. His nerves and muscles had no responses ready for this new demand. His whole body was attuned to saving life. There he was quick, efficient, at home. In battle he was lost in a strange world. He could heal wounds but he did not know how to inflict them. Stumbling up onto dry land he lunged clumsily with his musket barrel at a vermilion-painted face that separated itself from the confused blur of struggling bodies. The shouting Indian tried to wrench the gun from his hands, and another Iroquois flung himself on Rene's back.

Another volley of war whoops rang out above the bedlam and a second crowd of Iroquois rushed in through the reeds to take the Hurons from behind. The fight was hopeless. Eustace and his braves struck out furiously with their tomahawks but they were soon overwhelmed and borne to the ground by weight of numbers. The object was not to kill but to take prisoners for the torture fires at home.

But Couture was in his element. He was made for this. Bulling his way through a crowd of Iroquois he knocked three of the braves to the ground and sprinted off into the safety of the forest.

Jogues had been watching the hopeless battle from a clump of reeds in the marsh. As a priest there was nothing he could do in the fight. He could have escaped, but instead he came forward now and gave himself up. He could not desert his flock at the time he could do the most for them. He bent over Goupil who was lying on his back, tied tightly. Rene whispered, "O my Father, God be blessed. He has permitted it. He has willed it. His holy will be done. I love it, I cherish it, I embrace it with all the strength of my heart."

All the Hurons were on the ground by now and being bound by the Iroquois who were shouting like maniacs. Theresa and the boys were unmolested. Couture decided that he could not leave Father Jogues to his fate so he too came back to surrender. As he appeared among the trees some Iroquois dashed out at him and a chief raised his musket to fire. Instinctively Couture threw up his own gun and fired first. The chief fell with a bullet in his heart. The other Iroquois went mad. In a blind rage they knocked Couture to the ground, stripped him, jumped up and down on his body, and beat him with the stocks of their Dutch muskets till he was only a mass of bloody flesh.

Father Jogues, who had bluffed the Iroquois into leaving him untied, ran up to embrace and console poor Couture. The savages then turned on him and Rene and beat them as they had Guillaume. With their teeth they pulled out the nails of Jogues' and Goupil's index fingers and then ground the fingers to a pulp between their jaws. Finally, leaving their victims tied on the ground, they gathered exultantly around the Huron canoes to divide the booty.

Rene was a semi-conscious, bloody bundle of pain. Human violence was a new and horrible experience for him. He had lived in a world where pain was outside him and he had devoted his time to soothing it. Now the pain had come to him, and angry hands had mauled him. It was hard to believe that his gentle world had crashed to pieces in a few terrible minutes. But it had. The thongs bit deeply into his bruised flesh and told him it was true.

He had the presence of mind to notice that one old Huron, too feeble to be of much use as a captive, would probably be killed by the Iroquois. The man was not a Christian and Rene asked Father Jogues about baptizing him. After some questions from Jogues the Huron requested and received baptism. As Rene had feared, a few minutes later a Mohawk split the old man's skull with a tomahawk blow. Rene had helped the priest to send a soul to heaven. Did he realize how true a Jesuit brother he was in spirit if not in fact?

The next few days passed for Rene in a confused blur of pain and exhaustion. The Iroquois were eager to get out of enemy territory with their prizes as soon as possible. After the battle they had packed the bound captives into the birch canoes and headed for the Richelieu River. They paddled steadily through the hot day, pulling into shore at night to fall exhausted on the bank for a few hours of sleep. They reached the mouth of the Richelieu and knifed down the glassy-surfaced river southward toward Iroquois land, still keeping the same furious pace. The warriors were Mohawks, the fiercest of all the Iroquois, and their homes were many a day's journey ahead.

His sore and feverish body cramped in the bottom of a canoe, Rene tried to turn his mind and heart to God. The pitiless August sun beat down on his festering wounds. If he changed his position and disturbed the delicate balance of the canoe a Mohawk would shout at him and strike him with the blade of a paddle. His wounds were suppurating and attracting flies. His head throbbed with fever. He never realized before how easy it had been to pray in a comfortable room, with a full stomach. God must forgive the poor many things. And then how great must be the fault of the rich if they do not become men of prayer.

But Rene knew that worse awaited him at the end of this death journey so he redoubled his efforts at communion with the God he would soon see face to face. He offered his death to God now, ahead of time. Rene had attended too many patients dying in agony not to realize that the desperate concentration of the death struggle monopolized every last shred of the sinking victim's consciousness.

Jogues and he had been crammed into the same canoe. When he was not talking to God, Rene spoke to the priest in front of him —quietly so as not to irritate the Mohawks. In low tones they spoke of God's goodness in allowing them to suffer for Him. They spoke of the happiness of heaven to be bought so cheaply, and they wondered if their sufferings would be sufficient to merit some success for their blackrobe comrades still laboring to bring the Hurons to God. Always they spoke of God. With reality staring them in the face, there was no time for the conventional trivialities with which polite society masks the only thoughts worth uttering.

About the fourth day Rene finally mustered enough courage to whisper, falteringly, to Father Jogues the wish that had been hovering at his lips since the day of the battle.

"My Father, God has always inspired me with a burning desire to consecrate myself to His holy service by the vows of religion in His holy Society. All the time up to this hour my sins have made me unworthy of this grace. Nevertheless, I hope that Our Lord will be pleased with the offering which I wish to make to Him. My Father, I wish to pronounce now, in the best sentiments that I can have, the vows of the Society of Jesus, in the presence of my God and before you."

Rene blurted out his request and held his breath. Jogues was too overcome for a moment to answer. My God, who could be more worthy to be a member of the Society than this man? How few in the black cassocks are Jesuits as close to the heart of Christ as this amazing man already is? It is I who am unworthy to receive him. Chokingly, Jogues whispered back that under the circumstances he would presume permission to receive Rene's vows in the name of the Father Provincial. Rene's eyes filled with tears. When he could get control of himself he slowly and reverently whispered to Father Jogues the vows of the Temporal Coadjutor in the Society of Jesus. There was no question of his stumbling over the formula. Many a night in Paris and in Quebec he had made these words his prayer before going to sleep.

Huddled in a Mohawk canoe on a strange river in a primitive wilderness, on his way to a terrible death, his practically naked blood-caked body burning in the sun, Rene Goupil of Angers, Old France, finally bound himself to the Ignatian Company of the Lord he had so long served. He had never dreamed it would be like this. Jogues inconspicuously imparted his priestly blessing to his new brother in Christ and the two men sat silent, their eyes moist with happiness.

How the fashionable throng in the Tuileries' ballroom would have smiled pityingly at these two ridiculous wretches. The gay crowds at home in Louis XIII's "modern" and "reasonable" world danced on in their dream, while these two expatriates from civilization, huddled in a savage canoe, gazed at the glory of reality.

The fifth day found the flotilla on the broad expanse of Lake Champlain. Worn out at last by the strain, the Mohawk braves forced the Hurons to take up the paddles. A paddle was thrust at

Jogues, too, but he refused it. Rene, uncertain what to do, thought that in any case it was his duty now as a Jesuit brother to take over the work of the father, so he grasped the paddle and began willingly to dig into the water. But the Mohawks only used his compliance as an occasion to redouble their efforts to make the priest follow suit. They beat and kicked Jogues unmercifully. Rene was broken-hearted. He had done the wrong thing. Instead of helping he had only brought more agony to the father. Service was so simple in his desires but so complicated in execution. Rene paddled on, confused and wretched.

But at night, when the canoes beached and the toil-wracked travellers threw themselves on the grassy bank, Rene was in his element again. Confident, sure of himself, he moved about in his gentle world of kindness and mercy, doing what he could for the wounds of the Iroquois and the Hurons. He wiped pus from the raw flesh and opened throbbing veins for friend and foe alike. And both friend and foe received his ministrations with the same stoic, grim indifference. The grateful, appreciative smiles of Quebec and Sillery could not live in this wilderness where the Prince of Hate ruled supreme.

The eighth day of the nightmare journey found the long line of canoes driving steadily down the west rim of the lake. The brilliant green of the thick summer foliage gleamed in the sun and sparkled with reflections off the water. Mohawk scouts were encountered. They reported an Iroquois war party, two hundred strong, camping on an island ahead. The braves were on their way to wipe out the beginnings of the French fort which was rising at the junction of the Richelieu and the St. Lawrence. The warriors of Rene's fleet increased the beat of their strokes. Coming in sight of the island they raised the Mohawk victory chant and fired off their muskets in a salute to the sun god and the god of war.

The other Iroquois crowded excitedly around the canoes and clamored for a chance to "caress" the prisoners. The proud captors gave in, though this ceremony was not customarily performed be-fore the home village was reached. Appropriate treatment of the

detestable paleface captives might send good luck along with the
war party as it attacked the French fort.

The braves provided themselves with sticks and clubs and
hurriedly formed in two parallel columns stretching up the beach.
The prisoners were shoved into one end of the gauntlet and told to
run to the other end. As they stumbled along, the Iroquois, screaming insanely in a blood frenzy, rained a continuous hail of blows
on the naked bodies. Rene was in the middle of the line. Awkwardly
he blundered along, blinded with pain and sweat and the maddening confusion. His old wounds had reopened and mingled their
blood with countless new ones long before he stumbled the length
of the line. He could not pray. He could only think of that road
to Calvary and of the Man tottering weakly along sixteen hundred
years ago and forever.

The dazed captives were hauled up onto a hastily built low
platform and exposed to the whimsical cruelty of the whole savage
band. Screaming insults and taunts the Iroquois took turns beating
the victims, slashing their flesh, pulling out their fingernails and
slitting the skin lengthwise on their fingers. Sputtering firebrands
were thrust against the open wounds to cauterize them and staunch
the flow of blood. Rene was saturated with pain, but it was perhaps
sharpest in his sensitive surgeon's fingers. The diabolic faces grimac-
ing and screaming around him faded into a blurred picture of hell.
He was back at Paris in the Long Retreat listening to the earnest
Novice Master paint the terrors of eternal punishment.

The horrible afternoon became evening. Finally Rene was conscious that the pandemonium had died away. The pain remained,
beating against his brain with every throb of his pulse. The captives
had collapsed in a stupor all around him. The big summer moon
made a ghastly picture of their twitching, blood-caked bodies.
Rene begged God for strength to be true to his consecration, and
fell off into blackness. . . .

With the first light of morning the eager war party took to its
canoes and headed north. The Mohawks herded their half-dead
prisoners down to the water's edge and into the boats. The night-

mare journey took up where it had left off. The shining waters of the lake finally narrowed down to a swampy stream that cut its way south under the steep wooded sides of the Adirondacks.

On the tenth day the end of the lake was reached. The Mohawks cached the canoes and herded the stumbling prisoners along the forest trail that led to the villages. A three-day journey yet remained and the supply of corn mush had given out some time ago. Captors and captives alike were getting weak. So the Mohawks set off at a killing dog-trot to reach home before anyone collapsed from hunger.

Jogues and Goupil could barely walk, let alone run, and could not possibly keep up with the column. Their guard finally left them, to follow the column as best they could. Each night they would stagger into camp after most of the savages had gone to sleep.

Stumbling along the uneven trail during the day Rene tried to convince himself that he was looking after Father Jogues. But neither of the exhausted sufferers could be said to be caring for the other. They were too weak to even brush the clustering gnats and mosquitoes from their sores. Jogues begged Rene several times to turn back toward the lake. Maybe Couture could get away, too, and then both of them could perhaps make their way back to Three Rivers. Rene would not hear of it. The brother's place was with the priest.

"My Father, I will die with you. I cannot possibly desert you."

On August fourteenth, the thirteenth day on the torture trail, the Mohawks kept all the captives together on the march. Ossernenon, the first Mohawk village, was near. In the afternoon the party topped a rise and looked down on the green Mohawk valley. They dropped down the bushy slopes to the river and split the silence with the victory chant. Answering shouts came from ahead. The long line waded through the river at a ford and climbed the opposite slope. They came out on the open rise that was crested by a long palisade surrounding a cluster of huts that was Ossernenon. A screaming, shouting picture of hell was there to meet them. In the face of every man, woman, and child that Rene could focus his eyes on he could read only hate. God grant there be love in his heart until the blood was drained from it.

Again the welcoming savages formed a gauntlet and screamed for the victims to be sent through. Couture, the killer of a chief, was first. Rene was in the middle again. The captives had all been stripped naked except Jogues and Goupil. Jogues had talked the warriors into letting them keep a shirt tied around their waist.

Rene was dead on his feet. His tortured nerves and muscles could do no more. He staggered in between the screaming lines and was pushed along under the blows. He was drowning in an ocean of pain. He could not even bring his arms up to protect his face. Clubs, iron rods, and sticks hammered his face and head and shoulders. His nose was smashed, his teeth were splintered. His face became a red pulp. Somewhere near the middle of the line the waves of pain roared over him and blotted out the sun. The savages kicked his body out of the way and shouted for the next victim.

The demoniac shouts of the Mohawks were dinning in his tortured ears when he awoke again. He was up on another platform before the gates of Ossernenon. The blood-mad villagers were hacking off the fingers of the Hurons and of Father Jogues. The priest kept exhorting the Hurons—all of whom had been baptized by now—to keep heart and to remember the happiness the Great Father had in store for them. Despite his own pain, Jogues still had room for more when he looked at Rene. His brother's swollen face was a mask of blood. Jogues later wrote in the *Relations* how the only white to be seen in Rene's poor face was in his eyes.

The howling savages forced an old woman, a Christian Huron captive, to come up on the platform and cut off Jogues' right thumb. Each clumsy hack she made at Jogues' thumb joint pierced to Rene's soul. There was nothing he could do to help the Father. That was the worst pain of all. Then the executioners moved over to Rene and grabbed his right hand. His heart sank. He saw what they were going to do. His surgeon's fingers were going to be torn from him. A snarling Mohawk grabbed the right thumb and hacked through skin and sinews and joint with an oyster shell. Rene had only wanted the finger in order to heal wounds and soothe the miseries of the world—but they wrenched it from him. Yet, what was the finger—was he not soon to offer the whole body to God?

The blood spurted out of the hole in his hand. The agony pierced to the marrow of his bones and set his nerves, already surfeited with pain, to throbbing even more violently. As a doctor, Rene had often been astonished at the incredible amount of suffering the human body could stand. But he had never imagined that it could endure this. A smirking Iroquois snatched the quivering hand and thrust a white-hot rod against the gaping wound. The agony exploded inside Rene's brain and he lost consciousness again.

When you meet Rene in heaven he will not be able to tell you much about what happened to him through the horrible weeks that followed this terrible day on the torture platform at Ossernenon. At night the unconscious captives would be dragged from the gory platform and staked out on the ground in the form of St. Andrew's Crosses. Then it was time for the children to amuse themselves with the victims. Through the night they howled around the helpless men like fiendish imps from hell, throwing live coals and burning embers on the lacerated bodies to watch them squirm. Rene was too weak to move. He could not get the coals off his body. They burned his whole chest into a livid welt.

He was dimly conscious of another hellish day on the platform and an agonizing walk to the other two Mohawk villages with nightmarish days on the torture platform in each village. No part of his body was whole any longer. None of his countless lacerations had time to heal.

Then days began to separate themselves from nights, and the din of hell began to fade in receding waves from his consciousness. He was back at Ossernenon. He and Jogues were lying in an Indian hut. A Mohawk War Council had decided to leave the door open for a possible treaty with the French. The palefaces would be spared. Couture had been taken to the largest of the three villages. Rene and Jogues were to stay at Ossernenon in the custody of a chief who had lost a relative in the ill-fated attack on Fort Richelieu. The boasting warriors who had "caressed" the prisoners on the island two weeks ago had met disaster at the French fort. Their surprise attack had been turned into a route when Montmagny's troops and workmen had refused to be surprised. So Jogues and Goupil were sure to receive no lenient treatment from their guard.

Rene lay in the dark stuffy hut for weeks, more dead than alive. So God had not wished to receive the offering of his life this time. God's will be done. Suffering was no mystery if you only remembered that the complete story of the Crucifixion did not end on the First Friday—that it will only be complete on the Last Day. Rene's consciousness came and went in fitful snatches between spells of coma and utter exhaustion. He could not really pray. That is, he could not pray by focusing his conscious attention on God in any kind of reasoned sequence, but he prayed a more fundamental prayer of adoration.

Peguy tells us that the night is more real than the day, and that days are only fitful interludes in the underlying reality of night. And so Rene prayed. The night of his inner self that supported the fretful snatches of consciousness was directed adoringly toward God. The stones in the Cathedral at Angers could not speak their praise, but through the silent centuries the tall spires pointed in ceaseless adoration toward God.

When Rene could move he did his best with his mangled hands to care for Jogues' wounds and then his own. The brother must do his best to help the father. His yearning to serve had a new obligation now. It had not all been a nightmare. He was really and truly a Jesuit brother now. But it was very little that the poor maimed hands could do. Rene felt helpless and lost. And when he and Jogues were able to hobble around the village his wretchedness increased. The Iroquois was not like the Algonquins at Sillery. They lived and fed only on hate and war and torture. Gentleness and kindness enraged them. Rene was hopelessly bewildered by their deep malevolence. He could not breathe in a world that never smiled. God had made him for kindness and gentleness. The savages responded to his smiles with sneers. They rejected his offers of little kindnesses with a curse. They shouted their hatred at him. He was a squaw! He had no spirit!

Rene's heart withered within him. How could he go on living if he could not be of service to anyone, if his love was rejected? He could not understand. God must have some hidden purpose in it though. God's will be done. And so, rebuffed by the men he wanted to love, Rene gradually turned exclusively to God. His life on earth was already finished. There was nothing more he could do but suffer. Yet the body can stand only so much suffering. Even God died after three hours of agony. Rene's physical injuries had not yet healed and now this new agony of his spirit was too much. He wasted away. The poor butchered body kept but a tenuous hold on its spirit. On top of everything else the filth of the savage living conditions, the coarse food, everything sickened him to the soul.

God had to take him to Himself, but first He would come to him. Rene began to live almost entirely in another, kinder world. God was giving a foretaste of an unutterable joy to this son who had suffered so much for Him. Faith began to give way to the clear light of vision. Rene would be silent for hours, oblivious to all in this world, only his lips moving now and then.

This last was the final straw for the Mohawks. This despicable paleface must certainly be a demon or an evil sorcerer. Did he not spend hours with his eyes closed talking to the demons? They hated his awkwardness when he stumbled about the village at some work they had set him, they hated his swollen features, disfigured in the gauntlet, they hated his spiritless pleasantness. There was talk of killing him.

It was only to be expected that the Mohawks would hate Rene. These savages were of a primitive world where Christ's New Kingdom had not yet broken in. They were still minions of the Prince of Darkness, and this devil had been spawned in battle, before the world and its little wars had been formed.

His only virtues were those of pride, haughty hate, and the

twisted bravery of a cruel savagery. The only thing he remembered of God was the terrible wrath of the offended King. The sweet gentleness of a little girl in Palestine and the incomprehensible love of a young Man on a Cross were poison to his soul—this brutal brooding warrior of a lost battle. Could the Indians of Ossernenon be expected to be different from their master? Their god too was the fearful god of the storm and the terrible god of war. Rene and Jogues were their first ambassadors from that other Kingdom— that foolish Kingdom of gentleness and love. And Jogues, after being rescued once by the Dutch, was to come back to the Mohawks yet a second time as Christ's ambassador, and be killed. But that is another story.

Rene was on his knees in a Mohawk cabin one day playing with a little child. The chubby baby chortled with glee when Rene put his own cap on the little head. Only the Indian babies responded to Rene's love. They were not old enough to hate. He felt alive again when he could be with them. Taking the little hand in his, Rene traced the Sign of the Cross on the tiny head and breast. A strangled shout of rage burst from the shadows at the back of the room. An old Mohawk dashed over and snatched the child from Rene. He screamed and kicked at Rene. The Dutch had warned their Indian brothers that that sign was a curse used by paleface sorcerers. Now this child was doomed.

There was death in the madman's blazing eyes but Rene did not see it. Jogues, coming to the door to investigate the uproar, saw it. Later he warned Rene how his visible piety was mistaken by the superstitious savages, but Rene could not understand. It was incomprehensible to him that anyone could hate God that much. But the Iroquois was plotting his death for that Sign of the Cross.

One late summer afternoon Rene and Isaac were walking back to the village down the hill south of the gates. They had been up to their little retreat in the forest where they often hid from prying eyes to pray. As they came down the hill they were saying their rosary together. The last sun of Rene's life was playing long shadows past the palisades.

Two braves advanced to meet them and ordered them gruffly to hurry back to the village. Rene and Jogues walked on ahead. One of the two was the huge warrior who claimed to be the strongest man in the Mohawk nation. Jogues was worried by his furious scowl. But Rene, absorbed in his prayer, as usual paid no attention. The big savage made a sudden movement. Jogues spun around. Rene had heard nothing. The tomahawk came down with a sickening smash on Rene's skull. He fell forward. "Jesus, Jesus." Jogues gave him absolution. Two more blows thudded into Rene's brain and his soul was free. It was September the twenty-ninth, the Feast of St. Michael, the warrior who had first vanquished the Prince of Darkness.

Jogues was spared till a later day. That night the village rabble stripped Rene's poor body and dragged it around the streets. Jogues, broken-hearted, found it in the ravine and tried to hide it until he could get a chance to bury it. But the diabolical savages threw it further into the ravine and Jogues found only a few bones and the skull some months later. He concealed them at the base of a great tree, intending to bury them reverently when he could get free from the savages. It was never to be.

Richelieu died a few months after Rene. A century later his dream of empire in New France was shattered by the English guns on the Plains of Abraham at Quebec. But Rene had gone to New France to plant the Cross, not the *Fleur-de-lis*. And the Cross is still here.

Five years after Rene's death, Henri Arnauld, brother and disciple of the man who had been writing of a fearful God the day Rene sailed for Quebec, was installed as bishop of Angers. But a man from Angers had already proved with his blood that Arnauld's God does not exist—only the one God of love. And so the web of people and events in which Rene's life was set spells out its full meaning only in the light of Providence.

Let us leave Rene's earthly story there where we found it—in the ravine in a corner of the New World. What happens to his body matters not to Rene. He has long since been enjoying the gentle love of the God he so selflessly served for thirty-five earth years. Ignatius surely welcomed this incomparable Brother to heaven, this young surgeon who lived a life of heroic and humble Jesuit service long before he became a Jesuit.

Perhaps his life is a puzzle to us. But only if we do not understand how real his God was to him. A love story is incomprehensible only to him who does not know love. Christianity's glorious adventure is only for the lovers, not for those who merely dream.

### AMEN!!!

# Japanese Journeyman

BY NEIL G. McCLUSKEY, S.J.


*Brother Leonard Kimura, S.J. (1575–1602)*

**Declared Blessed** 1867

So THIS WAS what it meant to be a Christian! The young man, turning with difficulty amid the press of the crowd, let his shining eyes enfold the surrounding panorama. There behind him down the hill, lay the harbor whitened with the close-packed sails of hundreds of tiny boats, like so many gulls rocking with the gentle lapping of the waves. From the rickety bamboo docks by the Port of the Chinese, up to the military field and ascending across to the temple entrance, thousands of his fellow Christians, bee-like, had clustered on this hill to witness the crucifixion of twenty-six of their companions.

Young Leonard Kimura looked at the intent faces about him. Of regret he saw none; of sorrow little; of an infectiously exhilarating joy much. His glance continued to the brow of the stubby hill capped in a rough circle by the twenty-six crosses of wood.

There in silence they hung: Father Peter Baptist, the fearless leader of the Franciscan Friars and his five gray-frocked brothers. Who had not heard of their courage in captivity, or been thrilled mightily at the tales of their sufferings? And over on the far side was that group of his own countrymen, yes, including those three children whose boyish bodies looked so out of place roped to the heavy cross timbers. His eyes stopped at the cross of old James Kisai, the patriarchal Jesuit lay brother. How like the picture of St. Joseph he looked, thought Leonard. Here before him now hung John Soan, likewise clothed in the black Jesuit soutane. He and John had been companions in school—they were of the same age and John was standing on the threshold of paradise. A momentary envy gnawed at his heart. He blinked the mist from his eyes. With awe he gazed at the cross to Soan's left. For here hung the noble Paul of the Miki family. Head slumped with exhaustion, his Jesuit black proudly draped about him, Paul Miki still bore on his brow the stamp of the noble he was. And the youthful Kimura realized, as did every Japanese spectator, that this Jesuit scholastic could, if he had so desired, have garbed himself in the richest of silk kimonos, could have worn at his waist the two jeweled swords —the badge of the highest samurai.

An hour later it was all over. With the coldly professional dispatch of butchers the band of imperial soldiers had used their lances: the Catholic Church of Japan had at last come of age: the vanguard of the glorious army to die during the next forty years had flown heavenward. The date was February 5th, 1597.

As he retraced his steps down the now holy hill of Nagasaki, Leonard was lost in reverie. It all seemed so fantastic, so unreal. Like a bad dream! He stopped, turned and glanced over his shoulder. Yes; the crowd was melting away; there remained only those mute witnesses standing gaunt and twisted against an empty sky. Twenty-six Japanese Christians had died—just as in the stories he had read of the Roman martyrs in the colosseum. He resumed his way slowly but his heart was pounding out a new beat of pride even in his anguish. He was a part of this triumph.

It was his own grandfather who had welcomed Padre Xavier to Hirado that famous spring of 1551, and who had first bowed his head for the Padre to pour the baptismal waters that make one a Christian. Soon after his grandfather had packed all his household and goods onto two carts and moved away to Nagasaki. For already a community of Christians was flourishing there, and a tiny school had just been opened by the Jesuit missionaries. Leonard himself had been born at Nagaskai twenty-two years earlier. Like many another he had gone to the Padres' school and had loved those years of quiet and ordered happiness.

When he was twelve, though, the long days of calm snapped abruptly to an end. The old emperor [1] in his far-away capital at Miako had surlily yielded to the demands of the rapacious

[1] A regional hereditary ruler of sixteenth-nineteenth century Japan was called a *Daimyo* or Prince. The most powerful of the *Daimyos* was considered the overlord of the entire kingdom and was called the *Shogun* or what is here called Emperor. Ieyasu, generally called Daifusama in European writings, established the *shogunate* as an hereditary office in his family, the Tokugawa, who held that power until 1868. The shadowy *Mikado* had little actual power until that date, since his position as divine head of the Buddhist religion immersed him totally in spiritual contemplation.

Hideyoshi, his powerful general, and had issued a decree of banishment against the missionaries. Poisonous stories of the European Padres' real motives in coming to Japan had been dropped into the imperial ears. These strange-garbed men, it was alleged, came as spies—the vanguard of huge armies soon to undertake the conquest of the country. So the heavy foot of soldiery began to echo throughout the land.

After the first tremor of alarm, the Christians of Nagasaki had carried on life as usual. They had faithfully attended Mass each morning in the white thatched chapel and had openly thronged to the frequent instructions. Their Padres, with much more caution and many times in disguise, had come and gone from the village. Rumors of distant arrests and impending police searches had on occasion disrupted the even flow of village life. But the schoolboy Leonard had eagerly been initiated into the Confraternity of Christian Doctrine and the spice of danger during those years only added to his zest as he taught the catechism to the younger children of Nagasaki and of the neighboring villages.

So marked was his success as a catechist that after completing the course of studies at the Padres' school Leonard gave serious thought to applying for entrance into the Jesuit order. His effectiveness, he thought, in spreading Christianity amongst his people would be much increased as a Japanese priest. After much pondering and continual prayer he made his decision. The unsettled conditions all over the country, the increasing pressure upon all nonnative gospel workers made it impossible for the young man to enter upon the normal institutionalized years of study necessary for the Jesuit priesthood. He knew that God was beckoning him to share his precious gift of the Christian faith with his countrymen, still mired in the dark ooze of superstition and paganism. Well, he would offer himself to the Fathers for further work as a catechist. He could accompany them and could gain safe access for them to quarters barred to all but native Japanese. Perhaps at a later date, after religious calm had again settled upon the land, he could follow his heart's inclinations and become a member of the Company of Jesus.

Thinking back now, Leonard mused over that new life which opened for him that day. Those first years had been oddly exciting ones. God had been good to him. Up and down the length of the land they had traveled, he and sometimes one, sometimes two of the Padres. The news of their arrival always preceded them and when the Portuguese or Spanish "merchant" and his "servant" paused in their dusty travel before the first thatched hut on the fringes of a village, it was an eager crowd that usually pressed about them. Excited young mothers bearing unbaptized infants in their arms would beg in staccato fashion that the Padres would at once lave this or that ruddy wrinkled head with the saving waters. The village mayor would be there flushed with self-conscious importance, demanding quiet so that he could inquire of the good Padres what time the Mass would be on the morrow. Laughing bands of children would tug at the visitors' packs and importunately demand medals and holy pictures. Who could deny their fond boldness? Leonard would protestingly shake them off, meanwhile scattering his small treasures which quickly found their way into the grimy little fists. Oh, but he loved these sweet blossoms of his flower-country, Japan! These were the minutes whose reward lightened other shadowy times when he and his companion would lie for days cramped and cold in the high stands of reeds surrounding the paddy fields to elude the ever-increasing patrols.

Then there were times when they slipped quietly into a village forewarned that government agents were lurking in the vicinity. Only Kimura could move about the streets in safety while his European companion lay hidden in a safe house. The regular chapel remained dark and silent on these visits. The baptisms, the anointings, the marriages, the Mass all took place silently with uninterrupted flow in the main room of some Christian house. Once, he vividly recalled, the flow of visitors to the Ishida home in Shimabara had attracted the suspicious eye of an imperial inspector. A loud banging at the outer door, as a squadron of soldiers had forced their way into the house, gave the Padre Rodriguo just seconds to consume the sacred species and conceal himself fully vested beneath a layer of gourds in a huge wicker basket which lay in the inner garden. Heavy fines for the Japanese, certain banishment, if not death, for the Padre would have been meted out as their prize had they been caught. But God and His holy angels preserved these fearless commandos of Christ through trying years. With divine treachery they sought souls—no risk too great—no price too steep to pay.

And now as he reached the bottom of the hill he fell in step with his cousin, Sebastian Kimura.

"God is good, Leonard," the older man greeted him. "Praised be His name forever!"

The two walked on in silence. Close friends they had been even though a decade separated them in age. Leonard was proud of his Jesuit cousin who would have been an ordained priest in normal times but whose theological studies had been interrupted by this year's fierce outbreak of persecution.

"Cousin Sebastian, has God abandoned us? Is this to be the end of all of our work for His kingdom? Ah yes, it is beautiful to see the great souls of His martyrs taking flight to heaven, but what of the millions of our countrymen who still stumble and grope in the blindness of not knowing the true God?"

A troubled anxiety was mirrored in his clear eyes as the two paused before the gate of a dwelling, now used as a headquarters for the Jesuit missionaries.

"Have great confidence and be not troubled in your soul, cousin. God will take care of His own. The clouds will soon lift. Meantime, He expects us to continue to do our best to strengthen and console the others in these sad days. Praised be His Name forever!" The older man passed quietly into the shuttered house.

Night after night the blazing sparks from flaming Christian churches and mission stations leaped through the purple darkness like votive lights suppliantly signalling the dire needs of the little

Japanese flock. In the cold gray ashes of scores of God's former dwellings they knelt and pleaded. And God took care of His own. Just when the decrees of banishment were most cruelly enforced, the carnage and destruction at its most furious pitch, that same year of 1598, Emperor Taikosama, or Hideyoshi, was stricken and after a short illness, died. This brilliant schemer, a peasant become generalissimo through sheer acumen, who, as regent for Nobunaga's grandson had stolen the throne fifteen years earlier, was now about to be repaid in kind.

Hopes of the suffering Christians soared. The true heir to the imperial throne was still Nobunaga's grandson who had recently become a Christian. Taikosama, however, never had any thought of restoring the rightful heir and shortly before his own death, he had appointed as regent to succeed him the unscrupulous Daifusama, whom he had bound by every sacred oath to place his young son Hideyori on the throne. Ambitious and without conscience, Daifusama had no intention of keeping his word but dreamt of himself as the founder of a new dynasty: his own son Hidetada would follow him.

The double usurper was anxious to placate all who might prove friends. Accordingly at the beginning of his reign he showed himself favorable towards the growing Christian power. The former laws of banishment became inoperative. The new emperor sanctioned the rebuilding of several churches and issued edicts in favor of the missionaries. In fact, in 1603 when the ship from Europe bringing money and provisions for the year was lost in a gale, he advanced the missionaries large sums for financial support.

Consequently, the faith now came into its own. In eight months of 1599, there were forty thousand baptisms. The year 1600 saw the erection of fifty new churches and another fifty thousand heathen converted. Seminaries, hospitals, schools and orphanages sprang up as if from holy ground and by 1602 the number of Japanese Christians must have been nearly three-quarters of a million. A prodigy little short of miraculous!

That fall Leonard Kimura, one of the most versatile workers and experienced catechists the vigorous young Church had in its mission band, was able to fulfill an ambition long close to his heart. He applied for admittance and was accepted as a postulant for the Jesuit brotherhood. Why not the priesthood? For one thing, he was now twenty-seven years old and had been away from schooling for over a decade. The long exacting grind of priestly studies, even without interruptions, would remove him from the mission work he loved for a possible fifteen years—his cousin Sebastian after seventeen years had been ordained a priest but the preceding year. It was questionable whether the Church could spare this valuable worker, especially now during the peace lull when consolidation was vital for the unknowable future. Besides, a sense of his personal unworthiness for the exalted office of the priesthood almost haunted him. After much prayer and guidance he made his decision. In the fall he entered upon his six-months postulancy to be immediately followed by the two-year Jesuit noviceship.

Dim are the footprints one can trace during this next period of Leonard Kimura's life, for scanty, indeed, are the records. However, the training of the Jesuit novice in 1602 differed but in a few accidentals from the training of the Jesuit novice of 1952. With the postulantship behind him, Leonard received his cassock and was henceforth called "Brother." Shortly after this he and the other novices made the thirty-day retreat of St. Ignatius' Spiritual Exercises, the pivotal point of any Jesuit's training.

Alone in his armor of silence, the novice penetrates with his guide, Ignatius, to the marrow of reality: God, Creator, and Sustainer, operating in a universe charged with the overflow of divine love. The years Leonard had spent as a catechist, teaching the simple truths of creation and of the God-Man with His message of eternal life for all men, had well prepared the ground of his soul for the truths it now thirstily drank in. Far clearer now in his consciousness was the captivating vision of Christ summoning hero-saints to labor with Him in bringing souls to the life of God's kingdom. He was thrilled with the ideal of the Jesuit life he saw before him; eagerly he longed to be again bringing Christ and His message to his countrymen.

The months tumbled confusedly on out of sight, drawn by fleeting weeks and days. The stifling feeling of monotony is utterly foreign to the rigorous routine of a Jesuit novitiate with its wisely balanced proportions of prayer and reading, work and recreation made meaningful by its "Christo-centricity"—Christ the focus of every action. So whether Leonard Kimura knelt with his brethren at Mass each morning in the small chapel, or whether he plied shovel or broom during the daily working periods, or perhaps relaxed in the evening amid the easy aroma of religious brotherhood he knew he was living the fullest life God offers man. Happy and calm was his soul as he looked forward to pronouncing his Jesuit vows.

And so in 1602—very likely on some feast of the Blessed Mother as is traditionally the Jesuit custom—Brother Leonard Kimura knelt on the altar step just before receiving communion and simply surrendered his total self by vow to the service of God. Then, bearing the white wafer reverently upon his tongue he returned to his place, a full-fledged member of the Company of Jesus. During the fleeting moments of thanksgiving, he mutely poured out the gratitude of his heart. How worthwhile it all was now. How glad he was that he had come. Soon, he knew, he would be returning to the same work he had done before entering the noviceship but now as a Jesuit religious he would be able to accomplish far more for souls and for God's glory. In a few weeks an eager Brother Leonard Kimura rejoined the laborers who were exhausting themselves gathering Christ's harvest of souls while the time remained ripe.

A decade had passed and the sun was quickly sinking on the infant church. Maggots of worry had again begun to gnaw in the treacherous mind of the imperial usurper, Daifusama. Not entirely forgetful of the past services of his Christian princes, he decreed at first, banishment rather than death for both Christian and missionary. In 1613 he ordered a census of all Christians to be taken, and the next year commanded that all the missionaries be collected in Nagasaki for deportation to Manila or Macao; that all Christian churches be destroyed; that all Christians be compelled, under pain of banishment, to apostatize from the hated European faith.

The emperor's increasing hatred of Christianity was eagerly welcomed by many pagan daimyos. Ever since the first persecution of 1597 had signalled the imperial will in this matter, certain of these princes had unceasingly oppressed the faith in their own domains. Almost every year some Christians had been banished, imprisoned, and some even executed for their faith. But all this paled into nothing with the fury of the storm unleashed in 1612 which for thirty terrible years lashed and thundered and annihilated, furrow by furrow, the majestic harvest that was the Catholic Church in Japan.

The immediate effect of Daifusama's edicts was the banishing of some four hundred Christian nobles of his own court, and the deporting of one hundred and twenty-five or more European missionaries, in addition to scores of catechists and teachers. Twenty-three Jesuits, including Leonard Kimura, were among the fortunate missionaries who eluded the emperor's drag-net, preferring to obey the edict of the gospel. Fools everywhere. Always fools sprung from the Galilean prototype.

The decisive year in the history of the Japanese persecution was 1615. This was the year in which Hideyori, the son of Emperor Taikosama, raised his standard to wrest the throne from Hidetada, the son of the usurper Daifusama. The Christians, unfortunately for their own prosperity, supported the more rightful claimant, Hideyori, in the ranks of whose army there waved six banners bearing the figure of the Crucified Christ. On June 9th near Osaka the decisive battle took place. Just as victory was inches from their finger tips, the Christian army, through a quirk of fate, tipped the balance against themselves and were crushed. Hideyori's standard bearer, seeing Daifusama's army on the point of rout—Daifusama himself was about to commit hara-kiri—turned from the front rank to summon his master that he be on hand to accept the fruit of victory. As the Christian ranks successively opened to admit the standard of their leader, this appearance of flight released panic among the army which quickly dissolved into a terrified rabble, to be hacked down in thousands by their surprised adversaries. Daifusama wreaked savage vengeance on the conquered army and for several days torrents of blood flowed from the systematic butchery.

This was, however, but the prelude to worse. Daifusama died the next year and his son Hidetada became undisputed overlord with the title of Xongunsama. A hatred born in hell fired this human beast as he dedicated himself now to the task of cleansing the pestilential Christianity from all his domain.

Ruthlessly he forbade all Japanese, of whatsoever rank, under penalty of death at the stake, to have dealings of any kind with the missionaries. Any family receiving a missionary into its home incurred this death: father, mother and children. Moreover, not only the law-breaking host and his family but five neighboring families on either side would be punished in identical fashion: death at the stake.

The Japanese Christians were not the only victims of Xongunsama's fierce hunt. Imperial commissioners were still ransacking everywhere in search of the surviving leaders of the ill-fated Hideyori's army. Nagasaki, shorn of its ancient immunities, came to the fore in the government search. During the month of December in 1616, two high commissioners were sent to search for Naikidono, the son of Acachicamon, a prominent captain of Hideyori, who, they believed, had survived the battle and had taken refuge in the village. The imperial agents failed to unearth their man but in the process of examining the whole village they stumbled across clues pointing definitely to the presence in Nagasaki of an equally worthwhile prize, a Jesuit missionary. Among other spoils caught in the finely meshed net and taken to the governor's palace for further questioning in the Acachicamon affair, was Leonard

Kimura. Since he was garbed no differently from the others, and the charge was patently false, after routine questioning he, too, would have been released. However, Leonard knew that Nagasaki would be under close surveillance until the government hounds had sniffed out the Christian missionary. How many other Christian lives might be taken, what reprisals might be visited upon the Nagasaki families, he thought, once tortured lips had been made to blurt out further information.

Speedily he got word to his religious superior asking as a boon that he be allowed to surrender himself as a Jesuit religious in order to spare the lives of others including the precious life of the Jesuit priest still trapped and in hiding at Nagasaki. The permission was sorrowfully granted by his Father Provincial.

A day or two later, while undergoing a regular cross-examination, Leonard was asked as a matter of routine if he knew any Jesuits. "Indeed I do," Leonard replied, his eyes smiling: "and what is more I can turn one of them over to you at any time."

"What! Where is he now?" cried the excited judge, as he started off to summon a company of soldiers.

"There's little need for hurry or for any rushing about," Kimura gravely called after him. "You've already captured him. I am a Jesuit!"

In the excited din that ensued as he was loaded with fetters and dragged off in triumph to a dungeon cell, a soft radiance played over Brother Kimura's contenance. Floods of gratitude welled up inside him and over and over again he silently murmured "*Deo gratias*"—"Thank you, God!"—that he had been found worthy to suffer prison and, he hoped, death for Christ. "*Jesu-ita*," he thought; now truly could he be "like-Jesus."

Three years of strict confinement, even in the *Roja*, "cage," or the *Gokusa*, "hell," as it was interchangeably called, had not been able to stunt the great soul housed in the breast of Brother Leonard Kimura. His prison, surrounded by a high palisade, lay in the center of Nagasaki. It consisted of several filthy huts, completely isolated, where the prisoners were lodged according to their dignity or the nature of their crime. His cassock tatters, his frame hollowed, his scabbed body criss-crossed with vermin—his sole concern was lest his unworthiness might cause a martyr's death to escape him.

Heavy lay the cross upon all of Nagasaki. Gone were her churches and schools, gone were her shepherds and guides, gone was her peace and happiness. "Only the prisons," the people said, "are now the Church of Nagasaki!" And nowhere was this truer than in the cramped circle of *Gokusa* where lay Brother Leonard. Murderers, thieves, adulterers, hurled through its doors, were astonished at what they found inside the palisade.

Brother had quietly transformed this foul den into a quasi-monastery. No Trappist monks ever spent a day with greater religious fervor. Each morning the prisoners had one hour of mental prayer, another hour of vocal prayer, the litanies and a spiritual exhortation up until noon. In the afternoon, they had four hours of reading, writing or of manual work. Further spiritual reading from the lives of the saints, then one hour of prayer and the preparation for the next day's meditation completed this monastic schedule. All this was salted with three and often four days a week of fasting plus severe disciplines. On Friday, this strangely assorted group held five hours of prayer in honor of the five wounds of the Saviour. Each month they held the Forty Hours devotion to obtain perseverance and the graces vital for the hunted missionaries. Only God could have sired such men as these!

One gasps in amazement at such heroism, such generosity; and one must gaze reverently at the humble Jesuit lay brother whose own Christlike love of God and his fellows was the dynamo charging a like impelling love in the others. Brother Leonard in his austerities surpassed most of his fellows, fasting and disciplining himself daily, and quietly taking upon himself countless little tasks to ease the rigor of their imprisonment. The carefully smuggled bits of food and clothing which reached him, passed immediately on to the others. Right up until his death he shared his daily ounces of rice with an eighty-year-old beggar who crawled each day, begging, up to the palisade wall. Is it to be marvelled at, then, that this Jesuit Brother was able to baptize for Christ scores of persons from among the prisoners and guards, and to prepare most of the condemned to meet their God? Like a high-powered magnet he drew others and they came with a surprised, reluctant willingness.

But the fanatical emperor was still not satisfied with the pace of his extermination campaign, especially in the province of Nagasaki. Accordingly, in 1618 he named a new governor of that province in place of the disgraced Toan Mourayama who had just been denounced as himself a Christian. A sinister young man full of cunning and intelligence, whose hatred of the Christians rivalled the emperor's own, was this new governor, Gonroku—a horrible name which, like Nero's or Caligula's, will forever be stained with martyr blood.

Gonroku, learning from his spies that several missionaries resided in the country and that they continued to baptize, to instruct and to administer the sacraments, was in a frenzy. Every effort was unleashed to hound them out and terrify the people into complete renunciation of Christianity. But—Gonroku's task was an immense one. The seeds sown by Xavier had rooted themselves deep, deep in the brave hearts of the Japanese people.[2] The Fathers, dressed as Chinese or wearing the humble garb of servants, trudged bare-

---

[2] Over two hundred cruel years of persecution could not root out the Christian faith from the shepherdless flock of Japan. A few years after Commodore Perry's reopening of Japan to the West in 1853, Catholic missionaries discovered around 50,000 Christians isolated in little pockets throughout the country. Or rather these Japanese descendants of the heroes of Nagasaki and Miako discovered the missionaries. These latter were cautiously approached and by their answers to three questions were recognized as the legitimate successors of the seventeenth-century Japanese pastors. The questions were: Did they come from the Pope in Rome? Were they celibates? Did they honor the Mother of Jesus?

The historian Delplace pays high tribute to the Japanese in his classic work on the history of the Church in Japan. "We do not believe," he writes, "that in the whole history of the Church extending over nineteen hundred years there is a single people that has such a glorious record and such a long list of martyrs as the Japanese."

footed through the snows and muddy swamps as they bore on their shoulders the Mass vestments and sacred habits. Few in numbers, they multiplied themselves by sending in every direction catechists and messengers. Lay brothers, like Kimura, regularly baptized in place of the priests. The sick were visited, the children instructed, all of the faithful consoled and strengthened for even darker days ahead. The missionaries continually changed their dwelling place, concealing themselves sometimes under the ground, sometimes in the inner surface of walls where for long spells they were deprived of light and air. It was thus that they practiced, almost without interruption, their apostolic work. And it was for this that Brother Leonard and his companions in prison fasted and prayed.

The governor next resorted to heavy fines, public whippings, imprisonment. But the roots of a hundred years would not be budged that easily. The poor, the helpless became his first target. An old blind man was brutally beaten and imprisoned for singing Christian hymns by the wayside. Into the prisons by the hundreds he crowded them. The more he probed, the more solidly Christian he found his populous province.

In despair, he attempted other tactics. He would use sweetness and light. Only the missionaries, these were the criminals. Let the Nagasaki folk abandon this foolishness of Christianity and the emperor would gladly forgive his erring subjects. Soothing promises and honeyed words fell on stony ears. The sweetness curdled to a devilish anger. Gonroku had taken a mighty oath at court, in the presence of Xongunsama himself, that he would sweep Nagasaki clean of Christianity. His great lord had himself pointed the way with a personal order for the death at the stake of fifty-two Christians at Miako on October 2nd, and a few weeks later commanded the beheading at Yeddo of the Christian predecessor of Gonroku, along with several of his family.

Goaded into action, Gonroku, on November 14th, came personally to the village of Nagasaki. The faithful had armed themselves for new combats by austere fasts and much prayer. In line with

the imperial cue he picked his first victims. Four of Leonard's
prison mates, all charged with giving hospitality to the missionaries, were summoned to the hall of sentence. His own brother-
in-law, Andre Mourayama Tocuan, was among them. In an hour
they came back, embraced their companions, and tremblingly told
the news. Two days hence they were to be burned to death at the
stake. Throughout most of the long night, the four prepared themselves for death with fervent prayer. Leonard Kimura's leaden
heart was near to breaking. What agonizing pleas arrowed heavenward that evening from the disappointed Jesuit Brother, kneeling
in the dark on the cold flagstones. For nearly three years he had
lived on the hope of dying—for Christ. Would ever his chance
arrive?

Dawn glimmered and the first orange shafts pierced the gray
of the prison hut. Fingers of light strayed over the stubbled faces
of the condemned men—peaceful now, even serene, in sleep.
Kimura stirred in his corner from a troubled rest. He moved to his
knees and achingly it all tumbled back to him: four were to die but
he was to remain. His thin lips formed a prayer asking for resignation, for acceptance of the divine will.

After the group had finished the round of morning prayer,
Leonard's glance carried out the low window to the near-by hill of
execution. He sighed. Workmen were already jockeying the large
rough stakes into the pit holes. He counted them. Two . . . three
. . . four. . . . FIVE! His beating heart thumped wildly. Yes; there
were five instruments of martyrdom there now. He knew, for certain, even before his later summons to the governor, that the fifth
was to be his.

That afternoon the five men were led through the streets to the
prison of Omura and brought into the court. The knifelike face of
Gonroku glanced sharply at them. He addressed Kimura, demanding to know if he were of the Company of Jesus.

"You know it, my lord," said the Brother.

"Why, then," roared the governor, "being banished from the

empire, have you remained here?"

"To preach the faith of Jesus Christ which I desire to do until my last breath."

"Very well," the young man leered crookedly at him. "You will be burned alive for your stupidity and crime. You will die for being a member of this Company of Jesus and for preaching this treasonable faith."

In a daze, his heart singing, Kimura was marched back to his prison. Word had raced about quickly and the streets were lined with throngs of Christians—some weeping, some congratulating, some resentful—who crowded about Kimura and his four companions as they passed. Hurriedly they were thrust into *Gokusa* while the crowds milled ceaselessly about the palisade.

The next morning the crowds were so intense that the doubled cordon of soldiers could scarcely make a path for the condemned party on its way to the near-by hill of execution. No martyrdom in the entire history of Japanese Christianity has left a more touching picture than that of Leonard Kimura and his brother martyrs. From miles around the countryside multitudes, by the thousands, in their finest attire flowed to the spot as to a gala festival. Tear-stained faces, softened with the joy of faith, pressed about them whispering pleas of remembrance. No kings moving to coronation were ever saluted by more solemn concourse. First in line came Brother Kimura, who as a Jesuit and a missionary was the chief criminal. Then walked Jorge the Portuguese, Tocuan, Chooun and Takeya. Each bore a large placard attached to his shoulders proclaiming the crime: *Following Christ!*

As they traversed the dirt street, Leonard's voice rang out clear and strong.

"We go to die, fellow Christians, for the sake of Jesus Christ who first died for us. We die unafraid for He will be our strength and courage. Soon the fire will blacken and twist our bodies but that fire will cleanse our immortal souls and prepare them for eternal happiness with God and His Mother and the saints. Is it not better to suffer fire now and gain God, than to deny him here and be ravished with fire for eternity? Love God. Love God, and pray that we may not falter!"

The spot was reached. Rough hands secured them loosely to the five tall stakes. The momentary fright in his breast vanished as there flashed into Leonard's mind the recollection of twenty-two years earlier, when his friend and brother Jesuit, John Soan, with twenty-five others had been crucified on this very spot. He closed his eyes tightly and silently begged those valiants for a share in their courage. Vividly did memory reenact that earlier scene, fusing it into what his eyes now enfolded until the two seemed one: the harbor densely white with ships, the surging, praying mass of humanity flowing all about the hill. But now he, not Soan; now his own dear companions, not strangers, occupied the front of the stage. His heart seemed dizzy with stabs of fear lest he should falter, yet also with joy that at last he had been found worthy of offering his life for Christ.

Bundles of faggots had been piled all about the posts but through a refinement of cruelty to linger the torment, the faggots were six full paces from the posts. Minutes passed. Through the stifling heat and the smoke and above the prayerful murmur of the crowd, a new note arose. It was the high clear voice of Jorge chanting the Creed. Phrase after phrase of the sonorous Latin was lofted to the sky while the voice grew steadily feebler. It falteringly gasped out the *Et Incarnatus Est*—that tiny phrase summing up God's great love for man—and then abruptly ceased.

A hush fell over the vast throng broken by the sharp crackling of burning tinder. A scream of pain became a sob stretching into an agonized "Jesus, mercy!" Low moans issued from behind the acrid pall of roasting flesh and flaming wood. Hundreds of men and women wept openly. A slight gust from the harbor cleared the smoke momentarily and thousands of fascinated eyes were glued to the pyre where Brother Kimura swayed in torture. The witnesses—later they recorded it on oath—saw that grotesquely swollen figure lowering his rope-freed hands to the ground and gathering up red coals and flaming bits of wood to place on his head. With an effort he then straightened his head to heaven and in a tremulous choking voice intoned the psalm, *Laudate Dominum*— "Praise ye the Lord!" In a second, like a mighty organ roll, twenty thousand throats took up the sacred words and a paean of prayer sang the soul of Leonard Kimura to Paradise.

# Gypsy Come Home

BY WILFRED P. SCHOENBERG, S.J.

*Brother Benito de Goes, S.J. (1562–1607)*

IT IS February 24, 1603. Abdullah Isai with his three companions and several hundreds of soldiers stand on the banks of the river Ravi and peer into the shadows beyond. Across the sweeping waters a caravan awaits their arrival. It will leave soon for the fabulous regions of Badakshan and Turkestan and Tartary; Abdullah with escort is to companion it.

An expectant hush attends the vigil, for tongues of men move reluctantly in the early morn, before danger not at all. Harness metal tinkles softly. Cocks crowing from distant roosts sound like bugles demanding instant service in battle. In battle, yes, even the stupid cart-oxen sense it and they chomp nervously on their cuds and turn heavy shoulders apprehensively.

Men have pulled their cloaks of silence about their ears. They pace. They beat their arms like athletes in warm-up. They brood. For here there are no dock crowds to cheer them like sailors off to sea. No sunshine. No hoarse hurrahs. Only chilly stillness and waiting. Waiting for fire-signals from the caravan. Waiting for the cold splashing waters of the river-ford. Waiting for battle. . . .

One, just one, stirs in business and all watch him with affected indifference. Abdullah Isai is not a lank man. Nor short. He is broad in shoulders and broad to the heels. He gravely wags a big head and a black flowing beard that reaches his chest. One would never suspect his Portuguese beginnings, for to all who examine him he is Persian. A swarthy Persian merchant decked out in acres of cabaia, jewel-crusted turban and belt sword, besides a bow with arrows. He makes a grand display of wealth and sagacity, questionable virtues attributed to questionable Eastern merchants. He nods. He consults. He estimates his bags and pack camels. He is an actor. His part he carries off well and there is none to suspect. For Abdullah is a Jesuit Brother.

Abdullah's companions have taken less pains to disguise themselves. There is Grimon, who is Greek, and a Christian sub-deacon. Greek—nothing about him to say otherwise. There is Demetrius the merchant. There is Isaac, faithful Isaac the Armenian. His appearance needs no complements for he is Eastern to the eyes, penetrating, dreamy and narrow.

All Indians are the two hundred soldiers. They are armed to the teeth and wear the discipline of their trade. They wear it easily for they are troops from the imperial barracks. Abdullah has connections. Indeed, he has served these past six years as councillor at the court of the Grand Mogul, Akbar himself. And Akbar now provides costume and escort for Abdullah's epic journey partly in gratitude, partly as policy.

For Abdullah is shaping history. Rather, he is about to determine what shape history has taken. A gulf of three centuries lay between the Indias and China. In this dark, mysterious hollow, cries from the thirteenth century echo and re-echo, then drift down Himalayan valleys into imperial and ecclesiastical chambers. Ghosts of the Polos, first roving reporters of these forbidding regions.

Marco, son and nephew of the other two Polos, had entered Central Asia during the rule of the sympathetic Mongolian Khans in that misty thirteenth century. He had situated himself in the Court City, Cambulec, capital of Cathay, and there he remained in the service of the Khan for seventeen years. In 1292, weary of exile, he returned to his native Venice and shortly afterward set Europe afire with crackling tales of travel and adventure. His Cambulec and Chinkalan and Cathay became better known in Europe than the most proximate points of the East, and all the West buzzed its interest.

Franciscan missionaries bustled, bustled off to this now glamorous mission field and established flourishing Christian centers. The Pope caught the fever and dispatched one John of Corvino as Bishop of Cambulec.

Then came night. The Mongol dynasty fell to the unfriendly Mings and Europe was cut away. Cathay vanished like a continent of Atlantis. Centuries of darkness. Portuguese in the flow of time and Renaissance trade next touched the shores of an approximate land called China. "Where is Cathay?" they inquired. "Where

Cambulec and Chinkalan?" And there was no one who knew. Only China, the Portuguese heard; only China and Peking and Canton. Cathay remained a mystery.

When the sixteenth century yielded to the seventeenth, two events occurred which led to Abdullah's present status as globe-trotter. The first was Ricci's success in achieving Peking, China's capital. Ricci was a Jesuit, a scholar learned in the sciences of mathematics, human relations, and Cathayan geography. His mathematics served as passage to the Emperor's halls and his thirteenth-century geography told him that here was Cathay and Cambulec. But there was no one to believe him, not even his own Jesuit confrères.

The second event was the arrival at Lahore of a teller of fables in the genuine role of Persian merchant. This man of Persian bags assured all who would listen that he had just come from Cathay. "From Cathay!" Jesuits at the Mogul court gasped. "From Cathay!" the old fox replied. He had seen Christians in vast numbers, "followers of Isauitae." He had seen Christian kings and processions and ceremonies and seminarians and bishops. "The priests," he added waggishly, "wear hats like yours, only a little larger."

The Jesuits were already intoxicated with whiffs of adventure's wine. "Someone," they cried, "must take the trail to Cathay." Here was the opportunity of centuries. Here was triumph—whose would it be?

A certain Brother Benito de Goes was selected by Jesuit superiors to undertake this mission. He was particularly qualified for the task. Besides his native Portuguese and smattering of Latin, he could speak several Oriental languages—above all, Persian, the *lingua franca* of the East. He had once served in Portuguese armies, so well knew the craft and depravity of hostiles. He was prudent, and more than all else, courageous. A dove with the heart of a lion.

Find Cathay, he was told. Find Cathay he would try. He made his preparations. Beard, long hair—good. No more barbering. Darkened skin. Clothes and gems purchased with the monies provided by Akbar and the Portuguese government. Ring on his finger for stamping letters and contracts. Weapons. Pack animals and bales of goods for trade. Finally an alias. He chose "Abdullah Isai," meaning "Mr. Christian." His nationality, his purpose, his status as Jesuit he might disguise. His Christianity, never.

In his turban he stuffed letters from the Archbishop of Goa, a list of the Church-moveable feasts for the next seventeen years, commendatory letters to kings and vassals of Akbar. On his breast he wore a cross within which were texts from the Gospels. Benito was ready. Were the Cathayans?

The route to Cathay (planned by Jesuit enthusiasts in Agra) was the most formidable imaginable. No European had successfully negotiated it for over three hundred years—not since Marco Polo. None, except Brother Benito, would succeed in traversing it for another three hundred years—not till Victoria's England. It lay through fanatically Mohammedan strongholds, through the dizzy passes and plateaus of the Himalayas, through the Gobi desert, into the Great Wall of China, and so to Peking.

Cathay, according to assuring maps and plans, would be somewhere in the unknown void between the Himalayas and the Great Wall. The rest was for Brother Benito to discover. His instructions informed him that once he had verified prognostications and served his credentials to the Christian authorities in Cambulec, he was to proceed to Peking to report to Father Ricci. It was all as simple as finding Father Provincial's hat. And Benito left it at that.

As the morning mists of late winter drifted away the great search began. Benito's Kashgar caravan squeaked and complained into line and rolled away. Scores of merchants with escort, a long train of burdened beasts, camels and wagons. To the west. To the north. An endless passage of valleys, ridges and rivers.

Every advance step was made at the point of the sword. Robber nations infested these regions far remote from Akbar's imperial authority. Brother Benito carried eloquent military passes countermarked by the Grand Mogul himself, the self-styled "Slayer of Hostile Kings." But they were not worth a camel's grunt. For one thing, come skirmish time, Benito did not tarry for formal presentations. For another, neither did the brigands. So the Slayer of Hostile King's fine commendatory letters reposed in their grandiloquence and Benito, like his companions, took to the more significant language called force.

At all costs the goods of transport had to be protected. Particularly the eatables. Precisely these were the attracting magnets for Ali Baba and all his forty thieves of Kashmir and Turkestan.

In the deep narrow valleys pack-trains and wagons rolled slowly along while their escort skipped upper ridges to shoo away possible denizens of the crags. If these ridges were left unattended rogues of every kind rolled boulders onto victim trains beneath. Besides delight, the strategem afforded generous returns.

Shortly after journey's genesis, the caravan was attacked in a wooded plateau by loudly bellowing horsemen brandishing sabers and knives. Benito's brave defenders (from the imperial barracks) took so vigorously to their heels that it required several days to collect them. That settled it. On the first suitable occasion, de Goes promised himself, he would dispense with their services. Guarding merchant-goods was responsibility enough—he simply could not answer for two hundred soldiers besides.

After the first month, the caravan reached the marketplace of Attock and crossed the Indus River, at this point but a bowshot wide. Thence it proceeded to Peshawar and the Khyber Pass, immortalized by England's Kipling three centuries later:

> When springtime flushes the desert grass,
> Our kafilas wind through the Khyber Pass.
> Lean are the camels but fat the frails,
> Light are the purses but heavy the bails,
> As the snowbound trade of the North comes down
> To the Market-square of Peshawar town.

To plague of robbers now was added rigors of climate. Late spring snows mantled the mountains, like grain to the eye, but cockleburrs for the heel. To Benito especially the freezing nights became an increasingly great problem. Cold made almost impossible

his diary—and letter-writing by candlelight. Yet write he must.
While others tossed and snored in their tent-bunks he scribbled
away with stiffened fingers, and with hunger gnawing at his in-
nards.

"It is still Lent," he wrote, "and we are fasting. We get but one
meal a day, and though the cost is much, we get very little. A bit of
rice with ghee, some coarse cakes and some onions. If we can get
a little salt fish, we count it as a great treat though it causes thirst."

Cold and hunger were little. A heavier cross was hurry's impact
on the Jesuit's prayer life. "Owing to the difficulties and the tur-
moil of the journey, I am unable to observe the regular times and
forms of prayer. Hence I say ejaculations, communing with God
in my heart and thus I gain strength to bear this cross, which to
others may seem heavy but to me is light and pleasant."

In Kashmir, Benito had a turbulent scene with the local Rajah.
"You are a Christian mullah?" the Rajah asked not unkindly.

"I am a Christian," Benito said simply.

"Then renounce your law and salute the Prophet." The Rajah
creamed his words and served them slowly.

"My law is my life. One does not lightly dispose of life."

The Rajah threatened. He roared. "This Christian dog must die!
Tie him up and drive elephants over his heart!"

"Sire," Benito graciously bowed, "you do me a favor. Gladly I
die for the one true God."

And he was hustled off to the dungeons.

Such audacity was unknown even among these fierce mountain
men. "We cannot let him die," the court attendants told one another. "He is too brave." And others added that it was a pity such
a brave man would have to go to hell because he would not salute
the Prophet.

The Rajah, too, had been disarmed by this display of courage.
He fondled a bracelet and wondered how he could let him go
without losing face.

"Let him escape," said the advisors.

"No," decided the Rajah at length. "I will pay tribute to his great heart by giving him life."

And Benito, quite alive, rejoined the mourning Isaac.

Several days later, the Brother had another interview—less stormy, to be sure. This time he was judge and jury, and the defendant was a foot-loose hermit, a nomad who scavengered the Khyber Pass approaches.

Did the hermit know of Cathay, a community of Christians living apart? No, the hermit didn't. But yonder, about thirty days' march, there was the country of the Siah-Posh, so-called because its inhabitants wore black garments when they worshipped in their temples. Did these people have priests without wives and the Mass with bread and wine? No, there was no Mass. But wine—ah! Wine was outlawed by the Mohammedans but among the Siah-Posh it was the very song of life! Delightful!

And the hermit produced a sample with which he regaled the thirsty Benito.

Yes, Benito decided it was good, very much like the wine of his native Villa Franca do Campo in the Azores.

The garrulous old hermit babbled on—it was not often he had such a good listener. The neighboring Mohammedans, he said, most heartily despised these wine-bibbing Kafirs, and the latter with equal gusto returned the compliment. By tribal custom each went bareheaded and honor-poor till he had slain one Mohammedan. To qualify for marriage, he must needs have slain two, and, the hermit concluded, there was no dearth of weddings due to corpse-default. No one like a Kafir for throat-cutting! And he winked with pleasure.

Early summer days were dawning when the Kashgar caravan wearily dragged into Kabul. Promise was in the air, fat flocks in their folds, fruits flourishing in orchard and garden. The Kabul Valley was a smiling, friendly oasis in a truculent empire. Doubly welcome to the wayfarer.

Though not at journey's end, the caravan disbanded. Too many of the merchants were dismayed by dangers and hardships of the trail. Benito discharged his stout imperial escort—not without celebrations by all concerned—and accepted the resignations of Demetrius and Grimon. The former discovered new possibilities of money-making in Kabul and begged to be excused. The latter, Christian and holy subdeacon, had heart only for his wife at home. He must go back to the family, he said, and Benito agreed while he wryly considered the Church's wisdom in its celibate clergy.

Only Isaac, faithful Isaac the Armenian, was left him. By far the better part. For between Benito and Isaac a bond of affection had sprung up. To the very end Isaac was purse, staff and girdle for the Jesuit Brother. He was as pet to master, though Benito refused to see it in this light. Rather, he explained to Isaac, they were Jonathan and David in the giving hours of boyhood.

In Kabul, Benito and Isaac, like tramp dogs on forage, wagged from bazaar to bazaar searching for scraps of geographical gossip. "Ever hear of Cathay?" they asked. "Have you heard of a Christian city called Cambulec?" They often crossed paths with local characters and summarily pumped them for what they were worth.

In the course of these wanderings, Benito chanced upon a princess in distress, a real, live princess. She had a pretty name—he called her "Hajji-Khanem," meaning princess pilgrim. She was most charming. She was pious, too, and as she peeped over the top of her veil, wondrously beautiful. The years had spared her, for already there were some who could call her "Grandma." Her son was the lord and high mighty of Khotan, jade-rich kingdom east of Turkestan.

It would seem that Hajji-Khanem was returning from Mecca where she had paid her respects at the tomb of the Prophet. Coming through the mountain passes, her party had been pounced upon by those playboys of the boulders and stripped of all its goods. Now here she was in Kabul, grateful for life, but in a state of utter destitution. Her countrymen had coldly turned aside her appeals. Would the Christian Abdullah lend her, at generous interest to be sure, the funds she needed?

Benito, like the robbers, cannily pounced upon opportunity.

Plainly here was a lady worth knowing. Mother of a king. Sister of another king. What gates through central Asia would this gallantry swing wide? What bribes would it spare him? Indeed, the Christian Abdullah was most willing. Charity abounded but it did not forbid a human discernment from which all might draw profit.

He feverishly sold part of his merchandise, then hastened to the princess pilgrim.

"Here," he said, "are six hundred gold pieces. Take them, they are yours."

Only one demand did he make of her. The sum was to be returned to him in the form of "transparent marble," jade.

Of course the princess was delighted and she embarrassed the shy Jesuit with her thanks.

"Allah has sent you to me! May Allah reward you! Allah be praised!"

"Amen," said Benito. Mumbling his polite goodbyes, he left the field to Isaac.


The "Roof of the World" local savants called the stretch that lay ahead. Roof of the World it was. An empty wasteland of ice and snow and rock surrounded by the largest mountains on earth. It was not a plateau, rather a peak-high level of filled-in glacial wash, once valleys, now a table as lofty as Mount Blanc. In length it was a forty-day journey. Forty days of nightmare struggle, bitter frosts and bleeding lungs occasioned by the rare atmosphere.

Men and animals died with equal disinterest. Those who survived sickened with the means of survival, dried apples, onions and garlic. For such were the grim remedies prescribed. Garlic in abundance was strapped to the horses' backs and periodically halts were made to rub it into their festering gums. This, Benito was told, retarded circulation and so prolonged animal energies.

The approaches to this formidable hurdle were not less severe. First there was the Parwan Pass with seven smaller ones leading up to it. A sort of stairway built on a Paul Bunyan scale with God's own granite.

Inhabitants of the region, fair-haired, blue-eyed giants, were an uncompromising lot. Tribute they exacted, and tribute was theirs. At this time they were in revolt against the regional Khan and, like pirates before the mast, they scurried hither and yon for pillage and plunder.

Near Telekhan, once the great garden and corn market, (now queen city of these demon mountains), Benito's caravan encamped for brief respite. At once, even before campfires were lighted, a messenger appeared from the town. The governor of Samarkand, he said, insisted that the caravan hasten within protecting city walls. Hordes of Tartars were devastating the country and he, the royal and supreme governor (though he did not like to press the point) feared the more lest these scoundrels attack the caravan and carry away badly needed horses.

Into the town the weary merchants betook themselves. But to their dismay, they found more thieves within than without. They soon abandoned the den and the governor, like a possessive rooster strutted after them with numerous guards. It was his duty, he loudly crowed, to prevent the devilish Tartars from getting horses. For this, like any brave man, he would die. But alas! Scarcely had all cleared the city walls than on the horizon appeared—yes, Tartars! The plucky governor and his less assertive soldiers scattered like rabbits.

"We'll fight!" yelled Benito.

There was nothing else to do. Bales were piled into barricades, flint rocks scraped together for ammunition should the arrows give out.

When the Tartars arrived on the spot they decided to stall. Here was their booty. What need for haste? They sent forward envoys of peace who indulged pompously in meaningless double talk. But no one was impressed by this Tartar benevolence.

As soon as the messengers made off, the merchants determined to take advantage of truce by retreating. Leaving their bales they scrambled into the nearest woods, and from behind their trees they watched the robbers tranquilly approach and dive into bags of treasure. They were like rowdy kids in an unattended dime store. The quantity and sparkle cast a spell over them and, as they plucked, they whistled and danced.

Then their master arrived, chief of the tribe. He forced them all to put back what they had taken, called for the merchants and helped them to reorganize their caravan.

For these proceedings the Tartars had little taste. They split into bands and followed on the heels of the caravan to harass and nag stragglers. Several days later, as Benito lagged behind to attend to his prayers, four of these rascals ambushed him and like cougars crouched for the spring. Just in time Benito spotted them. Quick as a bird he tore off his jeweled turban, flung it as far as he could, and set spurs to his horse. While the hunters quarrelled over this glittering bait, Benito was away.

On the Roof of the World, five of Benito's horses died. He could ill afford to lose even one in this wilderness, but then, as Isaac said, he was more fortunate than most.

"Thanks be to God," answered Benito piously. But his mind was occupied with the future, the next two mountain passes, reputed to be the most difficult en route.

Wakhjir Pass came first. It was 16,150 feet high, with paths just wide enough for a single beast. To the left towering walls of unrelenting stone. To the right precipitate river canyons, the bottoms of which were lost in haze. One knew there was a bottom only when a companion slipped into the abyss; then shrieks of a tumbling human echoed against that other world and assured all of bottoms and unburied bones.

Once this summit was accomplished the trail dropped down into a valley of death. Six more horses rolled over and died. For five days torrential rains kept the travellers drenched. No fire. Almost no food.

And the end was not yet. Far from it. Another pass, Chichiklik, stretched like a challenge across the skyline. It was a gap, but a gap more lofty than the highest mountain in the United States and as high as two Rocky Mountains passes piled on one another. Along its crown lay deep snows and for six days the caravan had to plow through it. Several merchants perished from the cold. Avalanches buried others. Brother de Goes himself became gravely ill with fever and barely escaped the Pursuer Death.

Downward the trail became increasingly worse, for the most part now the boulder bed of a river with quick drops and innumerable deep pools.

To climax Benito's anguish, faithful Isaac plunged from a cliff into icy waters below. Benito leaped after him and finally dragged him onto a ledge. For eight hours he prayed and rubbed while all but himself despaired. "He is a dead man," they said. "Save your strength." But Isaac was not dead. He recovered and took again to the miserable path.

After a fifteen-day descent, the caravan pulled into a shabby little village. The horrors of famine and cold had left their mark. All but Benito despaired of going one step further.

"We cannot," the merchants groaned with fires of fever in their eyes.

"Someone must," snapped de Goes, and he began his preparations. He chose the best horse that was left them. He sacked a scant measure of rice and rolled his blankets. At dawn he was off.

For five more terrible days he raced against death. A lone, tragic shadow cast against forces as black as hell. On the fifth evening he sighted the gates of Yarkand, flourishing capital of Turkestan. Diffidently he drew near. Would his papers be accepted? If not, all was lost.

"Your passports," the gatekeeper mumbled in Persian.

Benito produced them and waited. It was like waiting for the surgeon's knife.

"Pass on," said the guard and he handed Benito his packet.

Benito trotted his horse through the short tunnel. He suddenly felt weak. His strength had vanished.

Ten days later the rest of the party joined Benito at his lodgings. He had sent a rescue expedition to gather them in, and all admitted his services. He alone, they loudly declared, had saved the caravan.

It was late November, 1603. Benito and Isaac had now been ten months in the mountains. They had completed a journey of 1,240 miles, a distance only as long as the Rocky Mountains from Mexico to Canada. The obvious marvel was not the distance negotiated, but the nature of their obstacle course. Hardly another route in the inhabited world bristled with such opposition. Passes higher than Pike's Peak, gorges as rugged as the Grand Canyon, rivers like the Snake, dens of robbers, hostile religious fanatics, Iron Curtains, colds and heats, treacheries, fevers, beasts of the jungles—all of these in the course of ten months!

People did not live in Yarkand, they adventured there. It was a Moslem nest crowded with fanatics and prophets. A Christian was about as welcome there as he would be today in the Kremlin. Probably less so, for popular as well as official sympathies were against him. Immunity came only from boldness, and Benito had to scrape together all he possessed.

Scarcely had he entered the city than his arrival was noised about. A "Giaour," hated Western infidel, was in their very midst! He had walked right in! It was the sensation of the year. Old-timers declared it an unprecedented event and there were many who said it was too fantastic to be true.

"He is not a Christian," they confidently repeated—just to re-assure themselves. "He is a Buddhist who acts like a Christian."

Others cried, "No! He is a Christian! The king will soon pluck his goose!"

The king, it must be said, was as intolerant in religion as the next person. Even more so. He had contrived a delightful procedure for conversion to his own persuasion. Horse-shoe nails driven into the skulls of dissenters.

Benito, conscious of this Mohammedan fervor, determined to feed the old bear in his den. Perhaps it was more like twisting his tail, but then, he would see. He armed himself with gifts and proceeded to the palace.

He found the king surrounded by an assorted collection of longbeards. Benevolent in appearance, he said afterwards to Isaac, but suspicious and vengeful as youth.

"Is this the Christian dog who dares to pollute the air of our city?" they whispered to one another. All stretched their necks to examine a freak so rare.

Benito spread his palms toward the ground and inclined his head.

"Your brilliant Majesty," he began, "I am your humble servant. I have brought your majesty gifts." He placed a watch, four mirrors, loaves of sugar, and a quantity of candy and fabrics before the king.

He beamed like a moon over his tribute and paused to observe repercussions. Then, with a nod to the spectators and another bow to the king, he swept out of sight. The long-beards, cautious as cats, watched with open-mouthed wonder. Incredible!

Come morning, a royal servant called on the Abdullah. He must inspect the foreign Rume's lodgings, he said, and his sharp eyes sucked out all Benito's belongings. In the pull came objects too strange for the Mohammedan's mechanism, a crucifix and Benito's breviary. He demanded them for examination in court.

"No, no," Benito pleaded. "Not these. They are all I have. Please allow me these and say nothing to the king."

So earnest was his begging that the servant professed himself deeply moved. "I promise to say nothing," he said.

And forthwith he sneaked off to the king.

Within the hour Benito was summoned to court.

"Bring the book and . . ." a shrug, "and all else." The messenger added it vaguely. It was, he knew, a lame effort to describe the unthinkable.

Benito hurried his subversive weapons to the palace, weapons just as subversive in some strangely "Christian" circles across the world.

"This," he said to the king, "is a Roman breviary." He placed it on his head, then kissed it.

"Let me see it," said the king.

Benito put it on his head again, and kissed it. He handed it to an attendant who, caught with the fever, also put it on his head, and kissed it. To the king—who put it on his head, and kissed it, while all the lords gawked with popping eyes.

"This is small writing," cried the king. "Can anyone read it?"

"Yes, Your Majesty." Benito took the book with customary ceremony and opened it at random. He solemnly intoned the first passage that met his eye.

"*Viri Galilaei, quid statis aspicientes in caelum?*" "Ye men of Galilee, why stand you here looking up into heaven?" Then he preached a sermon on the text. So stirred was he as he spoke that tears rolled down his cheeks and all the courtiers wept and sighed with him.

From the sermon till departure, the game was all Christian. Benito became the hero of the city, the toast of every party and banquet. At each he gave spiritual talks to which all listened with more than polite attention. He was exempt from the tax and from mosque duty, and even on Friday, the sacred day, could go about his business in perfect freedom.

Only the Mullahs and Buddhist monks, understandably, remained aloof. "Can it be," they asked, "that a man of intelligence belongs to a law other than ours?" And they begged him to be converted, at least so far as to salute the Prophet. For thus, they promised, the Abdullah would be saved from hell.

Besides salvation from the Mullahs' hell, there was other business to attend, the collection of the princess pilgrim's jade. Khotan, home of this beauty, lay ten days' journey south of Yarkand. Off the beaten paths, the region had an enviable reputation. It kept its Mohammendanism untainted. No "Giaours" penetrated this sanctuary and lived to tell of it!

As a matter of fact, till the late nineteenth century, Benito was the only Westerner who did visit Khotan and live to tell of it.

Others, like the German explorer Schlagintweit in 1857, entered but never came back.

Into this death-trap, where murder lurked around every corner, Benito boldly betook himself. A month passed. There was no definite word regarding his welfare. Only rumors, ugly rumors as tenuous as wisps of smoke floating back to Yarkand. Abdullah Isai, these reports would have it, was dead. He had been torn to pieces by jealous priests.

Poor Isaac's grief was boundless. For whole days he did nothing but weep. Benito murdered! His body bloody and torn, a heap of flesh in the dust! Was life worth living?

And out across the city, within gray walls of the Buddhist monastery, there was great rejoicing. For according to law, property of deceased travellers fell to the monks. The Abdullah—a week overdue, they gloated. Surely the monastery would be declared heir. And the monks beat the drum.

Then, of an evening, Benito came riding on his camel. Bags full of jade, choicest cuts as gifts from his Princess. Isaac in his ecstatic joy frisked everywhere. Now let those monks come snooping around! Hah! And all the triumph of Asia was in his laugh.


Agi-Afis was like a juggernaut. He moved slowly but his progress was certain. He was always sure of himself. That's why he was one of the richest men in the capital and could easily afford to bribe when bribing was expedient.

There was, for example, his determination to be ambassador to China. Merchants (and Agi-Afis was a merchant) could penetrate that proud land only under the guise of an embassy fetching homage and tribute. To direct this pseudo-embassy an ambassador was appointed by the king of Kashgar—for a consideration, to be sure. Agi-Afis understood all this very well. In a glowing anticipation of a sevenfold return, he posted a "gift" that would assure his appointment and began to lay his plans for the journey.

Of course he was right—Agi-Afis never reckoned in error. The credentials were his. Next he needed suitable leadership for his caravan, and this too was determined—Abdullah Isai. All that remained was the Abdullah's consent, and the juggernaut was sure of it.

Benito had been careful to keep secret his intention of proceeding to China. He knew his companionship was eagerly sought, but for one thing, he could not compete in bribe-bidding with the wealthy locals who clamored for inclusion in the caravan. Could he get a berth without an exhorbitant bribe? He would wait and see.

He had not long to wait. Agi-Afis soon appeared on his threshold. Would the Abdullah consider a journey to Peking? The Abdullah was not sure. Did the Abdullah know that the Emperor considered it beneath his dignity to accept gifts from foreigners without extravagant returns? Yes, the Abdullah had heard of it. This was common knowledge. The Abdullah would do well to accept so handsome an offer. Yes, the Abdullah was grateful, but the journey—it was long and tedious. . . .

In the end Benito consented, but it was perfectly evident to all that he, not the ambassador, was the one granting a favor. It was all bread for the sake of butter, but could it be otherwise? Benito doubted.

To Peking, then, he started on the fourteenth of November, 1604. His first break from travel occurred at Aksu, twenty-five days later, where he took time to visit its twelve-year-old king. Lacking erector sets and tinker toys, he brought as gifts the next best thing, bags of candy.

"Whee!" cried the royal Tom Thumb. He was completely captivated by this grave merchant who knew so well what boys liked. He clapped for dancers—melody, rhythm for the new found friend, the Abdullah!

Benito watched a score of Turki maidens brightly clad in reds, purples and greens. To please the court he kept time with the music and bowed graciously to the whirling performers.

"Now you dance," said the boy.

Benito danced, a fast, gay tango learned in his far-away home.

At forty-three, hard work this dancing! He soon tired and came huffing and puffing to the king.

"You must come tomorrow," the entranced little fellow commanded.

For fifteen days Benito made visits to and fro. To the boy king, to his mother, to his tutor. They were all entranced and insisted that the Abdullah remain with them. But Benito could not. Caravans, like tides and suns, wait for no man, anticipate for none. On Christmas Eve he again took to the deserts which for a thousand miles stretched before him across Asia.

"Abdullah Isai." Each syllable cracked out like a pistol shot. The master of Turfan reloaded and aimed again.

"Abdullah Isai!" he exploded.

"I am here," said Benito, stepping forward.

The sovereign coldly looked down on him and as deliberately measured his spirit. There was a great heart beating beneath that cabaia, he decided. The man was more than a lion—he was a dragon.

"You are about to travel through a country inhabited by Mohammedans," he observed. "It would be more prudent for you to drop the title of Christian."

Behind this worthy a hundred Mohammedans glared fiercely at Benito. They were ready to cut his throat on the spot and some already had knives in their hands.

"I am going to write down your name. Shall I leave out the word Christian?" the master of Turfan asked.

"Write down that I am a Christian!" de Goes cried out. "It is a title by which I am honored, that I have always borne, and no danger, not even the certainty of death, will make me give it up."

The silence was heavy like din, as realization dawned on Benito's hearers. Suddenly a venerable old man scrambled to his feet. He jerked off his turban and bowed very low.

"Honor to the faithful believer, to the brave man who dares to avow his faith!" And he bowed low again to the Abdullah.

That night winds swished through naked mulberry branches in

Benito's camp grove. Below, Isaac had his tent, and its flap fabrics rattled sympathetically with the trees. Isaac was not sleeping. He worried and tossed in his blankets till midnight, then crept forth to shake his apprehensions in a stroll.

Where will it end? he asked himself. It was perfectly evident that the merchants in the caravan were determined to squeeze all they could out of the Jesuit. He was legal game and it was open season. How long would he last? Nine months out of Yarkand—he was but a shadow of himself. The mark of doom was on his brow—no mistaking that.

Isaac brushed past the camel drivers' tents. Familiar odors, camels and the unmistakable perfumes of the Orient. A kind of odor-wash to conceal unpleasant effects of life without bath. Isaac sniffed the fumes indifferently. Redolence of home to him, but for the Brother, wasn't even this a constant reminder of his abandonment?

Now, that episode today. . . . Isaac could see the palace chamber. All the dignitaries of the desert oasis were there. A row of dour secretaries with pens in hand. The king himself poised like an inspired Pope in the act of presenting crosses to Crusaders instead of passports to these foreigners. It seemed to be his crowning day so solemnly did he nod and appraise his audience. Did he have many such audiences? Not in isolated Mongolia. No wonder he took it so seriously.

Brother Benito should have been killed in that crowd. That is if the ordinary train of events had occurred. There was some mysterious charm cast over him—what was it? Others had been bold . . . could it be God?

To what purpose did the great God lead Benito on? Already he knew with certainty that Cathay was China, that Cambulec was Peking.

Isaac with mind's eye reaped again the scene in that vast meadow. Two caravans meet, one from Peking, the other Yarkand. They stop to share news. Benito has questions. Cathay? Cambulec? A captain is found. He has lived with Ricci. He has a paper—where is that piece of paper? Here it is—in Portuguese. Benito's black eyes flash with excitement. He sees. He knows for certain—there is no Cathay!

Yes, a missing chain-link had been forged that evening in the twilight—two months ago—Benito for the first time had been loquacious . . . he had acted a little drunk. . . .

Ah, Isaac remembered each detail so well. Benito couldn't sleep. From dusk till dawn he squatted or paced by the camp fire, and he talked and talked. His boyhood, his life in the Novitiate at Goa, court life with Akbar. It almost seemed then that he would recover from his hardships—not of the trail, but hardships of the soul. Isaac sighed. There was the cancer, soul-cancer—Benito was doomed. Isaac was sure of it, though he continued to prod embers of the past for some glow of hope. And he found none before he slipped into his tent and fell into fitfull sleep.

The Gobi Desert, which alone now prevented de Goes from the Great Wall of China, is the conclusion of a desert-belt that stretches like a blight across the Old World. It is a sea of sand so fine that it runs through the fingers like water. Its surface is as smooth as a dam-intake and more neatly swept. Caravaneers, it is said, can trace on it even the path-patterns of the smallest insects.

On the eastern extremity of this no man's land lay the Jade Gate in the Great Wall, immediate objective of Benito's party. From Turfan it was normally achieved in two months.

Thus it happened that on a bleak December day Benito stood without and waited for the gates to swing favorably. He gazed around the approaches, idly, without seeing, little realizing what Moslem ceremonies would subsequently occur there in his memory. He chatted affectionately with Isaac. This, he confided, was the great moment of his life. China—Cathay—lay beyond those hoary walls! Journey's end. Ricci, a brother Jesuit, awaited him. And Jesus Christ in the tabernacle!

For four long years—they seemed like four hundred—no Mass, no Holy Communion, no confession. Not even church or altar, only idols and temples dedicated to devil-gods and prophets. A wave of longing trapped him like a beach derelict and flooded his soul. His lip stiffened and quivered. He struggled against the tears, but his heart was bleeding. There was no relief save in yielding.

Longer than a week Benito was left to cool his heels outside the Jade Gate. He was finally allowed to proceed, but only as far as Su-Chou, twenty-five miles within China. Here he frantically wrote to Ricci to secure imperial safe conduct and passports. His appeal went astray. He dispatched another. He was sick, he wrote, and funds were running low. Infidels and heathen had filched his precious jade.

Months, interminable and anxious, dragged by. A whole year, more than a year. Benito grew worse. Isaac hovered over him with all the tenderness and devotion of a mother, but it became increasingly evident that the patient would soon die. The prosperous Abdullah of journey's start had become a shell, a skin-bag of bones.

He knew he was dying. He hungered for his own, fathers and brothers to whom he had been drawn so closely in his first years of Jesuit life. He hopefully clung to all that was left him—his crucifix. He fingered the cold, hard little figure riveted to the crossbars, and this was balm for his heartache. He was not alone, after all. God was with him. God had spoken to him through the command of his superior. This had been his mission, to discover, and in doing so, to bear Christ into the darkness. Who could tell what seeds he had planted, what trails he had blazed in this ancient world that was perishing with him?

Dying, yes. Despite his crucifix, forsaken. No one to bring him the last holy Sacraments. No litanies for the dying. Indeed, he knew now that Christ's forsaken hour was the supreme agony in all His sufferings. He had often heard of Father Xavier dying like this on Sancian, of countless other Jesuits, forsaken and buried in unnamed graves. There was an emptiness in lonely death, a soothing emptiness like participation in mysteries. It was, he knew, a seal of approval. No memory stirring within him brought him so close to Christ and his brother Jesuits.

He folded his hands composedly, resignedly. In this last struggle he would not weaken. He could not lose faith now after having lived by it so long, so arduously. Let the Master but summon him. He was ready.

Then one morning in late March, Benito in a thin, tired voice called Isaac.

"Go to the market," he pleaded. "Buy food and give it to the poor. Inquire in the bazaars for a message. Help . . ." he whispered this very solemnly, ". . . help has come from Peking."

Isaac scratched his head and blinked in amazement. Was the good brother delirious? Help has come—what could he know about this? But humor the sick he must. He pocketed his purse and moodily trudged to market.

Within the hour Isaac was back. He tiptoed into Benito's room, took a peek, then motioned to a shadow at the door. The stranger crept in. He winked at Isaac, then began a little speech in Portuguese, a low Chinese sing-song voice—greetings from Father Ricci.

Benito understood—a Jesuit had finally come! He looked up into Brother Fernandez' face and pressed him to his heart while tears plowed down his wrinkled cheeks.

"Now dost thou dismiss thy servant in peace," he sobbed.

Brother Fernandez had brought letters from Ricci and Benito's hands trembled as he opened them. Over and over he read them and kissed them in delight. "See, see!" he cried "Father Matthew agrees. China is Cathay!"

The news was good medicine. Benito revived a little, then began to sink again. Eleven days later servants carried his thin remains to the grave. Two mourners followed. Lacking a book of devotions they prayed the rosary. And as they went along, kicking up little puffs of dust, no one looked up or paused in his occupations to comment on death and the hardships of life. For no one but the mourners really cared.

# Scaffolding to the Stars

BY JOHN P. LEARY, S.J.

*Brother Frank Schroen, S.J. (1853–1924)*

DUSK was stealing down the avenue again. Waters of the Chesapeake softly lapped the land, and the hulk of old Fort McHenry was blocked black against the west.

He scarcely noticed how lavender orange had transformed that drab gray Tuesday afternoon into an enchanted evening. For months now the neighbors had watched him from behind lace curtains and slits in the doorway. The surly quiet and the stare, the unspeakable stare, were so unlike the young Bavarian widower. Lucky thing that he had sent his little girl to stay with his sister. For something weird was going on in the house where Frank Schroen was living.

As night fell a sense of quiet gathered around leisurely old Baltimore, the blue gas-lights atop the poles, the clippity-clop of horse and carriage now and then upon the flat cobblestone streets.

Mrs. Fenel, from the second-story frame house across the way, was peering into the darkness. From her window for a long time now she had made her vigil each evening and watched her neighbor with his ouija board upon his lap, and later on with his slate and chalk. Etched in his own dim lamplight she saw his eyes close, his lips moving, his form taut and erect. She blessed herself three times and then opened her window quietly to see if mayhap the warm September air might not catch a few fragments of the tragic soliloquy over there. There was no sound in the stillness but the distant barking of a dog.

Across the way a piece of chalk in a man's hand was dancing along a board like some wild dervish. His own fingers scarcely moved. There was a chill, a fear in the room. Frank opened his eyes and read, "This is Mary, your wife, your dead wife, Mary. . . . You must help these to bring men to hell. . . . You must hate God. . . . I sold my soul to God and he damned me. . . . You are damned too . . . Frank. . . ." The voice drifted off hysterically.

Behind him he heard a low, hideous laugh. It frightened him

half to death. Surely he would go mad. What was he doing? What was happening to him? He looked at his gaunt trembling fingers, then wild-eyed, watched the chalk slip from them and begin to scratch by itself on the slate. He leaped to his feet and rushed into the night. Through deserted streets he staggered half-dazed, through long hours, heavily oblivious to everything save his own despair. There was only one way out of this . . . the bridge. Suicide! But he was afraid to do it, he knew.

Next day Fritz Herman took a second look at the boss. Those dark shadows under his eyes were becoming frightful. And the lips never seemed to stay still these days. He could notice, as they worked on a fresco together, how he twitched. Nerves, nerves, his features were becoming more distorted day by day. No good to say anything. He had asked Frank what was wrong before and been curtly told to attend to his own business. Let sullen dogs be or something like that, he thought.

The two of them worked quietly in the great cream-colored ball-room. As Frank Schroen moved along his scaffolding toward a pillar near the balcony he was aware suddenly of the stillness. He took the chalk from his pocket. As he formed the questions, the blood began to beat through his brain like a sharp little trip-hammer. "Who are you?" he said. "Who are you within me? Haunting me night and day?" A convulsion shook him. The chalk raced meaninglessly along the wall.

He waited and repeated his question again. His hand escaped control. "I am sin who has mastered good and God. . . . I am all the dead." Frank raised his sleeve and wiped the blue lettering away. He breathed more deeply, pursed his lips. "I conjure thee in the name of God, tell me who you are," he whispered huskily.

There was tumult in his ears. Slowly, tortuously the chalk wrote upon the wall, B-e-e-l-z-e-b-u-b. Without a word, deathly pale, he descended and walked out into the street. He did not feel the room quake nor see the swaying chandeliers. Fritz Herman watched his pipe fall to the floor and his coat from the hook. He grabbed both of them and ran. Those damned frescoes could wait until another day. That chamber was haunted or else he was going quietly nuts.

Frank stood leaning for some time against the grilled iron gate. What was he to do? There was Lady Simons, a spiritualist over on 32nd, who had sat through many a séance, people said. It might be good to see her and have this whole affair untangled. As the trolley lumbered along toward the east side of town he began to note the old familiar landmarks of his childhood, the board fences and stucco walls where he used to dabble as a kid, his dad's tailor shop, Carroll's grocery and meat shop, the barber shop, the ice cream store and there on the corner . . . the squat wooden Church of St. Michael's where he had prayed as a boy. Like a man in a dream he got off.

Before he knew what was happening he was mounting the rickety steps of that church. A wave of nostalgia gripped him for a moment, the holy water stoop, the leaks in the ceiling, the cracked angel hovering low around the altar. And there was the family pew where his folks and the thirteen kids used to attend Mass. He could make out a faint F.S. still visible in the dark stained wood. He had exercised his craftsmanship during the longer sermons.

Cap in hand, Frank Schroen walked to the front of the church. He stood there for a moment before the statue of Our Lady, then fell on his knees crying. Have you ever seen a man cry? It is sad. For he knew, kneeling there, how intimately he had lived with tragedy these long years. He had not been to church since Mary's funeral and before that not for six years despite her pleading. His faith had gone down the drain with the dangerous books he had read. He had thrown God out of his life and given his soul to enterprise. His success in art had only hardened him, made him more sure of himself: a man who could create as he could need hardly bend his knee to another. And so the tangled skein of motive and cross-purpose and deception fell loosely around him in the dimness of the old church.

When he rose hours later, he was stiff. A wan smile flickered across his features as he looked where tears had stained the brown carvings. No one could really tell what had gone on in the soul of the man. But it was a chastened and sad hand that lifted the brass knocker on the rectory door.

Before long he was telling all the story. His own happy background as a boy, then achievement, indolence and disdain, the dangerous curiosity, the books, wrong kind, the bartering, the possession by the devil, the questions and the horrible train of blasphemous, obscene replies. The whole sad tale of ten years past lay like a huge welt upon his soul. Every now and then the kindly Redemptorist priest would question him or speak a kindly word to make the ordeal less harrowing. The Father knew this stranger to be a man who was staggering beneath an awareness of guilt, a sense of sin. Sitting there this graying middle-aged priest was thinking how incomprehensible were God's ways and how boundless was the compassion of the Lord.

A week later, and the whole neighborhood knew Frank Schroen had come back to his senses. He had recaptured that blithe whistle on his way to work every morning. And though it woke up a few folks they didn't mind for they knew the man had found himself. He was civil again. He smiled at the bartender, passed the time of day with the vegetable man down on the corner, inquired after Mrs. Hamegar's crippled boy. Everyone had liked Frank when he was himself.

Out at Irvington in the suburbs of Baltimore he took a liking to Sunday afternoons spent in the garden of a little monastery. Those habited men intrigued him. They were Passionist fathers who had charge of the place and Frank had asked them for their counsel and help. He would sit on a bench beneath a grove of trees and talk for long hours with Father Frederick.

Frank would start out by briefing the monks on how it fared with Admiral Dewey. War hysteria of '98 was sweeping the country. Near-by Annapolis and Baltimore were aroar with movement as thousands of raw recruits were pressed into uniform. More battleships were shoving off. Newspapers had stirred up a strong popular wrath toward Spain. It was beginning to look as if Cuba and the Philippines would shake themselves free, Uncle Sam doing the shaking.

The monks would drift off then, and the priest somehow or other always got that conversation steered into some mighty deep channels. Frank began to look at Frank more closely and even in the warm pleasantness of this seclusion he felt terribly swept by a sense of futility. His past seemed to bear down upon him so relentlessly. He felt like a man emptied out and robbed, torn loose from what he so much wanted. Yet the priest could see how needful this laying bare of a man's soul was, for he knew souls; so, surgeon-like, he probed and lanced and let the wounds flow. They emptied out, they healed. A feeling of quiet grew into one of resolution.

His friends and family who knew him so well knew that Frank did not ordinarily act on sudden impulse. What he did he seemed to do tenaciously, stubbornly, as if when set he could not be changed. They could see too that, out of these bitter experiences he had been through, he was emerging a firmer man. Some of his brothers and sisters wouldn't believe the ouija story when he told them. That was to be expected.

His serious dark eyes seemed to slip almost into terror when he recounted at a family dinner a few weeks later his weird tale of possession. Poor Frank had been through a lot, they thought. Some kind of illusions had preyed on him, perhaps. But he knew otherwise, and, despite his wholesome normalcy now, there was a sadness, something different that set him off from other people. The neighbors got the impression too . . . that tired sag in his shoulders.

What God's designs had been in all this he did not know. Many people did not even believe in the devil; the supernatural was a phase of Christian dynamics, if it could be termed that, which progressive folks looked upon with about as much faith as they had in Red Riding Hood's grandmother. But, for him, he could never forget as he looked at his hands, still now and controlled, that Beelzebub had used them as his own, and that menacing, diabolical eyes had peeped at the world through the sockets in his head.

One day he asked Father Frederick, not unexpectedly, if he might enter the Passionist Monastery. He said he wanted to pray for others and to make up for his own dereliction. It was hard to rid his mind of what he had done and not done. Suffering had shaped him to a finer cast.

The priest waited for some weeks before he gave him an answer, put him off by saying he'd have to think it over a while. They were seated in the arbor. It had begun to grow dark. The afternoons were getting cooler now and the priest drew his coat more closely around his shoulders.

"I have been thinking over your desire to become a monk for several weeks now, Frank," he said. "I have prayed over the counsel I am about to give you. It seems to me that you should become a Jesuit Brother. . . ." He puffed a few moments on his pipe. "This, I believe, is what God wants of you. It is a way of life into which you will most easily fit with your talents and at your age. And yet it is an immensely meritorious way of life because it is so eminently supernatural in its character." Frank plucked a leaf that hung near his forehead and looked away.

He was silent for some moments, almost stricken at being refused. "So you really think I should become a Brother . . . a Jesuit Brother?" He stopped, "Now that you advise me, I begin to feel reluctant. I don't think I want to." His forehead creased in thought. "The step seems so final now, full of presumption for a man with my past." He paused again, took a deep breath, "And Father, I know nothing about the Jesuits. But they have a bad name historically, I know, for I have read Pascal and Voltaire." A whole train of reasons and arguments came rushing to his rescue. Wild possibilities thrust themselves before him and he struggled to save himself.

The priest ignored what he said. "Some time this week," he went on, "you should drop in to see a Jesuit Father over at Loyola College. He will be able to explain to you the more immediate details of the life. I am convinced, Frank, that this is God's will."

He smiled, though it seemed hard for him. "Some day you will be grateful for the counsel I am trying to give you." He had spoken that precisely, Frank remembered, not a spare word, just as if it had all been weighed ahead of time.

The priest arose with finality as if talking further or a prolonged discussion might weaken his resolve to see this fellow through as he had intended.

So Frank went home, a lonely, bewildered man. He prayed. He did not seem to want to become a Jesuit. Yet God wanted it. There were long weeks and months of conflict. He read all he could get hold of, decided not to go, to go, not to go. But what was there to stay for, he thought? That did it. There was a happy reluctance about his decision, once made. And thank God he felt peace for the first time in a long while.

In the following months he redoubled his efforts to build up the necessary funds for his little girl. He had decided now to go to the novitiate. His daughter, Margaret, must be provided for, however. The Jesuit Fathers had told him that his first responsibility lay in seeing that she should have all she needed to finish school and to give her also the care and guidance necessary for a young girl growing into womanhood.

By dint of months of overtime, some shrewd investments and extra painting on the side, he put a good sum in the bank under his sister's care. Then he realized that his life as it had been lived in his own apartment, doing what he wanted, coming and going as he pleased was done with—gone. Going down the sidewalk the last time was hard. No use kidding himself.

With lagging step and the stern anxiety of a man about to take the great step into religion, with misgivings popping up everywhere, Frank Schroen went along the dusty road to Frederick, Maryland. This was the Jesuit Novitiate he had fretted so much about in desolate hours. He felt a certain reassurance in the warm hand clasp and the smile of a young lad who met him at the door. But the door closed with an awful finality. In the parlor was Our Lady looking down at him from a heavy gold frame. Rather a gaudy oil job, he observed. No time to criticize now, however. His resolve sparked momentarily. "I'm going to stick this out," he muttered under his breath, "at least for a while . . . until I can't stand it, or they can't stand me."

It was not as hard as he thought. Within a few months he felt as if fifteen years of his life had been lopped off at one stroke. The regularity of going to bed and getting up, the three squares a day, the overflow of immense mental satisfaction added twenty pounds to his weight, just like that. He was thirty-five years old now, not so old, after all, he thought. And when the Novice Master told him one day that he was to help paint the chapel, he almost hit the sky with joy. They would not overlook what he could do. Quite the contrary, he would find out.

There were, of course, dark days too. That first year he missed his little daughter a great deal. Ties of flesh and blood couldn't be severed as easily as he thought. Letters from her became almost a necessity. In fact his longings were pretty obvious to Father O'Rourke, the Master. When he gave a short talk one day on Our Lord's saying that no man who put his hand to the plow and looked back was worthy of the kingdom of God, he noticed how melancholy Brother Schroen looked in the back of the room. That cheery round face wasn't meant to look bleak.

Because the old priest understood how Christ's commands to perfection were to be tempered with compassion, he arranged for the novice to go and see his child. And though she wept when she saw her father in a cassock, still he could tell by the look in her eyes and the pressure when she squeezed his arm, how proud she was of him. She wouldn't have had him do otherwise than he was doing. And Frank, after more than a year, could now see that before too long his child would be a woman, perhaps a nun, perhaps a fine wife and mother. He went back to Frederick content.

As the novices came along the road in two's, past the general store, they slowed down perceptibly, maybe to pick up the stray fragments of conversation drifting their way.

"Look at them Jesuits there, dressed like a bunch of old tramps."

"Pretty clean lookin' bunch of kids though, ain't they? And normal too, all considered."

"Where in blazes do the Catholics pick up all these men?" A pause.

"Well there you have your British for you, clubbin' the Boers; if it ain't them it's the Irish." A rumbling.

"Did you hear about this Italian guy named Macoroni? . . . They say he's tryin' to send codes without wires. Why we'll be flyin' through the air before long."

The novices quickened their shuffle to a clip. Funny what people thought, what they talked about "in" the world. The older fellow among the boys was laughing. Things hadn't changed at all in a year.

So from these and kindred unknown places in America, the Jesuits went on year after year, relentlessly putting their men through the training . . . Woodstock, Weston, Florissant, Los Gatos, Poughkeepsie, Grand Coteau. Most people had never even heard of them. And yet in the quiet of the rural valleys and hills in the U.S.A. and all over the world the military discipline and, above all, the vision of St. Ignatius went on being transmitted. Not so many foreigners any longer, but native-bred American boys learned in these houses built by the Germans and Irish, the French and Italians. And here the sparks were kindled so that other Cross-carriers might go forth and inflame the world.

Brother Schroen found the Society remarkably capable of absorbing all types of men and channeling their abilities in a competent and effective way. He began to share in a conception of his own strength when it was fused with that of his fellow religious, the brothers like himself, the scholastics preparing for the altar and the priests. None of them alone could so much as bar the way to hell against one soul. But in their numbers, their spiritual solidarity and the consecration of all their prosaic and glorious achievements to Christ, they could wrestle with the powers and principalities.

They could become the kind of daring cavalry Ignatius had

envisioned, moving from place to place where the need was greatest and the struggle most in doubt. The Jesuits were to be God's militia, the shield of the Church. And all the novices in the hills of Maryland thrilled to the picture their Master painted for them through the months of training.

At the beginning of what might perhaps be the most epic of all centuries, 1900, Brother Schroen knelt down early one morning and vowed his life on the altar of sacrifice. He scarcely conceived of his own role in this drama as monumental, and he was not wrong. What was it to the world, after all, that a young man got down on his knees and promised God to surrender his possessions, his affections, make an oblation of his entire self . . . forever? But he was thinking again in terms of a solitary man. Nothing had ever been of significance without God. And God, on His part, willed, he knew, to re-live His life in the disciples of each generation. Through the hands, the feet, the eyes and the heart of men, Christ willed to bring His influence to bear, to make effective the redemption.

So the Brother in whom Beelzebub had housed himself, clad in his black cassock, left Frederick and the recollection of the quiet corridors. He was about to begin an eventful quarter of a century. Long after his name was forgotten, his work would remain.

The elderly fathers at Frederick had not been asleep to the abilities and inclination of young Brother Schroen. His altar decorations at Christmas and the way he had transformed the plain old-fashioned window in the chapel lifted many an eyebrow. There was a sense of propriety, of artistic discretion and yet withal a daring, an aspect of bold original conception, about what he did. And he, for himself, was glad that God, through His Superiors, as Fr. Master devoutly reminded him, should choose to make use of his talents. Brother Kileen, with whom he had entered, was going to be the new cook at Loyola in Baltimore. Brother Finley was going to be the tailor at Georgetown over in Washington, D.C. And he? Brother Schroen was going to Woodstock where the philosophers and theologians studied. He would paint.

So, after Mass and breakfast every morning, the young Jesuits in training would see Brother Schroen in the chapel, or the library or the corridors, painting. One month, on a scaffolding, the next, crawling along over bare beams, the next, shading his eyes as sunlight filtered through white glass.

He began to observe the world around him with a new sensitivity and vision. He would need vision, he thought, to conceive the saints and God's Mother and God Himself as his superiors had decided he should. The clear paleness of an October dawn might serve as background for his Immaculate Conception; and he worked for days to catch the fleeting rapture of azure blue in an April sky.

You could frequently see him in the gardens or swinging off to the hills, notebook in hand, alert to the call of a thrush or the feel of warm spring mists upon his cheeks. Nothing stood in the way now of his cultivating a vast responsiveness:

The way that light streamed through a wooded hillside, the way stars fascinated in the darkness, how sunlight could set a lake on fire at dusk. He loved the whirring of crickets by a pond and the way a rose almost bled at high noon. He used to sit for hours watching the men around him laugh and talk and plan so that he might know the shades of meaning on a human face.

Years fled rapidly by. Stars up to forty-eight were being added to the American flag; before long a great trumpeting fellow, named Teddy Roosevelt, took over from the dead President. Came the unsinkable *Titanic* and it went down into the cold waters. Across the world Japan and Russia had sounded the tocsin of battle. From South Bend, Illinois (or was it Indiana, the papers said?) a band of boys started its trek to glory, making West Point bite the dust. On the screen, Little Nell and True Blue Calhoun had become the idols of millions. Came '13 and a slender, bespectacled professor from Princeton, New Jersey, walked into the White House to lead the country. Came '14 and an Austrian archduke was killed. War!

In the middle of it came Dublin's Easter Rebellion. Meanwhile the *Lusitania* went down and the Allies were calling for help. A year later the Yanks came marching down Fifth Avenue on their way over there. "Over There" and "A Long, Long Trail" and "Keep the Home Fires Burning" were household songs. Grief entered many a home, and where formerly men lived, now their comrades buried slashed bodies quickly in the fields of France. The Armistice, delirium, and peace. Came the wild twenties, the hectic, short-lived millennium; prohibition, bootlegging and gangsters. Wilson died broken-hearted. America was turning its back on the world. Up from oblivion, Dempsey and Tunney came, punching their way to fame. Aeroplanes, telephones, radios, automobiles, the bobbed hair, the derby hat, all had a spot in the passing parade of twenty-five stormy, reckless years.

Meanwhile, through the march of time, Brother Schroen went on quietly painting. At Georgetown University in the nation's capital, he remained for a long while, working ceaselessly on the library, the halls, parlors, corridors and entrance. Everywhere one saw the mellowed influence of his oils, the academic and the ascetic so ingeniously fused. Presidents and senators, judges, statesmen and ambassadors stopped to wonder at his madonnas, his crucifixion scene! The lovely play of light and shadow in his canvases, the apt profile, his vitality of expression.

Superiors were prevailed upon by Fordham next, and here in booming New York he labored on the chapel and St. John's church. Exquisite, thought the college men. Critics began to speak of his work with cautious reserve, to commend his economy, his clarity in conceiving, the warmth of execution which surpassed mere technique. They used to come to St. Ignatius' Church and watch him work there, observing him for hours with upturned heads. Many began to call his paintings "masterful." The gaudiness and pretentiousness of late nineteenth-century ecclesiastical art was missing, but not missed. With this man Schroen, color lived and the real in all its various aspects was beautifully captured. The saints looked like honest-to-God people, not fakirs or Egyptian mummies.

Philadelphia's huge Church of the Gesu succeeded finally in getting his services. And when he had finished, from all over the city crowds poured around the aisles of the church to look at his colorful medallions of the saints. While the papers next day came out frankly and lauded the results of his long labors, Brother Schroen sat in the large Jesuit recreation room and laughed uproariously at the movies and the antics of Charlie Chaplin. He made mental calculations on Mary Pickford too; there were certain features in his lady saints and his Lady which he must be careful of.

He was always like that . . . a great one for studying proportion, for balance and symmetry, a sense of wholeness in things. He even got a few hints on how things should and shouldn't be from watching Fatty Arbuckle.

Schroen's repute as an artist in only a little over ten years had surpassed what anyone might have thought when he was younger. The man understood feature; he knew how to appeal and how to select detail. Few could touch him in the delicate transfer of color to a canvas, a white wall or a curved ceiling.

Over in Jamaica the great cathedral was almost finished. Would Brother come and ornament the interior? It was a huge job, superiors knew . . . to commission this man to do what natives would look upon for year upon year as the prayer place and showplace of a nation. The Islanders were sensitive too. Even the poorer classes had an eye for color. Their likes ran strongly along lines of splendid display, so that an artist would have to use reserve sparingly if he were to please the people and not violate his own canons of proportion.

That was a long, difficult job. Day after day through the heat of the sultry afternoons Brother went on painting. Looking down now and then from his scaffolding he could see the little clusters of colored folk gathered to watch him, noisy in the early morning, pensive in the later hours. At times he felt as if what the Bishop wanted were too much and that his superiors in America should have been guided by more caution. But before he was an artist he remembered he was a religious man. Even should these paintings be miserable, covered over after the consecration of the cathedral, the source of unending ridicule and humiliation for himself, it was still God's clearly spoken will that he do them and, at this time, nothing else but them. His motives sustained him.

Finally the job was done. Men were tearing down the supports and scaffolding. The great church was a beehive of activity. Tomorrow would be the grand opening. It didn't look too bad, he thought, and still it was hard to judge when one was so close to his own work.

At daybreak, from all the environs of Kingston and distant points of the island, the processions wended their way through the cathedral. Hundreds of candelabra lit up the vaulted interior. Jamaica responded with a great burst of admiration. From mitred men down to lowly shopmen there was immense enthusiasm.

The newspaper asked a government engineer to write up the interior of the Church. Wrote Braham Judah:

The glory of the magnificent interior of the Cathedral is revealed in the expression of an extremely high art, superbly executed by the humble Jesuit, Brother Schroen.

The work is an embodiment of holiness. It impels a feeling of adoration as one looks into the depths of the Cupola. As if far away beyond the earth, the heavens open and within a circling cloud the Dove is seen, the emblem of the Holy Spirit, radiating beams of light.

We catch the deep inspiration of ecclesiastical art and we involuntarily admit as we read the words that "this is the Church of the Living God, the Pillar and Ground of Truth." The light descends, we see the beams broader and more clearly until at length they rest on the life-size form of the four evangelists enthroned on the four pendentives of the domes, their features illuminated and inspired with divine life and light.

Our eyes, slowly falling, rest above the altar in the sanctuary. We almost breathe a prayer, for there we find in wonderful allegory, the representation of the most Holy Trinity amid the seraphic beauty of the nine choirs of angels. This is magnificent.

Even where others did the work, Brother directed and conceived everything down to the statues in white Carrara marble and the wood carving in native black mahogany.

Back to America he sailed and the entreaties of Boston College next prevailed. The clear stillness, the white mists of New England became new incentive. Through all his toil the rotunda was gradually transformed, then the library, the parlors, the auditorium. It was the same old story, masterful work that would last and be treasured for a long time. Some of it was inspiration, a touch of genius perhaps, but most of his labor was sweat, he knew, and work . . . work.

One day 160,000 people picked up their Boston *Evening Transcript* of October 15, 1916, and read about all the doings over at the College. Said Lynde Hartt in part:

So used have you become to associating dull hues with the gothic, that you forget how gorgeous were the "Dark" ages and how daring the original color schemes their architects supplied . . . precedent and to spare for what has been accomplished here. Inside the great tower and offsetting the gray of stone pillars and arches, color gleams resplendent, with lavish use of pale greenish gold and a rich and all but redundant profuseness in design.

Gothic? In detail, perhaps not. In adherence to strictly medieval patterns, assuredly not. You recall Viollet-le-Duc's restoration of the Sainte-Chapelle, and remind yourself that it was not the least like this. The more you study these radiant decorations, the more it seems to you they reflect the spirit of the Middle Ages. And so they do, in a way little dreamed.

All the mural embellishments here, all those in the library, all those in the sumptuous assembly hall and plenty more besides are the work of a lay brother, who though not ordained, belongs to the Jesuit Order and labors for the salvation of his soul and to the glory of God.

Up yonder on his scaffold, you will see him, a very modern looking artisan in overalls . . . prosaic frankly, yet with a mission like the 12th Century craftsmen, whose skill in stone, wood and jewelled glass lives after them in the European Cathedrals, and was prompted by the same devout motive.

More time passed. The Fathers and Brothers could see how toil and intense concentration were making the artist an old man too soon. His passion consumed him and once more superiors relented. He was off for New Orleans this time. He must make this his best, he thought. Before many months the dim interior of Holy Names Church was quietly aglow. Arms lifted in benediction, the fairness of a maiden's face, eyes of supplication, ardent young men, martyrs silent in their agony. He reveled in this great armory of holy people which he was creating. Frequently when his imagination ran dry and contour became only a blur, he called for men and women to come and pose for him. The shrewd eyes narrowed as he sketched his models. In their immediacy he tried to recapture the marked spiritual something which should shine out through the features of a type. Seldom, artists observed, did he fail.

He stopped more frequently to rest now; sometimes he would simply lie still, flat on his stomach, looking down toward the altar. The Brother prayed there in the silence. Inside it was very still; he had not noticed it before. Outside he could hear the rumbling trolleys, the whistles, the hum of a city at work. He noticed, too, how heavily his own heart seemed to beat; the stabs of pain that filled his eyes with momentary surprise made him anxious.

Then the last pillar was finished. He smiled at the tributes that were heaped upon him. Jesuit fathers noted how his own sense of humor forbade him from taking temporary enthusiasm over his work very seriously. That laugh of his and the shrug of his shoulders made his task seem about as casual as dabbing a bit of paint on a kitchen chair.

Time to be on his way back to Georgetown, he thought. These warm, southern days were sucking his strength. So the worn figure in black sat down in the train. He heard faintly the stir of the depot, the farewells. His weary eyes watched the landscape spinning by, oh so fast. It was hard to keep up with it. The lids closed, the head tilted back against the green cushion. Two men behind him were talking about Coolidge and the election. Then a lonely blast of a whistle drifted out over the fields of Louisiana.

# Broken Strands

BY CHARLES A. WOLLESEN, S.J.

*Brother Dominic Collins, S.J. (1567–1602)*

FOURTEEN YEARS earlier Ireland's cliffs and breakers had been shatteringly destructive to the gale-driven Armada. Of that historic wreckage, ugly images, like bubbles sputtering in a cauldron of oil, renewed themselves by bursting in on the troubled surface of Jago's mind. Captain Jago was now charged with bringing another fleet, this time to bolster the invasion forces that Don Juan del Aquila had just pushed onto the Irish shore. As well land toy soldiers, the island's military experts had warned Philip of Spain, as dare to enter the southern tip with less than eight thousand men.

But Jago's supplement, joined with the other, barely equalled half that number. British forces, too, under Henry Carew's command were known to be driving toward Castlehaven. The Captain had no assurance that the devilish red eyes burning through the fog from shore might not be camp fires of enemies. The heavily laden ships, their canvas stretched, were roughing their dark passage in the North Atlantic as apt partners to the swarthy man at the helm of the foremost, gloomy in the forebodings of his mind.

Near him, as he anxiously stood his post, occasionally there passed a more than ordinarily tall figure. Almost every time it appeared, Jago's eyes followed and a gradual relaxation smoothed his features as if an old friend's proximity were teasing pleasant memories from his mind. As the figure circled again toward the prow of the ship where darkness cloaked him from view, Jago pictured the obscurity into which this remarkable Irishman had voluntarily stepped four years before. And the Captain was wondering at the strangely intransigeant mountains that rise between divergent vocations in life. Their great divide had not broken a decade-long friendship; but it had removed friend from view of friend. Now, as often, familiarity began projecting long dreams, trying to capture a glimpse of the mysteries on the other side.

Jago liked to think back to that day in Coruna when he had surprised this young comrade of his by slipping into his hand an envelope which bore the royal seal of Philip II. "News," Jago had congratulated, "the best you've heard since your captaincy of the cavalry up in France." Dominic Collins, the tall Irish military man, opened the packet and drew forth a royal appointment, countersigned and all, as Capitán de le Armada Real. All Coruna celebrated. The men in his Majestys navy saw in Captain Collins an officer of superior quality.

But now Jago was the one in command of the fleet stealing toward Ireland this night. The Irishman held no commission; he rode as a mere guest. The Spaniard, conscious by comparison of not being so highly qualified, straightened his ship on its course with an almost petulant jerk, and terminated his reflections on how time's crashing wheel had rolled over many things, changing all.

Dominic Collins had been circling the deck, not nervously or even in fear, but with more of the eager anticipation of an athlete ready for what he conceives to be combat of high and measureless calibre. As he reached the prow, he stopped, latched two large hands around the rail, and delighted once again in the creaking sounds of a vessel at sea, and in the rain the dark North drove against his cheeks. He was pinning his eyes on the distance, reaching mentally what his eyes could not yet distinguish, a tiny light or two that would reveal the coast of his homeland. Almost two days out of Spain, and according to his unofficial calculations, less than two hours yet to the salt sands of Castlehaven.

Castlehaven would bring him in contact with Father Archer, the Jesuit chaplain of O'Neill's Spanish-aided army, and into a new and dangerous phase of his life. But Collins, like Jago, found his mind pulled gently back to Spain, not to the beginning of his captaincy, but to the relinquishing of it. He remembered the evening so well. He saw himself slipping out of officers' quarters that night he decided to forego the military and sign himself over to an energetic little band of Christ's known as the Company of Jesus.

Compostella was the Jesuit house near by. In the parlor there, Father Thomas White understood much more than Dominic was narrating of military successes in France and Spain. But he paid keen attention as Collins told how old ambitions had become dwarfed by a greater, all-embracing desire to serve in the army of the world-conquering One. Something akin to contempt had settled on the lesser dun-colored callings; continuous, urgent, happy, sounded the vocation to Christ's army. Long reflection, a growing use of the Sacraments, attraction to bodily austerities, and all the while, as the priest knew, exemplary fulfillment of his naval duties, revealed the fingers of divine grace beginning to close about his soul. Francis of Assisi's simple devotedness for him outclassed the blaze of kings and courts. Ignatius of Loyola's prudent, dynamic persistence in battling for the Church outstripped the reaches of mere human achievement. He might not put it that way but that's how he had figured in the silence of a bivouac or in the pale dawn before a battle, and a day of heart-break and conquest. Could not he, Dominic Collins, be received into the Society of Jesus? Unworthy to become a priest, he desired but to give the best he could as a religious lay brother. Would the Father be so kind as to admit him?

Dominic huddled deeper now in the rain-coat he had thrown over his shoulders before coming out on deck, for he felt cold all of a sudden as he realized the near miss. That meeting had ended in disappointment. At the time he had not seen that further testing of his vocation was the priest's objective. He was aware only of his profoundest aspirations being blocked. The life of a Jesuit lay brother, Father White had warned, was a hard one. A successful, well educated man, a man from an illustrious family, would perhaps not be content in it. Had Captain Collins weighed well what a world of sacrifices it entailed? Had he thought of the priesthood, a state better suited to his level? Had he considered the other religious orders? The upshot of it all was that Collins returned to the Coruna naval base, a disappointed candidate.

The Ignatian ideal, however, tantalized him beyond sleep that night. The thought persisted that the ex-Captain of Loyola had fought through all obstacles blocking his path to a religious life.

From the siege of Pampeluna to the vigil of Montserrat Collins retraced the quest. There on the altar he envisioned Ignatius laying his sword, vowing allegiance to a divine King. With the sentry's footfall alone disturbing the night's stillness, Collins caught a suggestion from his family coat of arms hanging over his desk. "Vincit pericula Virtus"—Valor triumphs over every difficulty. His course was clear. In the heat of spiritualized, soldierly courage every stone of resistance must be shoved aside. He should live more Christlike daily till, time-tested, his vocation met with Jesuit approval.

A renewal too warm for even the ocean air to cool gladdened him as there on shipboard he again recalled the satisfaction of his entry a year later into the novitiate of the Society of Jesus at Compostella.

In many ways Fr. White had been right. The change was far from easy. Especially did the old military fire flare up when news reached the cassocked novice of Compostella that Hugh O'Neill, the Earl of Tyrone, had smashed a musket ball into the head of Bagenal and piled twenty-five hundred English corpses around him on the plain of Yellow Ford. Everything, a soldier could see, lanced toward a sweeping series of Irish victories. Every son of Erin, the impulse shouted, must in loyalty join up to follow one great victory with another and another, till Ireland in a great national shudder should shake the mongrel from its throat and stand free forever. A visitor called on Brother Collins. The Adelantado of Castile was asking him to assist in the invasion. Sword was being weighed now against vocation; the spectacular against the sacrificial; immediate domination against long-range spiritual victory. And Collins had, in the clutch, stood firm in his chosen vocation, sure that his service to his country and his Faith would be greater as a Jesuit.

The skein of his reverie snapped. On deck about him, shouting crewmen hustled. The coast of Ireland was washing near. If Carew's forces had reached Castlehaven, Collins might still have to be both soldier and Jesuit.

But he was glad, almost as much as Jago, when the hazy burst of lights flashing Del Aquila's welcome to the incoming ships re-

laxed the tension of uncertainty. Relay boats, come to unburden
the holds, were already bobbing out through the surf as Jago eased
the first ship into shallow water.

Collins felt the damp sand flex under the pressure of his feet
as he leapt from one of these smaller craft onto his homeland. Before he had time to ask questions, friends everywhere from Tyrone's camp were embracing him, slapping their hands into his,
assuring him they knew of his eagerness to see Father Archer immediately. They were aware of it and glad he had come to assist the
Jesuit chaplain and his homeland. But impossible just now, it was
their duty to warn him, was any passage through to that quarter.
O'Neill meantime would be honored with Brother Collin's presence. Would he come?

There was short time, though, to renew acquaintance with
O'Neill, or with O'Sullivan Beare, and Ireland's other patriots,
sworn to the defense of their country. The descent of Carew's
flying columns thundered war throughout Munster. Alerted generals and outnumbered soldiery hurled themselves into the onslaught. As the pressure of attack strained the little army's reserves
of manpower, Collins seemed at every soldier's side when needed.
His calm, the effect both of an old familiarity with battle dangers
and of constant union with God, he imparted to the determined
little army and increased their doggedness in the face of the English.

But the great numbers of Irish lads that he assisted at their dying,
and the many more that time's swift jealousy ripped from his aid,
warned of Tyrone's imminent defeat. Three thousand could not
longer hold out against an English army of seventeen thousand
trained troops, even though more Irish clans were attempting to
crash through from the other side. Tyrone and his Spanish recruits
were forced to fall back from Kinsale.

The dreamland hills of once peaceful Munster caught up the
shattered forces flying westward. Collins, in an old castle of Gortna-
cloghy, joined the chaplain, Father Archer. To meet a brother-
in-Christ at this juncture, joyously to experience the uplift of

mutual encouragement, softened the anguish of the defeat. The brother fell in as righthand man for the overworked priest. At the end of each day's effective coöperation in the work of Christ, splashed with sacrifice as it must have been, came the night's cauterizing hours of prayer.

English successes mounting, the risk of having capture cut short his priestly ministrations drove Father Archer eastward. Collins and he slipped down through beautiful Glengariff in mid June, climbed the rugged scars on the headland north of Bantry Bay, where Dunboy's gates cracked closed behind them.

Dunboy was now the eye of the nation, through it alone could the Irish see hope's fading outline. And in Dunboy, life was throbbing as violently as in a smashed fingertip. Collins, with doubly experienced skill, doctored up the weakened defenses and cared for the faithful defenders. From the ramparts, Commander Mac-Geoghegan and Collins carefully watched enemy forces swarming over the bulk of Beare Island just off shore. Hope leapt when a Spanish ship cut a wake toward the headland; lips again drew tight as its flag disappeared around the land's end. Now Beare Island began disgorging thousands near the base of the castle. British falcons began to blaze against besieged Dunboy.

"Collins," shouted Commander MacGeoghegan from the walls, "you get below and help my men who get stung by bullets. Up here, your black cassock is a number one target for fire."

Dominic was already bent over one of the first victims. Gently he laid the boy's arm over and around his own shoulders, and hustled the wounded lad across the platform toward the stairs. In the spray of stone chips that a cannon ball set flying, his head was bowed as if he already felt a martyr's crown settling surely upon it. He had long prayed for martyrdom. Dusty lips barely parted; no heart but God's heard the inner cry: "God give it. Or if it's too unworthy that I be, let works of charity, even here in Dunboy, win us His mercy."

Brother Collins was half-dragging his eighth bleeding, almost dead comrade down an inside passageway when a terrifying crash of stone and steel threw him against the wall. Screams and dust-choked groans were smothered as a cannon-battered turret collapsed, burying a pocket of Irish artillerymen. "Christ be with us," breathed Dominic. "Fast now, son, we'll be having God's plenty of work now."

By the time the first tower crumpled, the British barrage had been hammering for four hours against the walls. The priest had fled with O'Sullivan to get aid. MacGeoghegan, left in command, had long ago pressed every available man into the fighting. For his many wounded, there was no other relief but what Brother Collins could supply. The dying heard no lips but the Jesuit's, prompting a final act of love and contrition, a renewed profession of Faith.

After six hours' attack, the British ordnance had smashed the west front defense of Dunboy. Hundreds of attackers rushed in for the assault. The hopelessness of the struggle seeped through the very walls as the tide of fallen fighters flowed down to Collins. In sobs, the wounded Jago revealed the east post was weakening. It might hold for an hour yet, an hour and a half, but it could not last. Overwhelming English power was surging, now as if to crest the wall, now as if to crush it. Forty of his comrades, one veteran moaned, had in desperation tried an outbreak. All, every one of them, had gone down. Resistance was all but exhausted.

The setting sun that night crested the marred castle walls sadly, old MacGeoghegan felt, for it glowed not on the fine old familiar flag that had gloried there so long. High over the works, over mangled corpses and splotches of drying blood, an Irish wind furled the colors of Elizabeth.

Down into Dominic's inprovised cellar wards, quite suddenly, before he became aware of it, all that was left of the Irish forces came rushing, the living packed in there with the dead. There seventy-seven lives, trapped in a last hole of defense looked to Mac-Geoghegan for a commander's decision. Surrender would it be, or resistance till annihilation? MacGeoghegan, mortally shell-ripped, counting himself among the dying, judged that by opening negotiations an attempt should be made to save the remnants of his surrounded regiment.

And MacGeoghegan looked to the blackrobe. The Jesuit, by reason of his position as non-combatant, must be the man to carry word to Carew's forces. "Dominic," he asked, "will you go out to those devils? Say to them that my men surrender—surrender on condition that our lives be spared—but we will not stand to mercy —to English mercy—make that quite clear to them. Will you go in my stead?"

The question came, unexpected, to Collins as he was bending thoughtfully over a stretcher. In his noviceship days he had witnessed contagion like an acid burning ugly craters in the fleshy mass over which it boiled. Here, man's ageless penalty of suffering was cleancut as a sword, but equally cruel. It approached not as a feverish specter, but struck with cannon-ball directness. But, as a Jesuit, he was still pacing death's regions, whispering the Holy Name of Jesus to men drawing breath for the last time. High and worthy work!

MacGeoghegan had to repeat his petition: "Brother, will you act as mediator? Will you go to them in my name?"

A moment's pondering, not fearful, but thoughtful, worked the features of Collin's face. Here he was, a Jesuit, and that was sufficient warrant for the English to shoot on sight. A cassocked figure, coming even as a peaceful legate, might not prove secure against the recriminations of the priest-hunters. But more important, his going possibly would infuriate the English, would jeopardize the lives of all. Had the general considered that? He made known his thoughts to the dying commander.

MacGeoghegan left him free, but protested that the English could not dare so to violate diplomatic immunity, swore that there was no one he would rather entrust with such a mission than Dominic Collins.

The job of a peacemaker, Brother Collins knew, was one of those delicate and dangerous tasks that Christ commissioned His own to dare. He would go. Unafraid for what might happen to himself, he raised the white flag from the cellar, then lifted himself up through the opening in full view of the watching enemy.

That was the last MacGeoghegan saw of the Jesuit. Diplomatic immunity was shamelessly shunted aside. Even the granted guarantee of safety the besiegers violated. To have seized a Jesuit, Carew no doubt conjectured, would in the eyes of his countrymen shield him from the indelible stain of treachery. Collins was at once held, fit meat, presumably, to be thrown among the rats in the dungeon of Cork.

The history of the betrayed defenders of Dunboy is short. That night, strong guards continued watch over the cellar's exit. When, next morning, eighteen men came out and surrendered, Mac-Geoghegan, with the fierceness of a Brian Boru, took his position beside the nine barrels of powder and threatened to blow up the entire castle unless the English gave them all promise of life. The enemy retaliated with orders to open a new battery on the dugout and bury them all in ruins. The forty-eight Irish were now constrained to surrender unconditionally. Before the dying chieftain could stagger near enough to pitch a torch into the barrels of gunpowder, the English had entered the vault and quite expeditiously dispatched him.

Within a matter of days, crowds in the marketplace witnessed the execution of fifty-eight Irish victims. It was Carew's boast that out of Dunboy's one hundred and forty-three select fighting men, not a single one escaped, but all were either slain, buried in the ruins, or executed.

The great jaws of injustice were not yet crammed. The Jesuit prisoner at Cork knew they must soon close on him. Strangely, he was not loath to share the lot of his Dunboy compatriots, to face the same challenge thrown to Thomas More, Southwell, Campion, martyrs all.

The Lord President of Munster, in mid July, came riding into Cork. Dismounting, he descended from the scorched street down into the shadowed depths of the dungeon. There he attempted a smooth strain of friendliness.

"You're a light-hearted chap, Collins," he began. "I'm rather taken with you. You know, Her Majesty needs men with your education and experience. Did you ever think how you might use your talents in service to the state?"

Collins ignored him. How little of even natural nobility there was here, he thought.

Uninterrupted, Carew went on, "You want your life, I know, boy. And I've already taken steps to get you out. But you do realize, don't you, that you're in for the death sentence. All I can arrange as yet is a deferment of execution. But you yourself can do the rest. Come into service in our army. Use there, in Her Majesty's cause, your military skill and knowledge of Ireland. You know the leaders, you know the hideouts, and you are invaluable to us."

"You may as well proceed," was the downright reply, "with execution. I will in no way be drawn into any such service."

Shifting ground, Carew went on, "There's but one other hope for you then, sir. You profess to be something of a churchman already. Abjure the Papists and consent to the Queen's profession of faith. It will lead you to preferments in her Church. You might even get one of these Irish sees and settle down comfortably to an easy living. Refuse this, and the one alternative, you are aware, is your death."

"Death, then, let it be. All my life have I professed loyalty to His Holiness, the Pope at Rome. I have no intention of ever changing. And now, sir, if this discussion is over, please do me the favor of leaving me."

Left alone, Brother Collins slipped unperturbedly into his habitual practice of communing with God. He found it not so hard as he had anticipated to refuse what Carew regarded as "acceptable service," for his assignment would probably be nothing less than to cut the throat of O'Sullivan Beare or O'Sullivan Mor. That was too much like Judas' temptation to betray human blood in the service of the rulers.

His time approached when in October armed guards dragged Taylor past his cell to execution. That Irish chieftain had, like himself, persisted in refusing either to reveal the Irish plans or to enter into any collusion whatever with the foe, and so he was hanged in chains near the old north gate of Cork.

But for Collins a three and one half months' languishment in the seepy dungeon was broken only by questionings. A certain amount of prodding, commonly called torture, was plied to help the Irishman speak English. Sworn enemies of the Faith presiding, condemnation certain, the term trial must be elastically interpreted if applied. Through the trial, however, Dominic stood inflexible, professing openly that he was a Catholic, a member, too, of the Society of Jesus. To repeat his rejection of service in the English army, and to scorn servility in the Established Church was to aggravate the case. After protesting that he would never renounce either his conscience or his religious profession, the Brother reëntered his cell. It was now only a temporary stop-over on his way to the gallows.

But the government, for reasons of its own, was unwilling to sacrifice a man of Collins' calibre without a final effort. Tearful family appeals, they were aware, always rasp the surface of a tender heart. A trio of near relatives, therefore, soon faced the barred prisoner, and pictured the grief that flowed down the cheeks of a lonely old woman in Youghal. She had buried her face in her meager gray hooded cloak when they told her of her son's imprisonment. She loved him so. They hoped he would spare her. Would he not save her the pain, and save from opprobrium the Collins' name, illustrious in Ireland for generations past? By a mere word he could feign allegiance to the Queen; once free, he could drop the harmless pretense, they suggested, and make his escape to the continent.

His mother, framed against the door back home, seemed to stand before him. She must sorrow deeply, his heart told him. But he knew what course her Faith and constancy would have him choose. Neither he nor she would ever jettison all Christ's mystery of salvation by snatching the hem of the Queen's heresy-spun garment. His answer must be, No. Not the coldness, but the firmness of the cell's steel bars was in his voice: "No, what I am I must ever, even to death, profess myself to be."

The Jesuit was not astonished when the final sentence rang through the hall against him. Expecting no better, he heard the decree with composure, a composure suffused with joy: he was to be hanged, his entrails torn from out his living body, his corpse cleaved and quartered.

Such cheerful unconcern his enemies viewed as a challenge to their rage. It maddened them, this masterful self-possession. No longer now did they leave Dominic unmolested in his cell where rough fellow inmates acknowledged his guiltlessness and caught from his prayerful, encouraging lips the echoes of an ancient faith. They anticipated the end with days of unavailing torture. Official irritation flamed the more fiercely; but heaped-up sufferings did not smother the Jesuit's fire. It was prelude to martyrdom for him, heaven was already touching his burning fingertips.

Before the designated time, even on the Lord's day, the persecutors readied the gallows. On that brisk fall Sunday, the last of October—last October Sunday, incidentally, for the ageing Queen as well as for Collins—Cork prison gates heavily swung open to let the young cassocked prisoner, age thirty-five, pass through. Through the assembled populace, officers hustled him on his death-march to Youghal, the city of his birth. This time he viewed Youghal with hands lashed together behind him, and a halter dragging at his neck. His old parish church, now not many blocks away, hurled a long shadow toward him in the morning sunlight. The little Jesuit school of his boyhood days stood near too; and his home, now confiscated. Home, school, church, three-ribbed cradle of his vocation, now stood as sentinels for the birth of a martyr.

Lips of old friends he saw moving in prayer for him. One loving, tearless face was looking heavenward from the poor gray hood. Many were the loved and long-remembered sights that glowed about him, all unable, however, to diminish the central impression that beyond these, the arms of gallows stretched out toward him. Was it not, he mused, much like this for his Master Christ, as He long ago stumbled over Jerusalem's streets, was shadowed by the great temple, encircled by mobs of enemies and a scattering of loyal friends, yet steadfastly pressed through them all to reach His oft-dreamed-of Calvary?

Arrived at Youghal's gibbet of execution, Collins faced the somber structure resolutely and, dropping to his knees, touched his lips to one of the rough beams. Still on bended knees, he uttered a soulful prayer for his country, for the Queen, and all his enemies. A final craving for God's mighty assistance now that his hour had come, and Collins set his foot upon the step to ascend the scaffold.

Then, from the ill-constructed platform at the top, the Jesuit silently gazed a last farewell. The ocean breeze caught his cassock and threw great leaping shadows over the upturned faces. Suddenly, sensing the opportunity, as from a pulpit he spoke:

"You, who are my friends, we must look up to heaven. Your ancestors and mine, not a few of them, have given their lives in bold profession of the Faith. It is ours, now in our turn, to do the same, to uphold that Faith to our last breath. It is in the defense of our Catholic Faith that I wish to lay down my life."

So eager did he seem to swing into heaven on the death-rope looped around his throat. The crowd in part heard his words, in part were taken with wonderment at the mere sight of the figure above them. Simple Irish folk, plain and genuine as their country's moorlands or hills, gazed at a nobleman, one of their own, about to leave life as he had left title and fortune. Soldiers there, not doubting the sincerity they witnessed, wondered would they with such fearlessness face attack on their country and their faith. A small knot of foreign agents stood glaring at the man whom not all Elizabeth's power could swerve. Above them all there remained standing the Jesuit Brother, loyal to Christ to the last, exhorting his compatriots to remain unshaken in their attachment to the ancient Faith and to their allegiance to the Roman Pontiff. The defense of such a cause, they heard him saying, was glory.

It was glory and death. The Commandant, seeing the crowd swayed, bellowed, "Push him! Throw him off the ladder!"

A sudden, abrupt fall, and the rope snapped taut. It broke. The victim's large frame hit the ground. The frayed rope, sufficiently strong to have done its fatal work, trembled loosely above him. Deep searchings for breath were evidenced by the heaving breast. Without delay, disemboweling followed, and butcherly quartering. The blood-bespattered executioner, last of all, stood supporting the martyr's heart in his palm, and grotesquely chanting the popular formula: "God save the Queen."

# A Watch on Majorca

BY JEROME F. DIEMERT, S.J.

*Brother Alphonsus Rodriguez, S.J. (1531–1617)*
Declared a Saint 1888

$S$ URELY ALPHONSUS RODRIGUEZ, the Saint, will stand out from among the men presented in this volume like an old acquaintance in a crowd. Or so a fond fellow-Jesuit might hastily suppose. Actually, it is to be feared that Alphonsus has remained principally a family possession and secret of his order, a domestic hero. With a kind of obstinate, death-surviving humility he has shied away from proper recognition.

He began by keeping himself out of the records of his day. In the copious archives of the Spanish Jesuits over the period in which he was a chief glory of his province and a subject for pious talk in its houses, there are only two meager notices of him, remarking soberly that he was "very exemplary" and a "very good religious." And even when his hour of earthly celebrity did arrive—when he was elevated to sainthood in 1888—he shared the honors with (among others) two more of the Society of Jesus, Peter Claver and John Berchmans, and public attention went rather to his distinguished companions in canonization than to him. Since that time very little has been written about him. Often enough he is regarded as mainly a character in somebody else's biography—namely, in St. Peter Claver's. Finally, there is indeed a Jesuit named Alphonsus Rodriguez who has won some measure of renown among Catholics, religious particularly. But he is not our saint at all, he is the writer of a classic treatise on Christian perfection. Because of this coincidence of names, when our saint does come to be heard of, he is apt to be promptly mistaken for that other, the good Father, his namesake. Altogether a self-effacing individual, this St. Alphonsus. But then, most probably what we are talking about is not *his* self-effacement but *our* neglect.

We may find something humanly odd in that neglect. Ought not the persistent hiddenness of the man be covering over a good story? For surely one might reasonably suspect the makings of a good story in the life of one who was a Spanish Jesuit saint and lived from 1531 to 1617.

Why so? Well, first of all there is the huge and sumptuous back-drop of the sixteenth century to pose our figure against. In the very year Alphonsus was born, Henry VIII was declaring himself supreme head of the Church in England and Pizarro was conquering Incas and gold and silver in Peru. The former event calls up what vast and violent changes were rocking old Christendom from within. The latter calls up what an expansive movement of human enterprise and mastery of earth was opening out to Europe a great modern age; the far Americas were now heaving up from the mysterious waste of ocean to lie on the western horizon and give shape and scope to the new dream.

Even had Alphonsus remained the merchant he started out to be, we could easily imagine a romantic career for him. This was an era when the merchant was growing into an imposing giant; he was an Antonio whose "argosies with portly sail" came bearing fortune to him from the ends of an earth stretched out and filled with buried treasure overnight.

Nor is our fancy checked when we learn that in fact Antonio literally closed up shop and walked off from temporal goods and turned Jesuit at forty. For the Jesuits of the period, in their eager headlong beginnings, and in an epoch when God was lavish of saints and heroes, were providentially made to rise to the historic occasion.

They were staying or turning back the broad bristling advance of Protestantism in the Germanies. They were lurking under disguises and in priest-holes and braving the pikes and Tyburn gallows in England to salvage some of Mary's Dowry.

Moreover, for the losses in Europe they were making up, adventurously, perilously, with far-flung missionary achievements in the new worlds lately discovered or unlocked to Westerners. In Alphonsus' time, there were Jesuits engaged after Cortez in a new conquest of Mexico—for Christ. There were Jesuits plunging into South America armed only with the crucifix, and organizing ferocious tribes into fantastic lost Arcadies of Christian states in the wilds there. There were Jesuits in India living as Brahmins or argu-

ing theology before the Great Mogul. There were Jesuits on the
trail of Marco Polo, carrying the faith into ancient China, where
they inveigled themselves into favor by the marvels of the music-
box and the clock. There were Jesuits being decapitated or hung on
crosses in Japan.

All in all, taking vows as a Jesuit at such a time could lead to
strange consequences, quite worth the chronicling. Not without
reason Jesuits have found their way into legends and novels.

Again, the promise of a story in Alphonsus' life may seem better
yet when we learn that not only was he a Jesuit of the period but
a Spaniard to boot. Surely we have only to remark casually that he
came into the Society the year (1571) in which the Turks had the
might of their galleys broken disastrously at Lepanto to weave a
richly colored immediate setting about him. Having recently concluded a long crusade of wresting her own home soil from the
Moor, Spain was now in the proud glory of her Golden Age. She
bestrode Europe like a Colossus and was building up an empire
overseas. Within her was working a great ferment of culture and
learning. Cervantes, for example, had mounted his "foolish knight"
upon Rosinante to wander the roads into history, and El Greco
was painting at Toledo. More of concern to ourselves, Spain was
producing great saints and mystics, like Teresa of Avila and John
of the Cross.

While naming the latter kind of names, we might go on to mention Ignatius of Loyola, founder of the Society of Jesus; Francis
Xavier, great Jesuit apostle of the Indies; Francis Borgia, grandee
and hobnobber with royalty, who created such a stir by demeaning
himself to the ranks of the raw little newcomer among religious
orders. And so on, down an impressive roster of early fathers and
heroes of the congregation that Spain cradled and so helped grow
and show power. Spanish Jesuits went out of their homeland to
do resounding work for Christ in Europe and on the new mission
fronts. They also participated eagerly and with distinction in the
movement of learning and culture within Spain. We may single out
Francis Suarez, theologian and political theorist, for one. A con-

temporary of Alphonsus, he died the same year Alphonsus died (1617).

Gradually, from taking in the broad world of the sixteenth century, our camera has swung down to center on Spain. Now, moving in toward a close-up of our subject, it comes to be trained on the island of Majorca, a possession of Spain well off her east coast in the Mediterranean. Here Alphonsus had almost all of his Jesuit career. This fresh detail may keep up our hopes of a story, inasmuch as the Majorca of that time was a kind of island fortress, with fierce Moslem corsairs out of Algiers constantly prowling the approaches to the mainland. Perhaps we might also remark the bitter feuds that made the island a house divided and perilous within itself. A good number of Alphonsus' prayers and holy victories went to assure safe passage for Jesuits to and from the mainland through the pirates, and to undo the dark and childish hatreds between local families.

But enough of background. It is high time we were going ashore on Majorca and searching out Alphonsus and his story.

Let us set our time of arrival about the close of the century. Our approach to the island is from the south, between two guardian capes into the shining Bay of Palma. Sliding past the old Moorish signal tower of Fort Carlos and Castle Bellver on its conical wooded hill, we drop anchor in among the ships before the white city of Palma. It is a city invitingly gracious with palms and gardens and set off by the mountains to the west. Though its dominating feature is the great Gothic cathedral hard by the quay, the ancient port is Oriental in appearance as well as in brooding memories: all those steeples are like minarets that thrust up from mosquelike buildings into the fiery-blue sky.

Once we are ashore, almost anybody—the viceroy himself, should he happen by—can tell us where to find this Jesuit Alphonsus Rodriguez. We are directed up through the narrow twisting streets to the high part of the city and the Jesuit College of Montesion. We knock on the college gate, and it is swung open to us by the very person we have come seeking!

Doubtless we are taken aback at the sight of this bald and wizened old man, bent far over with age and infirmity, looking his serene welcome at us out of a startlingly deathlike (but not unsightly) countenance. That face is an old and strange record: a face with nobility enough in its arched aquiline nose and finely shaped forehead, but seamed with wrinkles, its bearded jaws sunken and toothless, and—most remarkable—its eyes even now brimming with the inevitable tears that have inflamed them and made bright permanent traces down the cheeks.

When we said that the man to greet us was Alphonsus Rodriguez, we were not merely taking a liberty of imagination. We had excellent reason to be sure it would be he. For—the horrid truth will out—at this time (around 1600) as over thirty of his some fifty years in religion, the great Jesuit saint, whose rank was that of "temporal coadjutor," held the position of college doorkeeper. It is to set down most of the outward incident of his Jesuit life to say that hour after hour, day after day, week after week, month after month, year after year, decade after decade, Alphonsus walked to and from a door which he opened to let folk in and out, or went about the college with the messages that came to this busy doorway. There, one might say, goes our story!

Indeed, a journalist might well flounce away in disgust at this point. But we shall stay and have a tale out of this old man yet. As will presently be seen, we have not been writing a grandiose preface to a story that does not exist, nor conjured up a vision of world-shaking Jesuit endeavor in order to shame the insignificant saint of a porter. What has gone before will work into what comes after. And in making the connection we shall by that very fact be interpreting the life of any ordinary Jesuit brother of today, who may be polishing a candlestick while his ordained fellow in religion is declaiming from some high pulpit. Alphonsus is not just an individual but a divinely selected type.

Nevertheless, for the moment we may well look with a secular eye at the contrast between what other Spanish Jesuits of the period were about and what Alphonsus was niggling at. With a purpose we may allow ourselves to feel the embarrassment, for a brisk and enterprising American, of having to write up Alphonsus; of having, in a sense, to make excuses for him as one might for his patched cassock and simple ways.

Yet hardly have we finished explaining carefully and apologetically that there is little humanly worth telling about in Alphonsus' history, than we must turn about and explain quite as carefully and apologetically that his life was one long succession of extraordinary events, events that will sound at first to a sober everyday citizen like the stuff of fairy tales. And that brings up an embarrassing difficulty of a contrary kind in writing of him.

It comes to us, not out of popular legend, which might be benevolent fabrication, but out of the solemn, painstaking memoirs of Alphonsus himself, that he was a peer of John of the Cross in receiving mystical graces. What is more, these graces included the spectacular kind of thing, like apparitions and prophetic illuminations, that is outside the solid substance of even mystical life and granted to the relatively few. Thus, for example, he would see different-colored roses materialize before him as he said his beads. Once, when toiling up the hill to the Castle of Bellver, Our Lady appeared to him and wiped away the sweat from his brow with her handkerchief. And so forth.

Again, from one end of his religious life to the other, especially in the night, Alphonsus received, as visible callers and tormentors, very devils out of hell. This also is on the written word of the man himself, a man as truthful as the saint that he was and instinctively distrustful of such visionary goings-on.

What a disconcerting contrast is to be found, then, within the very life of our subject! It is as though we saw one who by day was a ragged beggar on the street swaggering into the opera in formal dress and a top hat by night. Or as though a mild and commonplace clerk were found to be keeping a leopard in his flat as a house pet.

That is not quite all either. There are mannerisms of holiness and mortification in Alphonsus that we common-sense folk may find difficult to swallow. As difficult, say, as the rotten egg, for example, which he bolted down when it was served him by mistake, or the earthenware dish which he tried (as we shall see) to crumble and masticate on a certain occasion. What disgusting foolishness (you may ask) is this?

Well, let us deal with the problems as the proper moment arrives. Let us now begin at a beginning and see if we cannot make a story and something agreeably understandable of the old man who surprised us at the college gate. After having spoken with him and those that know and loved him, we may well feel that he is an old secret of the Society of Jesus too good to be kept to itself.

In 1531 (quite probably), on July 25th, the feast of the great patron of the land, St. James, Alphonsus Rodriguez was born to Diego Rodriguez and Maria Gomez de Alvarado as their third child—third of eleven as it happily turned out.

The birthplace was Segovia, a very old and storied city built on a plateau standing up from the bleak Castilian plain. Over nearby mountain slopes there moved flocks of sheep, whose wool the Segovians made into cloth famous in Europe. Quite the man of his town, the father of Alphonsus prospered as a wool merchant, and Alphonsus himself was to carry on his father's business for a very considerable part of his long life.

There was a lingering memory in Segovia of one Iñigo Loyola who had stopped there and made some lasting acquaintances. By the time Alphonsus was born, Iñigo was attending the University of Paris and attracting followers in his high enterprise for Christ. Among them were his room-mates, Francis Xavier, a fellow Basque, and Peter Faber, a former shepherd lad of Savoy.

Since he had the good fortune to be born into an ardently Catholic family, it is not too surprising that the little Alonso (Spanish for Alphonsus) exhibited just such early marks of piety as writers of the lives of saints are apt to dwell on with relish and unduly. For our part, we cannot refrain from mentioning the devotion he so notably showed Our Blessed Mother from his first years. When he came into possession of a picture of her, he would hide it next to his heart. And at times he would fix his bright dark eyes as though on somebody present and pray earnestly to Our Lady at the very top of his shrill young voice.

It was on an autumn evening in 1541, when Alphonsus was ten years old and the Society of Jesus (to reckon its age from its confirmation by the Holy See) but one year old, that the Society walked into Segovia and the life of Alphonsus in the person of Blessed Peter Faber. Peter, accompanied by another priest (Dr. Ortiz) not a Jesuit, was in town to give an informal mission. But first he came to the yellow house of Diego Rodriguez, the wool merchant, in the Little Market Square under the great ancient aqueduct they called the Devil's Bridge, to beg lodging during the days of preaching and catechizing. Characteristically, Diego and Maria were overjoyed at the chance of welcoming two such venerable vagabonds into the hospitality of their home. Ever afterward the memory of that visit was to be as cherished a family belonging as the chair the holy Peter had used, henceforth too sacred a memento and relic to be sat in?

Following the mission in Segovia, Diego prevailed on his guests to enjoy the relaxation of a retreat at the family's country villa, and dispatched young Alphonsus with them to attend to their needs. Of course this arrangement, which was so fortunate for Alphonsus, bringing him into familiar contact as it did with a saintly, gracious Jesuit and intimate of Ignatius, one who might give him knowledge of the Society of Jesus and enkindle his boy's piety to something better and more promising, was God's rather than Diego's. Later God would make an external grace of Alphonsus in his turn for the benefit of other young Jesuits or Jesuits-to-be, like that other Peter who became a saint when Alphonsus did.

During the sojourn in the country, Alphonsus learned from Peter, among other things, how to say the rosary. The rosary was to figure largely in his life. After his death it would be remarked how calloused his forefinger and thumb were from having so often made the little journey of prayer over the round of the fifty beads. Meantime, however, he would still have to wait for another Jesuit after Faber to educate him to the deeper uses of the rosary.

When the time of retreat was at an end and the two priests bestowed a final blessing on the family that had extended them hospitality, and made off, they left a desolate youngster behind. The wistful eyes of Alphonsus saw something of himself walking out of his life as Father Peter strode away over the plaza in his black soutane and wide-brimmed hat, to go about his continental business of salvation.

And yet within a few years the Jesuits were in Alphonsus' life again, although this time he had to seek them out. Since his parents had heard that the Jesuits had opened a college of their own at the great new University of Alcalá, they determined to send Alphonsus and his older brother Diego there. So the boys struck off for their higher education and arrived in Alcalá to find Jesuit "college" a euphemism for a miserable house that the former owner had literally been glad to give away. But there was compensation inside that appalling place worth travelling after in the rather surprising shape of Brother Villanueva, the unordained Scholastic in charge there. For all the peasant ungainliness of his short dark person, this young Jesuit had a spiritual attractiveness that was by now no secret but a wide inspiration to students and professors at Alcalá. From Villaneuva Alphonsus received the kind of schooling that was lastingly to count with him. For the scholar's kind the simple though practically shrewd lad had neither the bent nor the intelligence. And presently he no longer had the opportunity either.

This for a tragic reason. Within the very twelve-month of their arrival at Alcalá, the two boys were summoned home to Segovia and to a sad transformation of their former life. Their father Diego had died. When the family, bewilderingly without its late patriarch, cast about for a plan for its future, it was decided that Diego, the elder brother with the head for studies and professional success, should continue his university training, but that Alphonsus should help his mother carry on the family business of the wool shop.

Alphonsus was fifteen, but the boy in him was suddenly become a man.

At this very time in Rome, Ignatius Loyola was finding it necessary to establish another grade in his order, that of temporal coadjutor or lay brother. Men of this grade, in every way true religious and Jesuits, were to be busy about the many things of household management, thus freeing the rest for the one thing necessary of wholly spiritual labor. Of course, the prosaic manual work and the prayer of the brothers were meant themselves, not to stay at home, but to make for the success of the others' endeavor abroad and share in its divine honors and rewards.

Who would have thought, when Ignatius was creating this new rank of Jesuit, that the young Alphonsus of Segovia was in God's intention to be the great type and model of Jesuit brothers, the living rule of their grade? Rather, it seemed as though he were committing himself to a quiet lifetime of honorable industry as a merchant.

Year after year, the years all reeling away gradually like the wool being forever spun in the hand-looms of the factories of Segovia, Alphonsus purchased bolts of cloth for his shelves and took them down again to sell them. On reaching his majority of twenty-three years, he became at length legal head of the business. Though continuing his growth in piety, and practising so generous an honesty that errand boys sent to his shop were under orders to deal with him personally, he certainly made the business pay, and this in spite of days of economic unsteadiness. Alphonsus' whole character was to do a job well, whether for God or in bargaining with men.

In his twenty-sixth year, he fell in with the desires of his mother and courted and won the hand of Maria Suarez of neighboring Pedraza. The newlyweds moved into a house of their own. In time God blessed their union with three children: two boys, Gaspar and Alonso, and a girl, Maria. And when shortly after the marriage the Jesuits established a college in town and Alphonsus was able to have a spiritual director much to his liking and profit in Father Louis

Santander, rector of the college, life seemed to be shaping up ideally for the young man. Actually, only four years of such happiness and peace were to gather before tragedy began rending its way in, so that a new story of Alphonsus was in the making.

First two of his children—his oldest, Gaspar, and the light of his eyes, little Maria—and then his young wife, took sick and died. Nor did his mother survive long to be of comfort to him in his sorrows. The world of Alphonsus lay in shambles about him; in his early thirties, he was a widower with one small son.

At length his comfort was to descend from God. But God, ever a surprising person, had a strange way of bringing comfort. It was to make the temporal sorrow of Alphonsus the occasion for another more terrible sorrow, one infinitely more upsetting to his existence.

As Francis Borgia, who had recently preached in Segovia, was put on his way to discarding a dukedom for service with Christ by seeing what death had done to the regal features of Isabella, so Alphonsus found that the effect of the deaths in his household, of the vision of what fragile stuff time is, was to make him turn a startled glance full on eternity. And when his look came back to himself, he who had lived piously was profoundly horrified at his sins and the wasteful disorderliness of his life. His first "conversion" had taken place. This is something hard for us, with out comfortable nearsightedness in regard to God's holiness, with the shuffling compromises of our religious observance, to distinguish from fanaticism.

Alphonsus set himself to pray and to do penance as he never had before. He frequented the sacraments, being permitted to do the thing, unusual for his time, of receiving communion every Sunday and holy day. Eventually he found he must be about one person's business only, God's. Accordingly, with the approval of Father Santander, he gave up his wool trade, gathered together his savings and inheritance, and set up as a sort of hermit in the old Rodriguez house in the Little Market Square. His two holy sisters, Antonia and Juliana, who were to live just such a life to the end of their days, and who deserve to be by themselves( had we space) a story within a story, kept house for him and looked after his child Alonso. The boy was not a charge for long; soon he followed his mother, brother and sister into the grave. With the falling of this last blow, Alphonsus was free for God's purposes.

We do not know what previous graces of an extraordinary nature had come to Alphonsus. But two remarkable visions stand at the outset of his new life. In one, that showed Our Lord and twelve saints, St. Francis of Assisi—Alphonsus' patron, we are happy to say (there are Franciscan qualities in our Jesuit brother!)—stepped out from the group to ask him why he wept. He answered that it was for the gravity of his sins, seeing that even one venial sin is matter aplenty for a lifetime of tears.

In the other vision, a dove with I.H.S. in silver lettering on its breast flew into a dense high column of black and clamorous birds, tearing them to pieces. When the latter dream was brought to Father Santander for his prayerful inspection, he interpreted it to mean that Alphonsus would enter the Society of Jesus and that in it he would suffer many assaults on his virtue, from which, however, he would by Christ's help come away victorious.

For about three years, Alphonsus went through the grimmer and more external stage of the purgatory which lies just inside the gate of the way to real sanctity. He was preoccupied with bewailing his sins and with fiercely punishing himself for them, meanwhile frequenting the sacraments and practising vocal prayer. Then, as is normal, he entered on a happier, more interior stage of getting intimately acquainted with his God, and this largely through the exercise of mental prayer.

Very fittingly, it was the rosary, whose mysteries Father Santander now taught him to meditate while his lips were busy with the prayers said on the beads, that was to be the instrument of this new progress. Alphonsus' mother, wife and daughter were all happily named Mary. But it was Mary Immaculate herself who was after God and in God the great love and influence of his life. Besides spending by now four hours daily over his rosary, he had long

had the habit of doing the round of churches dedicated to Our
Lady. He began his practice of frequent communion on one of her
feasts. He was favored with communications from her. In an important apparition she, attended by his guardian angel and his
patron St. Francis, took his soul in her hands and presented it to
the Eternal Father. Once, when he had had the boldness to declare
that he loved her more than she him, she retorted promptly that it
was quite the other way around.

Among the mysteries he encountered along the circle of his
beads, Alphonsus quickly took special affectionate interest in Our
Lord's Passion. He was even allowed to feel a certain bodily participation in it. This kind of grace is of a piece with the other often
sensible and consoling favors that were lavished on him through
the years before he entered religion and even up till his first vows.
After the latter would come a terrible new purgation, God's doing
then and not the mere efforts of a whip in Alphonsus' own hand;
out of that purgation would come a maturer, brighter sanctity.

It should be mentioned further that with the more interior
spiritual progress of the last days in the world went an increasing
zeal for the souls Christ was in agony to save. In God's design Alphonsus was a great Jesuit missionary—but in a typically brother's
way, as a stay-at-home; largely by offering up, not the journeyings
over the globe of a Xavier, but interminable erratic footsteps about
a college on porter's errands. We may see a likeness here to the
Little Flower, the Carmelite who paradoxically earned the honor of
being, with Xavier, Patron of the Missions. It is in Therese's life
also that she won grace for missionaries by offering up footsteps
she took in a cloister garden.

Father Santander had foreseen a Jesuit career for Alphonsus.
After six years of penitential life in the world, at the age of thirty-
eight, Alphonsus attempted for the first time to make that fore-
vision come true. By now Father Santander had left Segovia and
Castile for Valencia, the garden city on the Mediterranean coast.
But Alphonsus' new director, Father Martinez, also emboldened
him to his project and tried to secure his admission—to no avail.

Not only was this Alphonsus Rodriguez too far along in age, but also, mostly by reason of his ruthless austerities, he was in a wasted, precarious state of body. No saints in that condition need apply, thank you.

But Alphonsus was not to be so easily driven off. Putting his affairs at home in order, leaving behind the remainder of his goods to be the support of his sisters, and fortified by a determination that another life *should* begin for him at forty, he set out for Valencia and for his old friend Father Santander. From the latter he got the fresh encouragement he needed and the advice to prepare himself to be received for Jesuit priesthood by resuming higher studies at the Jesuit College of St. Paul. And so, astonishingly, very like Ignatius Loyola before him, who at thirty-nine had sat on benches with children at Barcelona to learn some Latin, Alphonsus, even older than his accumulating years, went to school again. Meantime he was able to keep alive by alms and some tutoring positions that were got for him. But this preposterous venture of school was not to last. Not to mention the other difficulties, Alphonsus simply did not have the head for this bookish learning. Finally, Father Santander, along with Alphonsus, had to bow to the inevitable; he advised his spiritual son to seek entrance into the Society as a temporal coadjutor.

Just before this, however, Alphonsus was very nearly diverted from the Society of Jesus by a whim of his own—not that the devil may not have had a hand and cloven foot in it. An acquaintance of Alphonsus, apparently a likeminded one, became a hermit and was anxious to have Alphonsus take to the hills after his example. On a school holiday, Alphonsus paid the new solitary a visit and was subjected again to something more than persuasion to come and do likewise. Yet he would not before returning to Valencia and laying open the whole matter to Father Santander. The good priest, exercised at the disclosure, gravely told him that he feared for his soul's salvation because of the self-will he had manifested in following his own secret bent in this affair. Smitten to the heart by the warning, Alphonsus went on his knees before his director and made a solemn promise that never again would he do his own will. In this abrupt and generous resolve was enclosed his whole future religious life and glory.

When Alphonsus tried once more to gain admission to the Society of Jesus, this time as a lay brother, it seemed he was going to meet again with rebuff, and final rebuff. The same objections raised by the Jesuits of Segovia swarmed up against him. But at length, the Provincial, Father Cordeses, brushing aside the advice of his surprised consultors, announced: "Well, Fathers, I have had a talk with Alonso, and examined carefully into his life and purpose, and I really feel obliged to admit him as a saint. For I intend he shall be one, and a great one, and he will give great glory to the Society by his virtues and example." Alphonsus was in. The next day, in fact, he was taken into the Jesuit college as a novice.

There is a sequel to the incident of the hermit. On the very night of the day Alphonsus was admitted into the Society, his erstwhile friend came to his new lodging and banged on the shutters of his ground-floor room. When he put back the shutters, Alphonsus was greeted by a face contorted with rage and a noisy outpouring of abuse. He fastened the shutters again, leaving the hermit out in the dark.

Of Alphonsus' novitiate there is not much to tell. Spiritually, it was largely a continuation and deepening of the tranquil progress he had known in recent years. Six months of his noviceship he spent right in Valencia. Here it was that he made the Spiritual Exercises of St. Ignatius that steeped him in the full spirit of the order he had joined. Making them in view of the role he was committed to in religion, he determined to keep forever busy, outside of the time required for spiritual duties, at menial work. Henceforward he was Christ's handyman.

During this period his hatred for his body grew, though his opportunities to maltreat it diminished. The novice master saw to it that his previous austerities were cut down, even if what remained seems considerable enough to us. Alphonsus had to begin now what would become his joyful lifelong custom of asking monthly per-

mission to practise corporal penance. This permission, as eagerly
sought as some monthly allowance of money or candy, will doubtless look to many a modern like a license for gradual suicide.

Indeed, now that we have brought the matter up again, it will be
well to say an explanatory word about the mortification Alphonsus
was so given to from the beginning to the end of his life, when he
became so feeble he had to beg others to take the scourge to him.
The scandalous affair of the rotten egg, already alluded to, is involved here. Not to mention the business of the bitter and sickening gourds served up to the community on another occasion.
Alphonsus, the first to have a chance at the dish, had his gourd
eaten and was scraping his plate before the next man could literally
get wind of the situation and cry out, "There's poison in the pot!"

It is a fearful thing to fall into the hands of the living God—not
only as a sinner to be judged, but also as a candidate for holiness.
Once a man sets his face resolutely toward heaven—comes to react
sensibly, that is, to the Good News which is the Gospel—God in-
spires him to wage a strange civil war in which his soul is pitted
against his body and senses, and even against his inmost spiritual
self. Moreover, not content with this incitement of a person to
self-immolation, God may apply mysterious purgatorial fires of
his own to the soul. Further, he may permit or bring it about that
outward things and persons conspire annoyingly or viciously
against the peace and happiness of his chosen one.

In reading an account of a saint's life, we expect as a matter of
course to reach a chapter wherein the hero is shown—often following a period in which his activity went on smoothly and prosper-
ously—to be misunderstood, contradicted, ill-handled even by his
well-meaning friends and by pious folk. The fact must be honestly
faced up to: God is no more gentle in his treatment of his saints-to-
be than he was with regard to his own Son. Whatever is posted to
heaven must be stamped with the sign of the cross.

Probably we can understand mortification well enough provided
it be strictly penance, a scouring off of the traces of sin that remain
even after sacramental absolution. The satisfaction yet owing to

God fittingly takes the form of making pain of the creatures one turned to as rivals of God, and of chastising the body one pandered to by sinning. And certainly the crookedness of passion and will which is the dangerous after effect of sin can be hammered straight again only by mortification.

But really serious mortification cuts more deeply even than to the roots of personal sin. It is a ferocity of self-denial that cannot be understood until we remember that the body we have inherited has the birthmark of original sin. A Christian hatred of the body is an enlightened love of the body. Corporal penances aim, not at the suicidal effect of separating the body from the soul, but at drawing the body closer to the soul again as the obedient partner it is supposed to be. And that is benevolently to seek the true honorable interests of the body. Enslaved by Adam, the body was redeemed by Christ. Accordingly, our love of it is also redemptive and so, paradoxically, turns into mortification. That means causing the grace received at baptism to soak down from the soul through all our fleshy being, healing and transfiguring and making Christ of everything.

Still, not enough has been said. A saint begins by mortifying his body, but advances to a more terrible, rending sacrifice, the annihilation of all self-will. "Nothing, Nothing, Nothing" is the legend that John of the Cross sets over the path of the perfect that goes steeply up Mount Carmel. It is the true development and satisfaction of the created person to lose himself in God, in Christ, painful business though it may be to do so.

Now at length we hold the master-key to all the astonishing, even revolting mortifications and self-abasements of men like Alphonsus. The carryings-on of a lover are apt to appear sheer lunacy unless it is realized that they are the expression of love. A saint is earnestly involved in a romance with God. He loves himself and all creatures well enough to love them for God's sake alone. The divine love and substance is consuming him gradually into itself, while onlookers may see only the havoc thus wrought in the independent self, the searing, charring effects of the invisible flame.

Finally, if we are to give to self-denying love we have been talking about the concrete form it lives under in the present divine scheme of things, we must put the crucifix into the hand of the saint in our picture. Then, too, we shall discover the apostolic implications of that love. And then only shall we come to the last reason for mortification beyond reason, in the mystery of oneness with Christ Crucified.

The grace that was in Our Lord, who came with the name of Jesus, Savior, was a force that sped him on toward the Cross as his goal. And the grace we have from Christ enfolds the characteristic inclinations of that Redeemer-grace as the blood a son has from a father moves him to be his father over again. Christ's Calvary merited salvation for all humankind, the Christian's Calvary applies that salvation. The more the saints grow in holiness, the more and more is Christ in their veins, divinely impatient to be again baptized with his bloody baptism. Their own prudence and that of their confessors must forever strain at their desire of the Cross to keep it from plunging them to excess and folly. Even so, they are apt to be moved and allowed to do things that will pass for folly in the world. And certainly we, their admirers, even though our flesh as well as spirit be willing and strong, shall not safely dare to follow them in many of their actions—unless, of course, under divine inspirations of our own and with submission to spiritual direction.

The digression on mortification was a considerable one. Yet it was needed to make sense of Alphonsus in that self-immolation that constitutes the inner substance of his life. With him, as typically with brothers, that immolation is reduced to stark and simple terms. It is kept domestic and personal and is not permitted to "flash off exploit" and catch the world's eye.

We left Alphonsus in Valencia doing the first six months of his noviceship. At the end of that period he was put on a boat to go finish his noviceship and his life in the new Jesuit college on Majorca. There he was to be entirely cut off from Spain, his dear ones, his old life, not mainly by the waters between or the Algerian corsairs who infested them, but by the joyous self-exile of a will made Christ's through obedience. For a time, indeed, there was danger that this aging novice, already spent and tottering, would be sent back to the mainland and the banalities of secular existence. But after some understandable hesitation, it was decided to have him close better than two years of novitiate with his first vows.

Now came a decade or so of probation while the Society made up its deliberate mind whether or not to keep him for good. And meantime God arranged a special probation of his own that stretched, like a desert road harried by bandits, from Alphonsus' first to last vows. The consolations that had formerly rained out of heaven were now pent up. The lower nature Alphonsus might have fancied dead and buried came roaringly alive and struck at him, furiously and incessantly. God permitted Satan to try this man as, anciently, he had tried Job to see of what stuff his sanctity was made. The devils, literally in person, were let fall upon this poor brother, filling him with indescribable pain during his morning meditation and crowding his cell with horrors at midnight. He suffered lurid temptations against purity, innumerable scruples concerning his past and present life, apprehension of being turned out of the Society, fears of death and hell, diabolical apparitions and physical assaults.

Who would have imagined there was all this horrible and fantastic drama in the life of the decrepit and pottering coadjutor-brother, outwardly taken up as he was with the trifling humdrum of duties in kitchen and refectory, of assisting the brother mason on the new church, of attending the fathers on their ministerial rounds? Or rather, one might have suspected something. For the countenance of Alphonsus wore such an emaciated look of death that the students dubbed him Brother Anointed—the brother that has (actually he had not) received extreme unction and is mortally done for.

There was light in all this darkness, however, and a happy ending to come. Not only the devils but also Our Lord and Our Lady put in a personal appearance and comforted him. Much help came to him from the recitation of the Little Office of the Immaculate Conception. He seems to have begun reciting it at this time, but thereafter he continued at it so faithfully and recommended it so urgently in and out of the Society that he contributed appreciably to its spread in the world, thereby fulfilling a true important mission of promoting belief in the dogma, not then of settled faith, which it enshrined.

With the aid of Mary, therefore, and of her Son, and by virtue of his own unwavering fidelity, Alphonsus won free of his troubles. A holy serenity now possessed him and vastly improved his health, so that superiors were willing to give him his final vows. God and the Jesuits had quite definitively set their mark of approval upon him—although there would be other trials near the end.

Perhaps a divine crown to all this Dark Night he had just emerged from, and to his new coming of age spiritually, may be made of a vision he had a few years later on. It constitutes an experience that is no oddity in the records of mysticism. Christ and the Blessed Virgin came to his cell at night. So far nothing quite unique for him! The same august pair visited him on other occasions, making a heaven for the moment of that miserable, bare room—bare even to wanting a chair, so that Alphonsus must seat himself on his plank of a bed. This time, however, Christ entered into the brother's heart and Mary placed a second heart she had borne along in his right side and entered into it. May we not find in this vision an anticipation of the devotion to the Sacred Hearts of Jesus and Mary that would in time be entrusted to the Society? Apart from the apparition, we discover instances in the brother's writings of his attraction to the Heart of the Crucified.

Allusion has just been made for the first time to the writings of Alphonsus. Under obedience he set down his spiritual autobiography, admitting to the wonderful favors that have therefore to go into an honest account of him, and (more to his liking) recorded the thoughts on religious life that welled up from his prayers. What he wrote on were odd scraps of paper picked up around the house, which he religiously asked leave to use. Eventually these scraps, ennobled by the perversely scratchy quill which he would not exchange for a better, accumulated to make an author of him and have since been published in three volumes. From the sincere, homely pages of this work comes a charm and beauty that goes with the thoughts of a saint artlessly breaking through language, showing him as the ingenuous and captivating person that he was.

But to return to the events of Alphonsus' life. This time we have arrived at the point of being able to put into one sentence virtually the significant whole of his remaining years. Toward the close of the period of awful trial, and precisely in order to give him some saving distraction, he was made doorkeeper or hall porter at Montesion. At last we have gotten Alphonsus to his gate, his doorway to heaven, to the post at which he is rightly best known for having served with diligent monotony throughout a generation's time. Here he kept the sort of vigilant watch the Master had called for in one of his Parables. And seeing Alphonsus as a kind of sentry in a war none the less real for being spiritual, we may give a martial meaning to his long watch on Majorca.

He laid careful plans for acquitting himself divinely well at his new employment. There has come down in his own writings how he would hark to the summons of the bell as to God's voice (*Behold I stand at the door and knock!*); how he would open as to Our Lord —and by way of consolation, Our Lord did actually come calling, attended by Our Lady and angels! (*I will come in to him*); how he would not allow himself to feel impatient at violent tuggings on the bell; how he would never tell a father to whom he brought a message how long or deviously he had been tracking him down. And so forth. Out of what might seem petty meticulosity a saint was forming.

Perhaps the students at the college did not always appreciate his conscientiousness; one of his jobs as porter was to ring the bell for class, which he did with unfailing, clanging promptitude! Fortunately his conscientiousness *was* appreciated when on one occasion he kept a distinguished party of lordly ecclesiastics and town officials cooling their heels for a bit outside the gate. Precisely in order that these fine folk might be sure of accommodation at a college entertainment, it had been decided not to admit the populace before a certain hour. When bishop, viceroy and the rest arrived in advance of the appointed time, Alphonsus politely but firmly abided by what he understood were his orders and shut them out. To the relief of the rector, they chose to be edified.

During all the years of answering his door, Alphonsus found time for various little works of zeal. He gathered children about him in the entrance hall to teach them catechism. When the boys' Sodality was organized, he urged the students to join, and after that kept them up to their engagements by reading them spiritual books, teaching them the Little Office and the rosary, and giving them sound instruction either in a group of individually, often enough in the form of written advice. Naturally he was attracting candidates to the Society (though he did not make a practice of suggesting his own order to those who felt the call to religion) and brought them in already well on in their training.

The adult Majorcans did not fail to profit from this remarkable brother either. At the bidding of superiors or because he would be piously tricked into coming by being asked to carry in a needed box, Alphonsus was often present at meetings of the men's Sodality and was prevailed upon to give inspiring little talks. In time, others about town came seeking him, to be simply edified by looking or to obtain his saintly, shrewd counsels. His clients included cardinals, archbishops, clergy of various orders—a Franciscan prelate was delighted to find a Jesuit Brother Giles in him!—viceroys, nobles and common folk. People liked brother to accompany the fathers on their calls; his prayers were needed power by a sick-bed. They liked to come and watch him serve Mass—as much as the fathers liked to be served by him. Here at the altar, very obviously, rather than in the college entrance hall, was centered the whole of brother's existence. Here God not only gave him private visions, as of our Savior present in the host as a babe, but also, for the people's edification, let a ray of light fall upon him more than once out of heaven. Here might the people see the relation of lay brother to priest in the Society of Jesus movingly and deeply typified: the

brother is meant to serve the priest, but in the noble fashion in which
one serves the priest at Mass and thereby assists him in releasing the
Eucharistic energies over the earth.

Finally, not only outsiders were benefited by Alphonsus; his own
religious fellows had good of him also. Far from being without
honor in his own order, he became renowned throughout the
Spanish provinces. He prayed Jesuits out of spiritual and temporal
and bodily difficulties, he counselled them sagely—pointedly too,
as when he had to tell a superior not to preach to the Majorcans
in an elegant Castilian that was Greek to them. He was associated
with the novice master in the charge of lay-brother novices. He
was called on to speak his mind and heart during the occasional
spiritual conferences of the community and even to preach in the
refectory on certain feast days. It would not do him justice to
remember only the time his superior tested his obedience by asking
him to mount the pulpit and give a sermon in Greek. Nimbly rising
to the occasion, he launched into a series of Kyrie Eleison's until
he was told for pity's sake to have done.

While on the subject of his helping people, we had better mention (it was already hinted at and is of a piece with his mystical
graces) that there are miracles, of a quiet sort at any rate, throughout Alphonsus' life in religion. He himself was intensely reluctant
to be credited with miraculous power; he used such expedients to
disguise it even from himself as attributing remarkable effects solely
to some autograph writings of St. Ignatius, much as the Curé of
Ars hid himself as a thaumaturge behind the relics of the mysterious St. Philomena. Nevertheless, happily in league with his Father
Ignatius or not, our brother did perform his fairly modest wonders,
healing, touching the hearts of the dying, helpfully predicting
things like dangers from pirates should one go aboard a ship at such
and such a time, moving people to lay aside their daggers and ven-
dettas and be reconciled in church, stopping a tornado that was
smashing up the island, and so on. When a human will allows the
divine will to pass into it and possess it utterly, strange things are
apt to occur in the world. God is walking among men.

The incident of the bishop and the magistrates beating loudly and in vain on the college gate was one of the things that decided superiors to relieve Alphonsus, a dozen years or so before his death, of the position of door-keeper, and to put him, for as long as he were able, at other less onerous and responsible duties. His appearance was more shrivelled and worse than when he greeted us on our visit to Majorca at the start of this story. His hair had fallen away to a silver halo of extreme old age. He now had to joke (and make something of a play on the Spanish words in so doing) that God had at least given him fingers as well as teeth (conspicuous now by their absence) with which to grind his food. He became more and more the concern of the infirmarian.

It is a pleasure to record that he also became more and more the concern of a lively new coadjutor, one that became his successor as porter, Anthony Mora. This lad makes a cheering and touching picture as he goes about with his elder brother Alphonsus, whose declining years are brightened, however the saint might keep up his reserve of gentle gravity, by having him about and forming him. Those years are also, to be sure, somewhat flustered as this un-lettered Boswell of a companion seeks to pry into the holy secrets of the saint of the house. Tony will have his day to publish his findings when he makes his deposition at the process of beatifica-tion. He will even say too much and set going a historical problem. For because Alphonsus had toward the end, on the bidding of Mary herself, made and circulated copies of the Little Office of the Immaculate Conception, the young brother had gotten it into his head that Alphonsus was the original composer of the office!

Here room must be cleared for a Jesuit of considerably more note than our Tony who likewise came into Alphonsus' life in these last years. Only a scholastic as yet, this newcomer, Peter Claver, was putting in some of his training under this very roof precisely because he had asked to be sent here in order to be spiritually bene-fited by the saintly lay brother. In line with his purpose, he ob-tained permission to converse with him a quarter of an hour each day. Very shortly Alphonsus was his true novice-master. It was

Alphonsus, who, without telling his young friend about it, was experiencing illuminations and a vision in his regard that put it into Peter's soul to offer himself for the foreign missions. Before he left Majorca, he had made the decision which it was almost Alphonsus' destiny to inspire him to.

Later, when he went off to be the slave of the Negro slaves in the steamy Caribbean port of Cartagena, Peter took with him as his chief treasures a portrait of Alphonsus and a sheaf of his spiritual instructions. As Peter lay dying, a fellow Jesuit had to use his fists to keep those crowding into the room after relics from making off with the portrait that hung on the wall as the memory of Peter's supreme grace.

There were others whom Alphonsus dispatched by his counsels to the missions—one father, for example, to the Philippines; another (possessed also of a picture of his mentor) to Mexico: that Jerome Moranta who perished under the clubs of the Tepehuanes. Pages back, we promised that what we had sketched of the work of the Jesuits throughout the world in their heroic age would be made relevant to the humble tale of Alphonsus, door-keeper and home-body. The reader knows enough now to appreciate what a singular role this brother played in that far-flung work. Indeed, Alphonsus was made to appreciate this himself in a vision, as when in some marvelous intellectual fashion he seemed to be discoursing on salvation to every living man and woman. Nowadays we should be able to grasp even by way of a physical illustration how it is possible to take part in a campaign at a distance of thousands of miles.

It was not in God's intention to leave Alphonsus in peace even yet, for the weary veteran was still capable of some final progress. In His higher, inscrutable benevolence, God could not quite tolerate the honors that were gathering about His servant. Not that the servant wanted them! One of his most ghastly temptations was the devil's taunting him with being holy and forecasting his canonization. Nor was he alertly aware of them. He did not realize how his brethren were scrambling for his autograph on some pretext or other, or that pictures of himself were being made and passed around. Indeed, when he saw one of these pictures flaunting in public during a procession, he took it for a representation of St. Ignatius, and a pitiful botch at that.

Anyhow, God arranged for a humiliation, in fact a train of humiliations. It all began when Alphonsus was consulted by the rector as to whether he might safely put ten Jesuit fathers and scholastics on a boat to the mainland at a time of particular danger from the Moslem corsairs. On having recourse to God in prayer, Alphonsus was assured that the run, if now ventured, would be a "golden voyage," and on the strength of this communication duly relayed to him, the rector overrode the protestations of his consultors and sent the Jesuits aboard the *Velina*. His only regret was that all the Jesuits that would have to go from Majorca to Spain in the next twenty years might not be put on this charmed vessel.

Now it turned out that "golden voyage" was, if we may dare to put it so, a divine equivocation and stratagem—part of a larger divine plan. "Golden voyage" meant that the *Velina* was to be boarded by the Turks after all and the Jesuits outrageously handled and sold into slavery in Algiers; but that the Jesuits would be purified of spiritual dross in this fiery experience, would help souls in exile, and would at length be brought home safe and sound to a man. All of this God soon explained to Alphonsus and so it was to work out. But meantime a great hullabaloo was raised, the rector was dashed, the consultors were loud in their "We told you so!" And Alphonsus and his formerly accepted status (contested by some) of being directly in touch with heaven were thrown under suspicion. Alphonsus had even to explain the whole thing in a letter to Father General in Rome.

Presently another vigorous agent of God's trial of Alphonsus bustled into Montesion in the uncompromising person of Father Joseph de Villegas, the new provincial. The recent affair of the *Velina*—"golden voyage" forsooth!—had confirmed the hard-headed Castilian in his opinion that all this business about the holy brother of Majorca needed careful looking into and attending to.

Ironically enough, Alphonsus' rector (who, incidentally, quite understood by now about the ship disaster), in his very anxiety to have brother make a good impression on the provincial, contributed hugely to having him make a bad one. Brother must not be seen in the old, patched-up habit. Accordingly, despite brother's own wishes—he did not think it well to deck what was soon to be a corpse with new clothes—let him be respectably fitted out by the tailor at once. Unfortunately, because of either the tailor's mistake or the brother's stoop, the new habit hung lower than what the rule allowed for temporal coadjutors. Brother himself did not notice this but Father Villegas did—triumphantly.

To the acute embarrassment of the rector and the entire community—except the serene, even delighted, culprit—Father Provincial publicly and severely upbraided Alphonsus for his want of poverty in sporting his fine garment and for his irregularity and pride in wearing the long cassock of a priest. Nothing would do but that the tailor come forward with his scissors and cut away the offending surplus on the spot. In an ironic sequel to all this, the trimmings would be eagerly appropriated by members of the community as relics! Finally, the provincial scolded the brother for the impertinence of his spiritual writing and forbade him to do any more of it. In general, as is clear, he deprecated the veneration accorded this highly questionable saint.

God was satisfied. Alphonsus had weathered the trial gloriously. Indeed, he alone of the Jesuits of Montesion would not heave a sigh of relief when presently the provincial should take his leave. The humiliations he had been subjected to had left no sting. The prohibition regarding the zealous work of his spiritual writing (which he would take up again on the death of Father Villegas) did. But at bottom all was gain, he had reached a final eminence of union with his God. Just before the opening of the provincial's spiritual conference, he was struck by a flash of intellectual lightning out of heaven. In it he saw with new vividness how great was the divine will; how from now on his heart must be as its seal; how he must realize perfect conformity with it by abandoning to it a self-will utterly mortified. And indeed Alphonsus was henceforward mystically absorbed in God. It seemed to him that no longer did he himself act but God acted in him, seeing through his eyes, hearing through his ears, speaking through his lips, working by his hands—God, in a word, was, as it were, the soul of which he was the mere body.

Naturally, his third religious vow, which generated the specific form of his will's identification with that of Christ, is involved here. One cannot do even the hastiest life of our saint without particular notice of the remarkable thing which is his obedience, and without some frank consideration of it as a problem. If the opening pages of what the Acts of the Saints contain on Alphonsus be turned over, it will be remarked what immediate, anxious concern there is with his obedience, and this by way of reflecting the difficulties made of it in the process of beatification.

Already we have mentioned the occasion when Alphonsus, told by the infirmarian, who had been trying to get him to swallow some tasty preparation, that the rector himself had ordered him to eat the whole dish, began scraping the dish with his knife, with every intention of digesting earthenware. There are instances of the rector's telling him not to move when he was about to rise out of respect and of his accordingly staying put for hours or overnight, like a walking-stick carelessly thrown down and forgotten. Bidden at a late hour, as a test of his obedience, to set out directly for the Indies, letting nothing stand in his way, he was for trudging into the night without hat or cloak, descending to the harbor, and then, were there not a boat there bound for the Indies, to walk out into the water up to his face. And so forth, God help us. A superior had to think twice before setting in motion so doggedly literal an execution! Although a general of the Society has observed that superiors would be glad to be bothered only in such a way by their subjects, yet some apology or other seems to be called for.

Well, first of all, the ordinary acts of obedience Alphonsus performed *were* ordinary. To be sure, they were motivated by an extraordinary spirit of self-immolation and union with God, but we need not go into that again. With regard to the relatively few instances of sensationally literal performance, we may candidly assert that the obedience shown in them, however prompted by heroic virtue, is not for general imitation. Objectively, it is not even defensible as a saintly extreme of the blind obedience Ignatius calls for. Ignatian blind obedience means comforming one's very mind to the mind of the superior. But it is not normally a superior's mind that his orders be taken so literally, with no active response of attempting to interpret his mind.

Alphonsus, one of whose temptations was to argue this subject with professional theologians, might want to contradict us, favored as he was with mystic divine approvals of his obedience. These approvals may well have fallen on the supreme generosity of his dispositions in this matter, and perhaps even on a highly individual mode of obedience to which God was inspiring him. The "perhaps" seems to us rather timid and therefore tends to make excuses for Alphonsus necessary. It may be said that the lay brother, whose type he is, is meant to play a relatively passive role in religion and presume less than a priest to read between the lines of directions given. It may also be said that Alphonsus might reasonably suppose that the superior wanted his orders observed to the letter as an exercise in perfect obedience.

But doubtless what may be said most sensibly is contained in the following lines out of Father Martindale [1]: "The incredible naiveness with which he translated his theories of abnegation into act issue into anecdotes exasperating to all who cannot take these incidents in the concrete, as it were, incorporate with this man, this lay-brother. . . . It may be said that old men of this type—I will not say, the complete expression of the type, like Alonso—are not so seldom to be met with in the ranks of lay-brothers of religious Orders. Perhaps anyone who has lived in a larger house of some such Order—a house of studies, for example—will remember one of these gentle old men, full of profound spiritual insight expressing itself often in acts of the most pathetic childlikeness or

[1] *Captains of Christ*, pp. 149-150.

downright childishness. And such encounters come, I would dare to say, with a sweetness singularly refreshing to a mind in danger of sophistication, for the moment, by too much metaphysic or jaded, at any rate, by intellectual drudgeries. . . ."

We have seen the spiritual life of Alphonsus brought to a temporal consummation. It remains speedily to conclude the record of his earthly one.

There is one incident of his closing years that must be mentioned as typifying and crowning much of his work and destiny. On being told at recreation after dinner that a thesis offensive to Mary's prerogative of Immaculate Conception had been posted in the town, Alphonsus, for all his habitual silence and extreme infirmity, became greatly excited, got to his feet and exclaimed in a loud voice: "You cannot trifle with the Mother of God, who, although she is so gentle, nay sweetness and gentleness itself, has a Son who is very jealous of his Mother's honor, and angels without number who would take the part of their Lady, and defend her purity and high name!" Then he added, out of what he later admitted was knowledge from heaven: "One of the causes, among others, why God has sent the Society into this world was chiefly this, to teach and defend this truth in Holy Church."

As the end came near, the devils were permitted to settle on Alphonsus again, black fowl that the white dove must again tear and scatter. They came with instruments of torture such as were in the visions and trials of other saints. Once they flung him down a staircase and dashed his head on the pavement. The divine purpose they were being forced to minister to this time was not mainly one of purification. Now rather was Alphonsus being made to share, for the good of souls, the endurance of Christ when it was his enemies' hour and the power of darkness. An apostle was winning grace whose beneficence would outlast him. Indeed, as much was intimated to him: thus, he had a revelation of what wonders he would work on Majorca after his death; a revelation he could not bear comfortably this side of heaven.

A little while before the end, Alphonsus was freed from all diabolical annoyance—forever. He could now prepare himself for the last moment in peace and joy.

Shortly after midnight on the vigil of All Saints, in 1617, when he was eighty-six years old, he loudly invoked the name of Jesus and died. With a quite uncanny swiftness the news of his passing ran through the town and brought out a huge crowd in the night to the college. First the men invaded the cloister to do reverence to the body. Then at length, the remains were carried into the church and set on a raised catafalque so that more of the faithful, the women included, might see them, pray by them, touch rosaries and handkerchiefs and ribands to them. A baby boy was healed of a disease of the eyes at the application of the brother's hands. Alphonsus was no longer the Society's exclusive property; he belonged to the people of Majorca and the world. Finally the Jesuit Fathers got the church cleared and proceeded to a secret nocturnal burial of their treasure. The treasure, it might be expected, was to be dug out again in time, and made share the honors of Alphonsus' official sainthood. But that was for tomorrow and for God.

EPILOGUE

# The Brother Nobody Knows

ANONYMOUS

ACT I SCENE I . . . *Action opens in a large, modern factory. Several hundred men stand near rotating belts, hands occupied with wrenches, screw drivers, bolts etc. White fluorescent lights beat down on them. Noise. The roar of machinery. The shouting of men from control towers. An overalled figure comes quickly down the aisle and taps a man on the shoulder, beckons him. He goes to the phone. The din dies down. Over the wires comes a supervisor's voice:*

"It is a boy, Mr. Reardon. Mother and child both doing nicely."

THE MAN: "Thanks be to God, she made it . . . thanks, nurse, thanks . . . gee, I'm almost dead from worry. . . . Say, nurse, tell her it's O.K., just as she wants. . . . We'll call him Mike."

SCENE II . . . *Action opens in big city street. Fire sales, Neon lights pale in the smog, yellow cabs streaking through the traffic, women milling in and out of 5 and 10¢ stores, kids playing baseball, half on the sidewalk, half on the street. Mike Reardon, the babe of nineteen years back comes chugging around the corner in a "lizzie." He swerves to avoid a hit, sticks his head out of the window and shouts:*

"Get the heck out of the way."

*Draws up to curb and gets out, glowers at the barber grinning, leaning against his candied pole:*

"Darned lucky I have that St. Chris. medal with all the fools abroad in daylight."

*Puts out his hand:* "Well, Tony, I wanta say goodbye. May not be seeing you for a long time. I'm going away to be a Jesuit Brother."

(CURTAIN)

ACT II SCENE I . . . *Action set in a small chapel, early morning, first rays of dawn steal through the stained windows. In the pews are many men in black robes facing the front, kneeling.*

338

*A priest is at the altar. From the loft a young tenor is singing in Latin. Sounds good.*

*Mike Reardon dressed in black, too, gets out of the front pew, kneels behind the priest and reads from a paper in the silence:*

". . . O Almighty and eternal God . . . I, Michael Reardon, though most unworthy, relying on thy infinite kindness and compassion, vow . . . before all heaven and your Infinite Majesty, poverty, chastity, and obedience forever in the Society of Jesus. . . ."

*Communion. The mass continues. As Brother Mike leaves the chapel an old Brother pats him on the back:*

"Nice goin', Brother Reardon. You're going to be O.K."

BROTHER REARDON: "Thanks, Brother. Gee, it's a great feeling."

(CURTAIN)

SCENE II  . . .  *Action set in large athletic room. Lots of shouting high school boys running around in B.V.D's, girt in towels, the plentiful flow of steam from near-by showers. In left forefront of stage, Brother Reardon is taking in helmets, knee pads, soiled jerseys. The rough harmony of several barber-shop quartets soars above the din. The boys get dressed. The noise dies down. One by one they leave.*

*Brother comes out from behind his counter, locks the cupboards. Last boy slips on his jacket:*

"Say, Brother, won't you ever be ordained and have a first mass like Mr. Hansen?"

BROTHER REARDON (*putting on his cassock over his sweat shirt*): "No, Steve. I've gone as far as I'm gonna go. Never had a knack for studies. But this is a fine way to serve God, working with you fellows." (*Turns off lights and closes door*) "Couldn't be much happier than I am."

(CURTAIN)

SCENE III  . . .  *Action set in fair-sized dark room. Over on one end the fires of a huge furnace peek through slits in the door. At the other end forestage Brother Reardon, now middle-aged, fairly heavy, wrestles with a wrench and a pipe in a lathe. Around him are more machines, drills, paintbrushes. The smell of turpentine and crude oil drifts out.*

*From backstage a spectacled priest approaches and looks over Brother's shoulder.*

"Say, Brother, when you finish there could you fix the leaky showers on the third floor?"

BROTHER: "Well, as I've said before, I don't know much about these things, but I'll do what I can, Father."

PRIEST: "Fine, no one expects any more."

(CURTAIN)

ACT III   SCENE I . . . *Action set in large church at night. The shuffle of feet mix with stillness and the organ plays softly. A spare, white-haired man lights the candles. Brother Reardon. He smooths the cloth, straightens the floral-piece on the right and goes into the sacristy. A flick of his hand and the church is aglow. He bows to the priest. All bow to the cross. The procession wends its way out, a long column of pageantry.*

*He kneels by the door and puts his face in his hands. He whispers loud enough to be heard:*

"Dear Lord, I am weary."

(CURTAIN)

SCENE II . . . *Action set in paradise. A colonnade of white marble steps mounting out of view. Suffused light in forestage. Powerful white spots shooting from behind backdrops. Reflectors shoot back brilliance on upper steps. The figure of an angel leads Brother Reardon up slowly from the bottom. The backs of both are to the audience. No lights hit them directly. The strains of distant choirs and thousand-pieced orchestras filter down.*

*Then quiet. . . . The angel kneels near the top:*

"Father, build this man's throne high. I have been with him for seventy-eight years. He has been true. He has sought first the kingdom of God and its justice. For practically his whole life, no one has paid any attention to him. He got his name in the paper twice and that was when he was born and his obituary notice after he died. He has lived by FAITH.

"Lord, remember Thy promise to lift up the lowly. Place him before the great, above the mighty, let the rulers of the world feel honored to touch the hem of his cassock. Behold a man of faith and devotion in a hardened generation."

*The music swells. Brother and the angel rise and mount higher, out of view.*

(CURTAIN)